Sport in the American West

Jorge Iber, series editor

REMEMBERING BULLDOG TURNER

Unsung Monster of the Midway

MICHAEL BARR

FOREWORD BY LEW FREEDMAN

Texas Tech University Press

Designed by Kasey McBeath
Cover photograph courtesy AP Photo/Football Hall of Fame

Library of Congress Cataloging-in-Publication Data
Barr, Michael D., 1952–
    Remembering Bulldog Turner : unsung monster of the midway / Michael Barr ; [foreword by] Lew Freedman.
        pages cm. — (Sport in the American west)
    Includes bibliographical references and index.
    ISBN 978-0-89672-827-1 (hardback) — ISBN 978-0-89672-828-8 (e-book)
1. Turner, Bulldog, 1919–1998. 2. Football players—United States—Biography.
3. Linebackers (Football)—United States—Biography. I. Title.
    GV939.T87B37 2013
    796.332092—dc23
    [B]   2013022606

13 14 15 16 17 18 19 20 21 / 9 8 7 6 5 4 3 2 1

Texas Tech University Press
Box 41037 | Lubbock, Texas 79409-1037 USA
800.832.4042 | ttup@ttu.edu | www.ttupress.org

For Ginger, Anna, and Joe

For He will command his angels concerning you to guard you in all your ways; they will lift you up in their hands, so that you will not strike your foot against a stone.

Psalms 91:11

Contents

Illustrations

Foreword

lyde "Bulldog" Turner joined the Chicago Bears at just the right time. The two-way player, a 60-minute man in the parlance of the day, was a monster in the middle because he couldn't be budged at center and he was a monster in the middle on defense because as a linebacker he disposed of anyone running his way with the ball.

Turner was Chicago's no. 1 draft pick out of Hardin-Simmons University in 1940 (a handful of years after the National Football League player draft began) and he helped the Bears become the powerhouse team of the decade.

More evidence of Turner's impeccable timing arriving on the scene—through 1939 the University of Chicago Maroons were known as "The Monsters of the Midway" because of their south side location where the 1893 World Columbian Exposition was held. But the Maroons gave up football and as smoothly as a steal of home plate the Bears promptly became known as the Monsters of the Midway. They weren't located on the old midway, but they were monsters and Turner was one of iconic coach George Halas's favorites.

The numbers do not seem so large today, but being 6-foot-2 and weighing 235 pounds with sturdy muscles and quick feet might as well have been a grizzly bear back in that era. Fast, strong, with great instincts, and a student of football who studied not only his own assignments, but where all 11 men on the field were supposed to go, Turner was a perfect specimen. There was a reason why teammates and opponents called Turner "Bulldog" rather than Clyde. Bulldog had tenacity.

"Bulldog Turner was the best football player and smartest player I ever knew in my whole life," said Bears end George Connor. "He could do everything."

It is the stat men, the running backs and quarterbacks, who gain acclaim on "best-ever" lists, given the difficulty of quantifying the contributions of blockers and tacklers. Evidence to support compliments such as Connors' was trickier to unearth. Turner was a six-time all-pro center, but he also led the league with eight interceptions one year.

"Bulldog was as great at his position as any player who ever lived," said Ken Kavanaugh, another Bears teammate.

He was great enough to be selected for the Pro Football Hall of Fame in 1966.

One memorable Turner play occurred during a 1947 game between the Bears and the Washington Redskins. Turner intercepted legendary quarterback Sammy Baugh's pass near the Bears' end zone, then put on a burst of speed, escaped most Redskin tackling threats and culminated the play with a Chicago touchdown 96 yards later with Baugh hanging on his back trying to bring him down.

Turner was indefatigable and was an eight-time All-Pro choice combining offense and defense. He played with the Bears from 1940 to 1952 and Chicago won National Football League (NFL) titles in 1940, 1941, 1943, and 1946. The Bears also lost in the title game in 1942.

As someone who grew up in West Texas (Plains and Sweetwater), and played college ball at a school that was a long train ride or two-hop flight on a puddle jumper away from major cities, during an era when scouting was word of mouth, Turner was lucky to be discovered by the NFL at all. Trying to keep a secret, the Detroit Lions got to Turner and paid him $200 hush money not to say anything about their interest. They said the cash was to "fix his teeth." Turner's bicuspids were fine and the Bears won him anyway.

Turner and Baugh (another contender for best-ever) followed the same path through the same high school that may have fibbed about its name, Sweetwater. If they hadn't been fortunate sooner they might not have ended up ranch owners later. At one time Turner's spread was 1,200 acres and the hardscrabble land and unpredictable weather often treated him as roughly as NFL pass rushers and fullbacks did.

A Texan to the soul, Turner was the son of a cowboy, born in a cabin on a ranch, took up the national sport of the state, and when he walked away from football, he took up the romantic profession of the state. Both the football sport and the ranching profession were tougher than the movies made them out to be, and Turner had to stay tough his whole life to get by. Yet those were the worlds he chose and he said he never regretted it.

But Turner recognized at a young age through poverty that life could be tough and that opportunity called only rarely. While at Sweetwater, Turner picked cotton for an after-school job until he grew envious of the athletes who wore spiffy sweaters with a fancy "S" on them. That's what inspired him to take up the sport that provided him a college education.

Not that he followed a straight path to Hardin-Simmons. Turner may have been the only Sweetwater student who dropped out of high school, yet still wanted to attend college. (He received his diploma later that summer.) He tried to convince schools to take him in exchange for his football savvy. He hitchhiked to Oklahoma with 10 cents and a candy bar in his pocket and then went hungry for five days when he got there. After finding his way to Hardin-Simmons in Abilene, he showed witnesses just how tough he was and got invitations to play pro ball.

There was uncommon perseverance in the man when he was forced to plumb it, and mixed together with his other traits, gave Clyde that unyielding Bulldog nature. It made him hard to push around, a useful capability in the trenches on a football field.

"I knew everybody's assignments and I could play every position on the field," Turner said.

He could, and sometimes it seemed like he did. Turner boasted with a chuckle that his yards-per-carry average was 48.0 because that's how far he went on his one chance to tote the pigskin from scrimmage. Turner also ran back kickoffs and punts, although as a big man, he was an unlikely suspect in those roles.

Yet Turner never made much money in the game, as his heyday

was during World War II, and he never saved much. He became a rancher, not a gentleman rancher, but one not so different than the typical Texas rancher, whose life depended on how the land, the weather, and livestock treated him. It takes a stubborn streak to cope and Turner had that. Ranching is a 24-hour-a-day job and that wasn't a stretch for a man who packed so much into 60-minute hours on the gridiron.

He coached the New York Titans for one year in the early days of the American Football League, but living in New York City was a bit like renting in a foreign country. Turner and Manhattan folk may have spelled words the same, but that didn't mean there wasn't a communications gap.

Turner at heart was a homeboy. He may have played football in Chicago for years surrounded by skyscrapers, and where modern trends came early, but Bulldog was a Texan and the wide open spaces and the dust always felt more like home than the asphalt and the noise.

Clyde Turner had been back home in Gatesville for a long while when he died at age 79 in 1998.

Lew Freedman

Preface

n 1976 an Iowa state trooper stopped a speeding motorist on I-29 between Omaha and Sioux City. Hoping to avoid a ticket, the driver let it slip that he was a noted professional football personality.

"You wouldn't give a ticket to Bulldog Turner of the Football Hall of Fame would you?"

The trooper kept writing. "Bulldog who?" he said without looking up. "I don't care if you're Elvis. You were speeding, and you're getting a ticket."

"I can see you're not impressed," said the motorist, as he flashed his enormous Hall of Fame ring.

The trooper just kept writing.

The ticket was issued, and the motorist went on his way. The trooper went about his business but couldn't get the episode out of his mind. He was a football fan, and that name, Bulldog Turner, had a familiar ring to it. The trooper had heard that name somewhere before. He was certain of it. Later that day the trooper checked the records and found that, sure enough, the motorist was indeed a gridiron legend from a bygone era. He played for the Chicago Bears from 1940 to 1952 and really was a member of the Pro Football Hall of Fame. He was 57 years old and lived on a ranch near Gatesville, Texas. At the time he worked in sales for the Interstate Steel Company of Omaha,

Nebraska, but in the 1940s he was the best center and the best line-backer in the NFL. The name on his driver's license was Clyde Turner, the name his momma gave him, but in his day sports fans knew him as Bulldog—the toughest man on the roughest team in professional football.

Then, like the Iowa state trooper, we forgot.

Acknowledgments

No book about the life of Bulldog Turner would be possible without the help of Pat Turner, Ilene Turner Hairston, Ed Sprinkle, J. R. Boone, Cotton Davidson, Jack Pardee, Jay Black and the Texas Sports Hall of Fame in Waco, Dr. Merlin Morrow, former athletic director at Hardin-Simmons University, and Bulldog Turner's scores of friends and neighbors throughout Central and West Texas. Many thanks.

Thanks also to the following providers of inspiration and encouragement: Coach Ron Barr, Lana Janssen, James Wilson Brazzil, Wes Gilbreath, Sr., Charles Wise, Patricia Bosquez, Bobby Hodge, Ken Dyson, Howell Otis Cearley, Jr., Tommy Joe Ford, Robert W. Caster, Dr. Evelyn Farmer, Dr. James Pohl, Dr. Billy Ray Brunson, Alan Weihausen, Bob Alexander, and David Johnson.

REMEMBERING BULLDOG TURNER

Chapter 1

The Short End of the Stick

The ramshackle ranch house sat a hundred yards north of State Highway 116 and a quarter mile east of Cowhouse Creek, in the valley between Hard Bargain Mountain and Rattlesnake Ridge. It was a two-story wooden structure, of typical ranch house design, surrounded by slender, delicate bluestem, scrawny mesquites, broom weeds, and prickly pear, and built on a gentle rise between the rocky creek bottom and a cedar and live oak–covered chalk hill behind it and to the east. In March the sweet spring rains in this part of Texas transform the Cowhouse Valley, for a few brief weeks, into a green carpet as far as the eye can see, with spectacular clusters of bluebonnets, purple horsemint, and Indian blankets more beautiful than an impressionist painting, but come July the heat and the lack of moisture will incinerate the grass, kill the flowers, and turn the countryside the color of dry cow dung. By August the Cowhouse slows to a trickle. Between the ranch house and the hill, a Farmall tractor rusted in the shade of a tin hay barn of crude construction. The ranch house itself was big and roomy, once a grand lady, but by the 1980s, bleached of color by the brutal Texas sun, she was old and cracked and gray and in need of serious repair. After almost a century of doing battle with the Texas heat, wind, and rain, the ravages of time had finally gained the upper hand. The covered porch that extended across the front of the house creaked and sagged, the roof leaked, the screens were rusty, and the walls—inside and out—needed a fresh coat of paint in the worst way.

The roof over the porch sheltered a lively assortment of darting dirt daubers, bouncing daddy long legs, and several colonies of angry red wasps. The largest wasp nest was as big as an iron skillet.

There was no indication from the outside that there was anything special about this house or the large, gray-haired man who called it home. Farmers and ranchers drove by the place every day without knowing that the unpretentious old gentleman who lived there was an NFL legend and one of the best professional football players who ever buttoned a chin strap. Yes, there were whispers among the younger crowd that he was once a professional athlete. Perhaps he played Major League Baseball, and he had that great nickname. But often the people he encountered in everyday affairs at the Guaranty Bank, the cattle auction, or the feed store thought of him as just an old Texas cowman who had fallen on hard times. There were rumors that he drank too much and had trouble paying his bills. At least that was the talk over coffee with the morning crowd at Andy's Restaurant—that is, when the superintendent wasn't being second-guessed or the football coach vilified. Even the old man's friends and neighbors who knew of his career in the NFL never understood or appreciated how great he really was. He played so long ago. Few memories reached back that far.

And yet if his neighbors had only known, they would have stopped and even paid admission, to go inside that weathered old house. What awaited them, if they were football fans, was something akin to a deep religious experience—like trying on Jim Thorpe's floppy leather helmet or smelling Red Grange's sweat socks. Scattered about that old ranch house were dusty silver trophies, championship rings as big around as golf balls, pictures of the owner with movie stars, Franklin Mint medallions stamped with the owner's likeness, and other priceless souvenirs from an NFL career that every player dreams of but only a few ever experience. A gold Hall of Fame blazer, size XXXL, seemed out of place as it hung in the bedroom closet next to the work shirts and khaki pants. On the walls were faded black-and-white photographs of the owner with the gods of football—Jim Thorpe, Bronko Nagurski, Harold "Red" Grange, Slingin' Sammy Baugh, Don Hutson, Doak Walker, Bobby Layne, and Johnny Unitas—staring down through the ages.

The owner, Clyde "Bulldog" Turner, was himself a football god on equal footing with all the others. He rose up like a dust devil from the dry West Texas plains to become an early NFL superstar and one of the greatest professional linemen of the pre-television era.

But the everlasting fame and immortality that came so easily to those other gods never stuck to Bulldog Turner because the positions he played rarely made headlines. Had he played quarterback, running back, or even receiver, like the other gods on his wall, he could have been famous all across America. He could have been set for life. He could have made a good living endorsing breakfast cereal, beer, and cigarettes. But Bulldog played center and linebacker, while the recognition, the glory, and the money went to players who scored touchdowns. Today even casual sports fans know of Thorpe, Baugh, Grange, and Nagurski, but some of the greatest football players of all time are virtually unknown because they played before television, and they didn't play in the backfield. These days not many people remember Pudge Heffelfinger (the first man to play football for money), Fats Henry, Ox Emerson, George "The Beast" Trafton, Frank "Bruiser" Kinard, Cal Hubbard, Ed Healey, Adolph "Germany" Schulz (the first center to deep snap the ball with a spiral), Link Lyman, or Mel Hein. Like those legendary linemen from the first half of the twentieth century, Bulldog Turner is a ghostly character from football's leather helmet days.

Let's be honest: There is little glory for offensive linemen. They always get the short end of the stick. Their work is done in the trenches in violent physical encounters rarely noticed by spectators. Even today an offensive lineman, even a great one, is the most invisible man on the field. He gets no attention at all unless he makes a bad snap, jumps offside, holds, clips, or commits a felony in the off-season. His name is never called unless he screws up, and he never gets his name in the paper. Sportswriters compose elegant verse in iambic pentameter describing every spin and juke of the running back on his way to the goal line while snubbing the man who threw the block that made the whole thing possible. A lineman is the nameless, faceless Goliath with the dings on his helmet and the blood on his jersey. His career is spent perfecting the art of *not* calling attention to himself. His livelihood depends on his ability to be inconspicuous, because any attention drawn to him on the field can only be negative. The better he performs, the less visible he becomes in the tangled mass of arms and legs along the line of scrimmage. Even the refs get more attention.

In the middle of it all, surrounded and shielded from view by giants, is the center. Except for a protruding arm on the television screen, he is barely noticeable. The only time he gets his picture in the paper is in a crowd shot. There are always opportunities for men who carry, throw, or catch the ball to be spontaneous and creative, but a center strives for monotonous, repetitive efficiency. He cannot afford to be colorful. He has to keep his wits about him in highly emotional situations. In the midst of chaos, he has to remain calm and stay focused. He cannot afford to be sloppy in his delivery. A center touches the ball on every play, and if he doesn't do his job exactly right and with perfect timing, everything breaks down. All this he must perform flawlessly while smelling the breath and fighting off the brutal attack of a 260-pound nose tackle whose actions in just about any other venue would constitute a crime.

In addition to being mechanically correct, a center must have a poker face and the patience of a kindergarten teacher. Defensive linemen and linebackers study the center's every move. The slightest twitch, a sideways glance, or the flair of a nostril can betray the snap count and give the advantage to the defense.

"Well, you know as an offensive center you'd never get your name in the paper unless you make a mistake," Bulldog told a reporter in 1995. "If you throw the ball over the kicker's head or something your name would be mentioned. Otherwise, if you do it right, your name will never be mentioned."[1]

Even when he did get his name in the paper, it was sometimes for the wrong reason. Bulldog had a hard time catching a break with reporters. "One time we put in a running play off of a punt formation," Bulldog recalled, "and on this play, I was supposed to snap the ball wide so George McAfee could catch the ball on the run and have a fast start. Well, we tried that fake punt and it failed. I laid that ball right where I was supposed to, right in George McAfee's hands, but they caught him for a loss. The next day the newspapers said, 'Due to a bad pass from center, McAfee had to run the ball.' It doesn't seem like there was much justice there."[2]

"An offensive center's not going to get any publicity unless you make a damn mistake," he said again. But then he quickly added without a hint of insincerity, "I never made any."[3]

The men who played beside him and against him agreed. No man played his positions better than Bulldog Turner. For years he terrorized and mystified the rest of the NFL. At his defensive position, outside linebacker, he was the ideal combination of size and speed. As a general rule, big things move slowly. Not so with Bulldog Turner. He was big for his era and fast for any era. A reporter described his style of play as a "smashing, driving, roving, fearless defensive game in which he appears to do the right thing by instinct." Even when opponents ran away from him he routinely ran down ball carriers on the opposite side of the field.

And yet he may have been his best against the pass. Despite his size, Bulldog Turner could cover a receiver like a thick coat of West Texas dust. He is still the only linebacker to lead the NFL outright in interceptions (eight in 1942). Receivers underestimated his skills at pass defense, and he fooled quarterbacks, especially in the early years, with his ability to defy the laws of physics. It did not seem possible for a man that big to move that fast. He had four interceptions in five NFL title games and 16 total interceptions in his illustrious career before quarterbacks wised up and stopped throwing to his side of the field.

But it was at offensive center that he is best known, and at that position he was near perfection; one of the very best who ever played the game. He was a ferocious blocker, a superb pass protector and a flawless deep snapper. Only his idol, Mel Hein of the New York Giants, was his equal at center. Hein was the first center named to the Pro Football Hall of Fame and the only interior lineman to win the league Most Valuable Player (MVP) award. Just to draw a comparison to the great Giant center was an honor. But Hein was on the downside of his career when Bulldog became a Chicago Bear in 1940, and Bulldog quickly left the aging star in the dust. In his day Bulldog was the best center in the NFL by a country mile. There was no argument about that. No one else was close.

Offensive center is a difficult position to play, but Bulldog made it look easy. In addition to snapping the ball to the quarterback in the

T formation, Bulldog could deep snap the ball in the punt formation with uncanny accuracy, and under all kinds of conditions in all kinds of weather. "You have no idea [of] the pressure on a center," Bulldog explained, especially when deep snapping to the punter. "Centering the ball on a dry field is no problem, but get it on mud, or snow, or just wet grass, and you've got to be careful. And when you're playing in the rain, you've got to just baby that ball back to the punter."[4]

From most of the 1940s Bulldog was the best center and the best linebacker in the world. Of course the question is: How do you measure greatness in a lineman, a position that is statistically immeasurable? Just ask his teammates and his opponents. They'll tell you. They knew he was the best. He showed them every Sunday.

In 1940, Bulldog Turner was a 21-year-old rookie starter for the Chicago Bears, one of the greatest teams in NFL history. In his career he was All-Pro six times. At least twice his All-Pro selection was unanimous, placing him in the elite company of immortals like Sammy Baugh and Don Hutson. Bulldog played in the first two Pro Bowls. During his 12-year career, all in Chicago, the Bears won five divisional titles and four NFL championships. He was a member of the 1940s NFL All-Decade team as chosen by the Hall of Fame Selection Committee. In 1966 he received the highest honor, short of heaven, that a football player can get—a place in the Pro Football Hall of Fame in Canton, Ohio. Bulldog was the eighth offensive lineman to be so honored.

"People ask me if I have any Super Bowl rings," Turner once said. "I say, 'No, but I have four championship rings. It's the same game.'"[5]

Besides the Pro Football Hall of Fame, Bulldog is a member of the College Football Hall of Fame in South Bend, Indiana, the Texas Athletic Hall of Fame in Waco, the Helms Foundation Hall of Fame in Alta Loma, California, and the Hardin-Simmons University Hall of Fame in Abilene. In 1950 the Associated Press conducted a poll of Texas sportswriters to select the greatest Texas football player of the half-century. Sammy Baugh was first, Doak Walker was second, and Bulldog Turner finished third. In 1957, *Pro Football Magazine* listed Bulldog as the center of its all-time professional team. In 1969, sportswriters selecting the All-Texas college football team for the past 50 years named Bulldog to its first team. He was the only member of the squad who did not play in the Southwest Conference. In 1975 sports fans from the Lone Star State selected the all-time Texas professional football team. At center, Bulldog won in a landslide. He appeared with the rest of the team on national television on Monday night, November 10, 1975, at halftime of the Dallas/Kansas City football game at Texas Stadium in Irving. When he retired as a player, the Chicago Bears honored Bulldog with a rare and elite ceremony reserved for a few select men who played for that much storied franchise. The Bears retired his number. Today number 66 hangs in the Grand Concourse at Soldier Field beside number 34 (Walter Payton), number 51 (Dick Butkus), number 40 (Gale Sayers), number 77 (Red Grange), number 3 (Bronko Nagurski), number 41 (Brian Piccolo), number 42 (Sid Luckman), number 28 (Willie Gallimore), number 5 (George McAfee), number 7 (George Halas), number 56 (Bill Hewitt), and number 61 (Bill George).

Not only was Bulldog blessed with size, speed, and talent, he was as durable as a cedar fence post. In 12 full professional seasons playing both sides of the ball he did not miss a single regular season game. He played with broken noses, bruised ribs, pulled muscles, sore knees, headaches, concussions, and hangovers. In 1945 he was in the army and played in only two games for the Bears. It took a world war to get Bulldog Turner out of the lineup.

In his book, *Pro Football's 100 Greatest Players*, George Allen, Hall of Fame coach of the Washington Redskins, called Bulldog the fourth greatest offensive lineman of all time behind Jim Parker (Colts), Forrest Gregg (Packers), and Mel Hein (Giants). The coach admired Bulldog's hands—especially the sneaky way he used them to hold and get away with it. As an offensive center Coach Allen gave Mel Hein the edge over Bulldog primarily because Hein was a single-wing center, which meant he had the more difficult job of snapping the ball to the tailback who was four yards behind the line of scrimmage. Bulldog was a T formation center so he snapped the ball directly to the quarterback.

At linebacker, Bulldog was better than Hein and one of the best who ever played the game. Coach Allen said Bulldog Turner "[m]ay have been the best linebacker against the pass I ever saw." Bulldog was a versatile athlete who could have played many different positions. "If he'd played running back, he might have been one of the best," George Allen wrote. ""If I hadn't put him among the greatest offensive lineman, I'd have to list him among the greatest linebackers."

Bulldog was one of those rare athletes who could knock a 230-pound fullback stone cold at the line of scrimmage or run down a speedy halfback in the open field. "Turner played with reckless abandon," Coach Allen said. "He didn't just tackle people, he destroyed them."[6]

Just about anyone who carried the ball in the NFL in the 1940s was hammered at one time or another by Bulldog Turner and had a story to tell about it. The sensation was like running headlong into a large oak tree. "This one game I went out to block Bulldog Turner of the Bears," remembered Pete Marcus of the Washington Redskins, "and he whacked me across the head with a forearm chop. I was seeing Venus, Mars, and Jupiter all at once. They carried me off. I didn't wake up until the second half."[7]

In a game in Chicago, O. E. Smith of the Packers once carried the ball on a wingback reverse. Most of the Bears went with the flow, but Bulldog read the play perfectly. When Smith turned up the field, Bulldog met him in the hole and knocked him into the middle of next week. Even his eyebrows hurt. Then Bulldog spoke, and it was like the voice of god. "In those days," Smith recalled, "you could get up and run again after you were tackled (until you were pinned to the ground). But Bulldog Turner threw me on the ground and whispered, 'If you want to make it in this league, don't get up and run.' I never did."[8]

Bob Snyder, Bulldog's teammate, had this to say when asked to identify the greatest football player he ever saw: "The best passer I ever saw—the best passer who ever lived in my opinion—was Sammy Baugh of the Redskins. The best running back I ever played against was Cliff Battles. The strongest running back I ever played against was Bronko Nagurski. But I think the best football player I ever played with or saw—this is going to sound strange because he did not play a glamorous position—was Bulldog Turner.

"He was just an outstanding football player. He was a great blocker, a good pass defender, everything. I used to do the punting for the

Bears, and I never had to move my hands *that* far to take the snap. He could have played almost any position. He couldn't have been a scat back, but he could have been a fullback, a guard, a tackle, and he was probably the best football player at his position I have ever seen. I don't know of a weakness he had. He was a complete leader, a team leader. He was never injured, and of course, he played both ways, linebacker and offensive center."[9]

Clarke Hinkle (Hall of Fame 1964) was a bruising runner for the Green Bay Packers who had the distinction of being the only man alive to knock Bronko Nagurski out of a game. Hinkle listed Bulldog as one of the toughest men he ever faced.

"After Nagurski," Hinkle said, "the most powerful was Bulldog Turner. He came along in 1940, I believe. He used to rattle my ribs a lot, too. I lit into him to protect myself, as I had to do against Nagurski. Ah, that Bulldog, he weighed 245 and had a twenty-one inch collar, was a great blocker on offense and on defense was as fine a linebacker as ever played the game. They talk about Dick Butkus, but I'm not sure Butkus could carry Bulldog's shoes."[10]

After Bulldog's rookie season Hunk Anderson, a Bears assistant coach, paid Bulldog Turner the ultimate compliment. "If every player in the league was declared a free agent tomorrow," Anderson said, "and I had first crack at anybody I wanted, I'd pick Bulldog Turner. . . . If I had two choices, I'd take Turner and Sid Luckman."[11]

Frank Kimbrough, Bulldog's coach at Hardin-Simmons and a man who rarely spoke in superlatives, said, "Bulldog Turner is the best center I've ever coached. He is the best man I've coached at any position."[12]

"Bulldog was the best at his position I ever saw," added teammate Ed Sprinkle. "He had great natural ability. He had quick hands and feet. He was smart. He talked like a cotton-picker, but he knew every assignment on every play. He had a great work ethic he learned from his parents back in West Texas. No one worked harder than Bulldog. He was a competitor. He had a passion for the game. He could anticipate. He could snap the ball and explode into a man like no one else. He was the most athletic big man I ever saw . . .

"Once up in Green Bay I was playing offensive guard, Bulldog was next to me at center. Across the line from me was a rookie defensive lineman who was supposed to be a young hotshot. Well, our first play from scrimmage, Bulldog snapped the ball, cut across in front of me and planted his helmet in that player's chest. When that young man opened his eyes again and took a breath, he was lying flat on his back looking up at the sky and trying to figure out what day it was. Bulldog just knocked him for a loop. Well, I was a little upset with my teammate. 'Bulldog,' I said. 'That's my man.' 'I know,' he said, with a big grin on his face. 'I just wanted to be the first to welcome him to the NFL. He's all yours now.'"[13]

"What kind of man was he? If you were his friend, he was the most loyal person you'd ever want to meet. He had a good heart. He was my friend. I owe my career to him," Sprinkle said.[14]

"On defense he backed up the line behind me on the right side, and not too many plays went around us," said Sprinkle. "He didn't feel he had a peer on the football field."[15]

"Bulldog believed he could handle anybody," Sprinkle added. "He was cocky, but he could back it up. He had great confidence in himself."[16]

"I didn't fear anybody," Bulldog once told a television reporter. "I loved to play football. I didn't play for money. I played for the thrill—like the thrill of catching a big fish." People who knew him agreed. Ed Rozy, Bulldog's friend and longtime Chicago Bears trainer, once said Bulldog "didn't give a damn about anything but football."[17]

Bulldog played the game with the joy and enthusiasm of a child, and off the field he had a friendly and outgoing personality that could be misleading. Early on some people misjudged him because he had a mischievous smile and didn't look mean enough to play football. His blond hair was the color of a bale of hay, and his eyes sparkled like the sunshine bouncing off the clear water of Cowhouse Creek. He was friendly, and like all really tough men, he had a gentle nature. Everybody liked him. "I really don't believe I had an enemy off the field," he said.

But on the gridiron he was as rough and tough as any man who ever played the game. And when there was trouble, on or off the field, Bulldog always ran toward it—never away from it. Beneath the hair and the smile and the pleasant persona beat the heart of a warrior. "I hate everybody when I walk on the football field," he once said. "I wouldn't even speak to my best friend [Sammy Baugh] in a game and we graduated from the same high school in Sweetwater, Texas. Yeah. Sammy'd wink at me when he was calling signals for the Washington Redskins, but I'd just glare back and do my best to rack 'em up."[18]

"I can see that big face in front of me right now," remembered Sid Luckman, the Bears' quarterback. "When he walked on the field, he was all class. He was motivated. He played both ways and he was a vicious football player. . . . He looked out for us. If there was trouble, Bulldog was there."[19]

Off the field he laughed, joked, sang songs, stayed out all night, drank too much beer, spent money freely, and never took himself seriously. He had a voice like thunder—a booming West Texas twang—that arrived at his destination several minutes before he did. He knew the first name of every bartender in downtown Chicago. Bulldog was a product of the West Texas cowboy culture. When it was time to work, he gave it all he had, but when the work was done, he believed he had a license to raise hell. He drew his pay and made a beeline to the nearest honky-tonk for drinks and a good time. And he might not stop until all his money was gone.

J. R. Boone, Bulldog's teammate and friend said, "There's nothing Bulldog wouldn't do for fun. He liked to drink beer and have a good time. He would take off his boots and run barefoot through the bar. He would use a toy gun and act like he was robbing the place. And he had no fear of the tough guys.

"He enjoyed telling funny stories," Boone remembered, "especially after a few beers. Every time he told a story he would change it up and embellish it. His friends knew the stories were just for entertainment, but for others not acquainted with West Texas ways it was difficult to know if he was telling the truth or pulling your leg. He enjoyed the mystery of it."[20]

"In the evenings Bulldog liked to go to a place called Helsing's Lounge up in Chicago," Ed Sprinkle recalled, "and after every home game we would go to a place on Clark Street called The Cottage for drinks and dinner. Bulldog liked to drink, and sometimes he drank too much. He was a tough man, and could get into a brawl once in a while. He knew how to fight. He used to box in college. But he was so big, most people were afraid to fight him. He had hands like catcher's mitts, and he was impossible to intimidate. He told me about some scrapes he had when he first came up to Chicago. He provided a lot of entertainment, on and off the field. But when I got there in 1944 I kept him out of trouble. I could reason with Bulldog when no one else could. We had a deal. If Bulldog was getting too rowdy, I would say, 'Bulldog, you are getting out of line.' 'Am I?' he would say. And after that he would settle down, or we went home."[21]

Still, his late-night escapades were legendary, particularly in the early days. Sid Luckman called Bulldog "the champion party boy. When he started celebrating he made no secret of it. He'd haul out a banjo and sing out some Texas tunes that would wake up the echoes for miles around."[22]

But when Bulldog played football, he was all business. On the field he was completely focused on whipping his opponent. And he relied on more than natural ability. In addition to his great athleticism, he had a deep understanding of the game.

"Before we played the Bears," recalled Coach Jimmy Conzelman of the Chicago Cardinals, "I thought of a special formation so I called a secret practice. I locked all the doors and had the windows covered. Well, came the day of the game, and we sprang that spread. Bulldog Turner of the Bears looked across our line, grinned, and said, 'Oh, here comes that spread again.'"[23]

Soon Bulldog's teammates recognized his football savvy and his leadership and deferred to him to make certain decisions on the field. "I remember the day this happened," Bulldog recalled. "We got a penalty and we were having a little officials–players conference. So I told George [George Wilson, the Bears' captain], 'You get the team in the huddle. I'll take care of this decision-making here.' Which was a real bad, cocky attitude. But that's what I felt about it. I knew what was going on in the game and I'd studied our reports and I knew what to expect. I also knew which penalty to take—whether to take it or refuse it."[24]

And he was not afraid to violate the sacred code that says only the quarterback speaks in the huddle. He was full of ideas and quick to share them, although his advice was not always well taken. Sid Luckman, the Bears' quarterback, sometimes began calling plays by yelling "Shut up, Bulldog."[25]

At the same time there was a calmness about the man that amazed his teammates. He was never skittish, and he never showed evidence of tension. He usually got ready for a game by taking a nap. C. W. Smith, Bulldog's teammate with the Bears, said Bulldog "could sleep at any hour, right up to within seconds of an important game."[26]

Bulldog was a natural at a very violent sport. He had an uncommon combination of size, speed, quickness, and athleticism that only comes along once in a great while. His speed was shocking, especially for a big man. He caused quite a stir when he came into the NFL in 1940 because his kind had never been seen before. He was a unique athletic specimen and every coach's dream; a lineman who could block like a bulldozer, run like a halfback, and catch like a receiver. In his prime he could run 100 yards in 11 seconds on grass in full pads and cleats. He could have been a Hall of Fame fullback. He made his case on December 3, 1944 in Pittsburgh when the entire Chicago backfield was ejected for fighting. The coach sent him in to play halfback. He carried the ball one time—for 48 yards and a touchdown.

And no one practiced harder than Bulldog Turner. He studied the game, and he mastered the complex system of plays and formations used by the Bears. He knew all 11 assignments on every play in any formation against any defense. He shunned the standing time linemen sometimes have during practice and routinely worked out at every position except quarterback.[27] Versatility was a requirement in the old days when men played offense and defense.

"I knew everybody's assignments and could play every position on the field," Bulldog remembered. "One time in Pittsburgh we got in a fight and two or three of our players got kicked out, leaving us shorthanded, and Halas [George Halas, head coach of the Bears] let me go in and play halfback. Gene Rozani, our quarterback at that time, called a real fancy play named Twenty-Two Behind. I come on up through that line with the ball and just kept plowing my way and finally got out in the open and scored. It was a 48-yard run, and that's the only time I ran from scrimmage. Walt Kiesling was the Pittsburgh coach at that time, and he was mad. He thought we were making jest of him by using me at halfback, but we weren't. We had run out of players, that's all. After I scored that touchdown, Halas put me back at safety to field a Pittsburgh punt, and I caught the ball and did a little dee-do and started up the sidelines. I went right over to their bench and got tackled. And as I was lying there, Kiesling came up and kicked me right in the butt just as hard as you ever saw. He thought we were making fun of him, and boy, he let me have it. It was a very unsportsmanlike thing to do."[28]

Bulldog Turner was uncommonly versatile, but he played at a time when all players had to do many things. Specialists and prima donnas came later, with television, free agency, no-cut contracts, big salaries, and two-platoon football. "They got guys now that signed up to just go in and rush the passer on 3rd and 25," Bulldog said. "That's the only play he plays on."[29]

That kind of specialization was unheard of in 1940s. In the old days pro football was a working man's game that paid blue-collar wages, even for superstars, and there were no benefits. None. Players were paid by the game with checks so small they could be cashed at the dime store. And the paychecks stopped when the season ended. When a player retired, there was no health insurance, no pension, and no severance pay.

As great as he was—and there was no greater two-way lineman in the history of professional football—Bulldog Turner never made much money in the NFL, and the money he made slipped through his enormous fingers like dry West Texas sand. When he retired, the attention went away. Even the iconic nickname faded from memory. The general public, even the NFL and the sports world, forgot about him. He lived out his last days in relative obscurity at his old ranch house on Cowhouse Creek. His only steady income was a Social Security check. The mighty NFL, flush with billions from television contracts, took care of its TV stars but turned its back on the founding fathers who built the game. Bulldog sold some of his most prized possessions, even most of his ranch, to keep creditors away. He did not receive a pension from the NFL until the last few years of his life. While mediocre athletes with signing bonuses became instant millionaires in the age of television, Bulldog Turner, a first-round draft choice, a unanimous selection to the Pro Football Hall of Fame, and one of the early superstars of the NFL, sold chunks of his ranch, his priceless mementos, and his signature to pay his medical bills.

But while he lived, Bulldog Turner never looked back and never complained. Life was a party. "I had me some great times," he said. The money wasn't important. And in some ways he was fortunate, and he knew it. He was almost overlooked in the stark isolation of his home in Depression-era West Texas.

His world was a near desert. Even today few people live there. It is a quiet place. The only sounds out in the countryside are the soft whistle of the wind, the shrill bark of a coyote, the gentle whirr of a wind turbine, or the steady rattle and hum of an oil rig. Although West Texas has beautiful cities and a diverse landscape, most towns are still tiny dots on a map separated by vast distances and miles of wide-open empty spaces. For much of the year the environment is hot and dry, like a summer afternoon in hell, and more to the liking of lizards, scorpions, and snakes than humans. The wind is never still.

West Texas marks, some say scars, everything and everyone it touches. No person is indifferent to it. It either attracts or repels. To some men, like Bulldog Turner and Sammy Baugh, it was home—a place they always returned to. They couldn't be really happy anywhere else. They felt hemmed in by the mountains and claustrophobic in the city. Other men despise the place and fight like hell to escape. Once they get out, they never want to see West Texas again. They are driven to be successful because failure means they might have to go back.

But for naive West Texas schoolboys of the 1930s, energized by testosterone, reared in a society that emphasized manliness, and already well acquainted with sweat and hard work at home, football was a natural fit. There was something glamorous, romantic, heroic, even sexy, about the game. And for the lucky ones, football was a way to escape a life of picking cotton, plowing fields, fixing fence, praying for rain, and eating dust.

In time West Texas became football country and a breeding ground for professional football players in spite of, even because of, its austere landscape and harsh environment.

Must be something in the sand.

Chapter 2
A Tough Row to Hoe

veryday life in rural West Texas has always been a tough row to hoe, and it was especially so when Bulldog Turner grew up there in the first half of the twentieth century. Daily existence was a throwback to the 1800s. The sprawling ranches and tiny one-horse towns were bleak and remote outposts, cut off from civilization. There was little communication with the outside world. There was no electricity, no piped-in water, and no flush toilets. Many West Texas families burned dry cow chips to generate heat in the winter, there being no wood for fuel. An old copy of *Life Magazine* was a treasure. A bath was a luxury. A bath in clean water was extravagant. People looked at the pictures in the Sears and Roebuck catalog for entertainment; then used its pages for toilet paper.

There was little money in circulation. West Texans traded produce or services for the goods they needed or purchased essentials on credit against the fall cotton crop. In a credit-based economy, a family protected its honor and its good name because without them, there was no credit. And without credit, a family could starve. In the 1930s a nickel was as big as a wagon wheel.

Life was tough, even in the best of times. The Great Depression came and went before West Texans found out about it, and even then they hardly noticed. Their daily grind was scarcely interrupted. The people worked six days a week, sunup to sundown, then went to church on Sunday and sometimes stayed all day. In addition to its spiritual purpose, church served an important social function in this lonely and desolate part of the world. Church was a place for adults to relax, visit, and gossip. Young people courted at church. Church was a respite from work and the closest thing to entertainment to be found in some parts of West Texas where amusement of any sort was hard to come by.

Then in the early years of the twentieth century, West Texans discovered high school football, a sport that fit perfectly with that part of the world. Football was a tough, gritty, and masculine game that quickly gained popularity across the state, especially after the Waco High Tigers, coached by Paul Tyson, won four state championships in the 1920s. For players, football was an outlet for physical activity, and it satisfied a desire for competition. Teenagers need a sense of belonging. The football team satisfied that need. To a few young men with athletic ability, football was a means of self-expression. For the community, football was a spectator sport that was fun to watch. The players were performers and celebrities.

The entertainment factor connected the school to the community. Small isolated towns with little going for them took pride in and identified with the local high school football team. In time football became an extension of the school and a part of the community. Football gave tiny towns in the middle of nowhere a source of pride and an identity far beyond their borders. Many people who have never set foot in West Texas know of the Dumas Demons, the Sweetwater Mustangs, the Breckenridge Buckaroos, the Brownwood Lions, the Hamlin Pied Pipers, and the Winters Blizzards.

The shortage of amusements made high school football a hot ticket in West Texas. In a lonely world starved for entertainment, high school football had no competition. In the fall it was the only show in town. Football was a diversion from a world with too much dust, sweat, and work, and not enough joy and excitement. Even though the grandstands were rickety and the playing surface was more sand and stickers than grass, the football field was an entertainment oasis in the middle of the desert.

Then the Rural Electrification Administration brought electricity to West Texas in the 1930s and 1940s, and a wonderful transformation occurred. High school football moved to Friday night. With the games now played under the lights in the cool evenings during non-working hours, attendance soared. The lights on the football field became, quite literally, a beacon in the darkness. The bright yellow glow was visible for miles, attracting millions of flying insects and guiding spectators to the field like a light from heaven. Visitors coming in for the game never had to ask directions to the football field. All they had to do was follow the lights.

As its popularity grew, football became an important source of revenue for the school and the community. Schools benefitted from ticket sales and concessions. Visitors bought gas at the filling station and ate at the Dairy Queen.

Soon Friday night football became a much-anticipated social event. Cultural, ethnic, religious, and political differences were forgotten, as least on Friday night, when everyone pulled together to support the team. West Texas farmers and ranchers spent long lonely hours at work, and they relished any opportunity to fraternize with their neighbors. They could relax and forget their troubles, at least for a while, at the football game. Moms and dads encouraged their sons to play football to keep them occupied and out of beer joints. For youngsters, the football stadium and the church were the only respectable places they could have fun. Any other form of entertainment was sinful or illegal or both.

To the community and the school, football was much more than a game. It was serious business—second only to water in West Texas. Season tickets were passed down from one generation to another or became prized bargaining chips in nasty divorce settlements. There were rumors that premium seat tickets were won and lost in high-stakes poker games or used as collateral to secure loans at the bank.

For coaches, jobs were on the line. Coaching careers were made and destroyed by the success or failure of 11 teenage boys. No one complained when test scores at the high school were low or dropout rates were high, but when the football team went 3-7, heads rolled. Every Friday night, then again at the coffee shop on Saturday morning, the coach's performance was picked apart in minute detail by just about everyone in town. In no other profession was a man under such intense public scrutiny. A popular basketball coach who never won a single district championship could have the gym named after him when he retired. A mediocre superintendent could die at his desk. But the football coach had to win or pack his bags.

To the young men who played it, football was a ritual with an unusual importance attached to it. Football could elevate one's social standing and allow a poor young man to rise above the others. A nobody from the wrong side of the tracks could become a hero if he could score touchdowns. Football was also a confirmation of an important phase in a boy's life. Just like a young Comanche brave became a man by killing a buffalo, a teenage boy confirmed his manhood on the football field.

Of course teenage boys never thought of football in existential terms. To them, football was simply a way to get girls. Guys liked girls, and girls liked guys who played football.

On March 10, 1919, just as football was making the transition from the brutal and bloody "mob" sport of the early days into a socially acceptable event, Clyde Douglas Turner was born in a ranch shack on the high plains of far West Texas. The nearest mark of civilization was the tiny town of Plains, the county seat of Yoakum County, not to be confused with the ghost town of Plains in Borden County or the town of Yoakum in Lavaca County. The town of Plains (Yoakum County) is located 50 miles southwest of Lubbock on State Highway 82 between the ghost town of Tokio, Texas and Lovington, New Mexico, about 13 miles east of the New Mexico state line. In the 1920s there was a courthouse in Plains but only three sides of a town square. There wasn't enough town to make up the fourth side.

Plains comes by its name honestly. The countryside is dull, colorless, featureless, and dry as a mouthful of sand. The entire expanse of Yoakum County is nearly flat, and even today the population density is only about nine people per square mile. As late as 1900 only 26 people lived in the entire county. By 1920, the year after Clyde Turner's birth, the county population had exploded to 500 people and 21,000 cattle.[1]

There are huge tracts of land in this part of the world that humans were never meant to inhabit. A man can fence this land but never tame or discipline it. Sooner or later the forces of nature will rise up to

put man in his place. The wind blows like a sandblaster across the na-
ked landscape without breaking stride. At times the evaporation rate
is twice the rate of precipitation. In this part of the world the temperature routinely hovers above the 90-degree mark for 100 days or more
a year. The sizzling summer heat is so intense that it can make a man
see things that aren't there, especially elusive pools of water that appear on the horizon then vanish without a trace amid the heat waves.

It's a good thing that West Texans see water in their fantasies because they encounter so little of it in real life. West of Interstate 35 (a
standard dividing line between East and West Texas), average yearly
rainfall drops to below 30 inches, and the farther west one goes, the
less it rains. Out on the high plains a half-inch rain is front-page news
and can cause flooding in low-lying areas. Only the heartiest vegeta-
tion can survive in the desert-like conditions. Just the sight of a tree
is cause for excitement and has been known to inspire poetry. Years
ago the lack of water was even a religious issue. The Baptists, whose
methods of operation require a certain amount of standing water,
often resorted to baptism in a muddy stock tank.

Of course when it does rain, the plains come alive. The smell of a
West Texas rain after a long dry spell is intoxicating. The grass, what
little there is, turns green almost before your eyes. Farmers swear
that after a good spring rain you can hear corn grow. It makes a low
popping sound.

There are people who like this empty, lonesome, and remote part
of the world, but not many. Most humans naturally prefer trees and
green grass. And even those people who claim to like the rural areas
of West Texas admit that aesthetics is not a factor. What they enjoy
is the solitude, the peace, and the slower pace of life. West Texas is
like whiskey. One has to acquire a taste for it. And it is not really the
taste when it hits your tongue but how it affects you that makes it
appealing.

The modern world teaches us to be comfortable in defined spaces,
but the area around Plains, Texas has little definition. It is not unusual
for first-time travelers on the high plains to feel ill at ease and disori-
ented. One direction looks like another. There are no borders or reference points. Much of West Texas is a whole lot of nothing. There are
rivers with no water, towns with no people and roads that go nowhere.

Distances are hard to judge because the ground is so flat. There is not a hill or hump in the earth to impede the view to the horizon in any direction. It is said on the high plains that a man can see forever; then stand on a can of tuna and see another hundred miles.

There is a reason that West Texas was some of the last open country in the lower 48 to be settled. People had to be tricked into going there. When land speculators had trouble attracting buyers, they lured naïve and unsuspecting customers to West Texas communities with false promises, cruel hoaxes, and grandiose names like Sweetwater, Big Spring, Big Lake, Springlake, Lakeview, Happy, Pleasant Valley, Garden City, Roaring Springs, Eldorado, Eden, Veribest, Water Valley, and Goodland, but towns with names like Notrees, Needmore, Plainview, Duster, Cactus, Sandhill, Loco, and Levelland are much closer reflections of reality.

In Old West times, criminals and desperadoes came to this godforsaken place to escape the law. Nomadic Native Americans passed through—quickly no doubt—on their way to the next watering hole. Almost no one lived here then. There was not enough water to drown a man, nor a tree to hang him.

Even today the high plains area is primarily agricultural and rural, with some of the lowest population densities of any region in the continental United States. There are no people, no trees, and no water in large parts of West Texas, just a panorama of land and sky. Much of the country is spectacularly barren; as empty as a beer joint on Sunday morning.

West Texas is all about survival. It is no place for soft or delicate things. Even the plants and animals have to be hardy, resilient, and proficient at self-defense. Any animal too slow to run has armor, claws, or fangs, and almost every plant has some kind of protective shield that will stick, sting, stab, prick, pierce, blister, burn, or irritate any human who touches it or animal that tries to eat it. And West Texas teaches patience. Farmers and ranchers wait with resolve and determination for the next good rain that might not come for six months. A cactus only 12 inches tall may have taken a half century to get there.

The people who live here now are tough, resourceful, and independent, just like the Native Americans, the outlaws, and the pioneers who came before. They work hard and play hard. They spend a lot of time alone, which makes them peculiar and a little crazy. Their isolation from the rest of the world produces some unusual habits and distinctive ways of expression. They entertain themselves and those around them with humor, tall tales, and music. They appreciate the simple things in life. They'll drive a hundred miles on a bad road for a cold beer and a chicken fried steak. They like their space. They are friendly but standoffish with strangers. The mystique of the Old West still lives in this part of the world. West Texans don't trust government, and they carry guns.

One of the few geographical features that breaks the monotony of the landscape around Plains, Texas is Sulfur Springs Draw, which cuts through the middle of town. Ranchers once watered their cattle in the puddles along the draw. Then when West Texans bought cars and trucks, they used the draw as a roadway to eastern New Mexico. The draw is the headwaters of the Colorado River, but massive pumping of underground water for irrigation and for town use has caused the water table to plunge like the stock market in 2008. Sulphur Springs, along with every spring in Yoakum County, has run dry. Even when the spring did flow, the water had a foul taste and smelled like rotten eggs. Today Sulphur Springs Draw is a city park.

The Dust Bowl hit Plains like a nine-pound hammer, but the town's designation as the county seat, along with the discovery of oil in Yoakum County in 1936, saved it from the fate of that other town of the same name in Borden County. Today Plains has a stable population of about 1,500.

In the early years of the twentieth century, Willie Lloyd (Bill) Turner met Ida Faye Rushing at a church social in rural Yoakum County. Both Bill and Ida were West Texans born and raised, and like most West Texans of that time, they grew up fast and married young. They said their vows on March 4, 1917 in Tokio, Texas. Clyde Turner was their second child.

"I come from Yoakum County," Clyde explained, "way out in West Texas where my dad was a cowboy. He worked for big ranches. They had to be big to make a living, because that wasn't too good a country up there. No trees or nothing."[2]

But a man with a family needs a more stable profession, so Bill took up farming. Then in the early 1920s the Turners moved to town.

"I was born in a little cabin on a ranch in 1919," Clyde recalled, "and when I was three or four we moved into a town called Plains."[3] Bill ran a combination service station and grocery store in Plains. There was a great advantage to being in the grocery business during the Depression. At least the family always had something to eat. Ida was a school teacher, and she had a small but steady paycheck.

Bill Turner's family was from Brownfield, Texas where his father had a good business repairing wagons. The Turners migrated to Brownfield from Olney, just west of Wichita Falls, but little is known about their travels before that. Some family members say the Turners came from Northern Ireland through the Carolinas. We do know that Bill Turner was born in Taylor County near Abilene and that the name Turner is English. In Old English a person's name often reflected his occupation. Turner means "one who uses a lathe."

Ida Rushing's family came to West Texas from Tennessee. The Rushings raised cattle on a section of land near Tokio. Ida was born there in 1893. She was smart, and she was tough. She could cook, sew, pick cotton, dig post holes, string barbed wire, and kill rattlesnakes. She was an educated lady, with a degree from Texas Women's University in Denton, and she could ride horses and work cattle as well as any man.

A section of land is a square mile (640 acres) and may seem like an empire, but such a ranch is tiny by West Texas standards. The biggest ranches in this part of the world measured their acres in the millions and were bigger than some European countries. But the Rushing place was small. It had no surface water, and without an Aeromotor windmill to draw water from the aquifer, a coyote would die of thirst on a hundred sections. Ida's family scratched out a living on that little place until oil was discovered there in the 1930s. During that decade, drought and dust storms tormented West Texans and turned this part of the state into hell on earth, but oil revenues made the Great Depression a little less depressing, even at ten cents a barrel.

West Texas and hell have always had things in common, and beginning in 1930, the lines of distinction blurred even more. During the spring and summer of 1930 almost no rain fell on the high plains. The Turners were used to drought, and it took a lot of dry weather to get their attention. The average yearly rainfall was only 16 inches in far West Texas. This part of the world had been subject to cycles of rain and drought for thousands of years. But this drought was unprecedented. Months went by, and not a drop of rain fell. Tanks and streams dried up. The ground split open so wide, a horse could break a leg in the cracks. Bees flew around in a confused state, unable to find enough moisture to make honey.

Then the winds came. It's always windy on the high plains, but not like that. And the supercharged wind combined with drought and some unwise agricultural practices caused environmental catastrophe. Native prairie grasses were drought resistant but they had been plowed under to plant cotton and corn. With the surface laid bare, but without moisture to keep the plants alive that held the soil in place, the winds picked up the loose, powdery topsoil, lifted it into the atmosphere, and dropped it by the ton on St. Louis, Kansas City, Philadelphia, Cleveland, Washington, and New York. That winter the snow in Boston turned red. All across the southern plains, massive dust storms blocked out the sun and turned high noon into midnight.

> A dust storm hit, and it hit like thunder;
> It dusted us over and it covered us under;
> Blocked out the traffic and blocked out the sun.
> Straight for home all the people did run.
> So long, it's been good to know you.
>
> *From "Dusty Old Dust" by Woody Guthrie*

The Dust Bowl produced unusual phenomena not seen before. Sand blowing at blinding speed across barbed wire created static electricity causing the wire to spark and glow. The electrical charge exchanged by the simple act of shaking hands could knock a man to the ground. Cattle ran around in circles until they dropped dead—their lungs were filled with dirt. People were known to get lost and die of suffocation on the way back from the outhouse. Chickens mistook daytime dusters for nightfall and went to roost. Ships 300 miles out in the Atlantic could see an auburn haze in the western sky. Radio evangelists, preaching from powerful megawatt transmitters in Acuña, Mexico and other locations south of the Rio Grande, predicted the end of the world.

Dust in the air was not unusual on the high plains, but the magnitude of these storms was beyond belief. Dirt particles, as fine as talcum powder and propelled by high winds, penetrated every tiny crack of the house on the north and west side. When a big duster hit, families hunkered down inside and gazed at each other in despair as a dusty fog filled the room and settled gently on the furniture. At suppertime, the Turner kids drew pictures or played tic tac toe in the dust that quickly covered the kitchen table. Ida always waited until the last minute to set the table to give dust less time to settle on plates, glasses, knives, forks, and spoons. She kept lids on the pots until the last minute. Still, dirt got in the food before hungry kids could get it to their mouths. Every food item on the table, cabbage, turnip greens, and even buttermilk, had a gritty taste. The day after a duster, Ida cleaned the floor with a corn scoop.

The lack of water drove away the birds, and without birds to keep the insect population in check, bugs multiplied exponentially. Spiders invaded houses looking frantically for water and shade. Scorpions crawled inside boots left on the floor. Women killed centipedes by the bucketful.

The drought killed most of the crops on the Plains. Grasshoppers took care of the rest. The grasshoppers came, a vision right out of the Old Testament, and descended on West Texas in an ominous flying cloud. In some places the insects were so thick they clogged radiators. They stripped leaves and bark from trees and ate clothes on the clothesline. They devoured gardens in a few minutes. They even stopped trains. Their pulverized bodies made the rails slick, bringing Santa Fe Railroad traffic to a standstill.

But even in the depths of the Dust Bowl, West Texans kept their sense of humor. It was about all they had left. They told the story of a cat blown off its feet in a high wind that rolled across the plains like a tumble weed all the way to Oklahoma. It was so dry, they said, trees chased dogs. A farmer fainted when a raindrop hit him on the head and had to be revived by throwing a bucket of sand in his face.

Still, the Dust Bowl shook West Texas to the core and turned many families into high-plains refugees. Some people followed the desperation road to California, while others, like the Turners, moved east just far enough where the grass was a little greener and the rain fell a little more often. In the early 1930s, Bill and Ida moved their family, three sons and a daughter, to Sweetwater—a small town on the lower plains 40 miles west of Abilene. Nolan County, of which Sweetwater is the county seat, is named for Phillip Nolan—a wild horse trader and freebooter killed by the Spanish army in 1801. The town of Sweetwater began as an Apache campsite. After the Civil War, buffalo hunters used the area as a base camp because the water in Sweetwater Creek, unlike many gypsum streams in West Texas, tasted particularly sweet. In the 1930s Sweetwater was known as a whistle stop on the Santa Fe Railroad. In more modern times it is renowned for harvesting the wind and rounding up rattlesnakes.

Sweetwater was not a big town, but it afforded the Turner children opportunities they would not have had in Plains. For one thing, Sweetwater had a big fancy high school, called Newman High School, after rancher James F. Newman who donated the land. For another, it had football. The team played on a field that was once Rancher Newman's private horse track. (The Mustang Bowl remains there today.) The high school first played the game in 1909. That year the Mustangs played Big Spring twice and got walloped both times. The school played a limited schedule throughout World War I, and then got serious in 1919. Sweetwater has been a hot bed for high school football ever since.

The Turner children were a good fit for this sports-minded town. None of them shunned work or feared hell. All were athletes.

The oldest, Lloyd James (Jay), was born on November 28, 1917 in Big Spring. In 1937 he played freshman football at Hardin-Simmons, but he got married and left school. He was also an amateur boxer and a very good one. Tutored by the former professional fighter Bobby Clark, Jay won state titles in both the Texas Amateur Athletic Federation and the Golden Gloves heavyweight division. He looked slender for a heavyweight, but his punches arrived like a sledgehammer and as sudden as a West Texas windstorm.

In the summer of 1940, Bobby Clark took Jay to the TAAF boxing tournament in Abilene. Jay won the heavyweight division by a technical knock-out (TKO) over Len Joeris from Texas A&M. Then in the finals at the state meet in San Angelo, Jay defeated Gilbert Stromquest of Austin by a unanimous decision.

Jay fought in a contest that Flem Hall, sports editor for the *Fort*

Worth Star-Telegram, called the most exciting bout in Golden Gloves history. On February 17, 1941, before 7,000 raucous fans in Fort Worth, Jay faced Aubrey "Fatty" Martin of Milford in the State Championship for Golden Gloves. For two rounds Fatty barely threw a punch. He had no time. He was too busy picking himself up from the canvas. Jay knocked his opponent down four times in the first two rounds, but each time Fatty took a nine count and got to his feet. Then in the last round Jay walked into a wild and wicked right hand. The blow staggered Jay, but he stayed vertical and won the fight by a decision.

The morning after the tournament in Fort Worth, Jay met with Fred Browning, a wealthy Fort Worth gambler and businessman, who owned a large percentage of Lew Jenkins's contract. Jenkins, from Sweetwater, was the current light heavyweight champion of the world. Browning wanted Jay to turn pro, but Jay declined the offer, along with the opportunity to represent Texas in the National Golden Gloves Tournament of Champions in Chicago in the summer of 1941. He was a cattle buyer with a wife and two young children to support. He never fought again after winning the state Golden Gloves championship.[4]

Jay Turner was the picture of youth, health, and vitality until the morning he could not stop the blood gushing from his nose. Over the next two years he suffered a series of blackouts, nosebleeds, and blurred vision. In spring 1945, he traveled to Scott and White Hospital in Temple for diagnosis and treatment, but on the return home he got sick while driving through Mineral Wells. He checked himself into the hospital there and died a few weeks later at the age of twenty-seven. The family always believed that head injuries suffered while boxing led to high blood pressure and heart disease that caused his death.[5]

Virgil Lee Turner was born on April 9, 1925 in Plains, Texas. His father called him "Dugie," a derivative of "doggie"—cowboy slang for a longhorn calf. As a teenager Dugie was a Golden Gloves boxer (middle weight), a track and basketball star and a record-setting, 164-pound, single wing tailback at Newman High School in Sweetwater. Dugie was good enough that Coach Frank Leahy gave him a shot at making the football and boxing teams at mighty Notre Dame, but Dugie left South Bend after a few months to join the Army during World War II. PFC Turner was a machine gunner in the 242nd infantry unit—later assigned to the Rainbow Division, 7th Army. In December

1944 the Army rushed the infantry regiments of the Rainbow Division to Europe to counter a possible development believed to be brewing near the Ardennes in Belgium. Those units, including the 242nd, went into action almost immediately, with no artillery support or backup, defending a 31-mile stretch of the Rhine River during the Battle of the Bulge. On January 9, 1945, in heavy fighting along the Rhine, the Germans overran Dugie's forward position.[6]

While the rest of the Rainbow Division slugged its way across Germany, liberating several concentration camps along the way, including Dachau, Dugie Turner and the other POWs from his unit were up to their dog tags in mud and filth at Stalag IX-B, near Bad Orb, Germany, about 30 miles northwest of Frankfort. The camp held prisoners from France, Italy, Serbia, Russia, and the United States. For 86 days his family back in West Texas did not know if Dugie was alive or dead—only that he was missing in action.

Then in early April of 1945, just as the U. S. 44th Infantry Division approached the outskirts of Bad Orb, the Germans guarding Stalag IX-B suddenly vanished.[7] The liberators moved in and were shocked by what they found. Many of the POWs were in bad shape. Dugie weighed just 137 pounds, down from 190 when captured. For his actions that winter the Army awarded Dugie the Good Conduct Medal, the World War II Victory Medal, and the Bronze Star.

Most of the large daily American newspapers routinely printed long alphabetical lists of soldiers returning from Europe and the Pacific, and the hopes of the Turner family soared when Ida read the name "V. Turner" one day in the newspaper. Still, she was not completely sure it was her son until Dugie walked through the front door on May 4, 1945. His first words to his mother were, "What's for supper? I'm starved."[8]

The uncertainty of Dugie's wartime situation only magnified the Turner family's grief, since Jay was dying in a Mineral Wells hospital. But Jay seemed more concerned for his brother than himself, and the family says it was a desire to see Dugie again that kept Jay alive, at least for a time. Jay died on April 15, 1945, two days after he learned that his brother was alive. Dugie did not find out about his brother's death until he got back to West Texas.[9]

After the war Dugie played football at Hardin-Simmons University in Abilene where he was one of the top rushers in the nation. He averaged over 100 yards a game in 1946. At Hardin-Simmons he shared a room with Dan Blocker, a good-natured, 300-pound West Texas cowboy from O'Donnell (between Lamesa and Lubbock) who later played Hoss Cartwright on the popular TV show "Bonanza."[10] Dugie married Betty Lambert from Sweetwater on May 29, 1946. He earned a bachelor's degree from Mary-Hardin Baylor College in Belton, Texas and spent the rest of his life teaching and ranching. Dugie died on June 1, 1979 and is buried in Greenbriar Cemetery near Gatesville, Texas.

Daughter Ilene, the youngest of the Turner family athletic dynasty, was born on October 18, 1927 in Plains. In high school she played full-court basketball when she wasn't herding cows and picking cotton. In 1945 her team at Hermleigh High School beat Highland for the district championship. Ilene, a forward, was high scorer in the championship game with 18 points, and she made the all-tournament team. Later that year Hermleigh played in the Girls State Basketball Tournament in Hillsboro.[11] Ilene married Lee Roy Hairston, a handsome West Texas cowboy, on March 4, 1947 in Sweetwater. They raised three daughters on a ranch along the banks of Dodd's Creek just west of Gatesville.

But the most unlikely athlete in the family was Clyde. In junior high and high school he was skinny and slow. He had none of the physical characteristics that would one day terrify running backs and intimidate receivers in the National Football League. The people in town knew him as Jay Turner's little brother. There was certainly no outward sign that he would one day become a football legend. As a boy he worked cattle, picked cotton, did odd jobs at his father's store, and went to school. In those days there were no organized sports at all at the school in Plains. Clyde never even saw a football until, at age 13, he saw a picture of one in a Sears and Roebuck Catalog. Until high school he never expressed an interest in the game.

Plains, Texas, had no television, magazines, or daily newspapers. Some families had crystal radios, but weak batteries restricted their use to short periods of time. That mattered little because most radio signals pooped out before they reached Plains. The small amount of sports news that penetrated the vacuum around Plains was about Joe Louis, Lou Gehrig, or Babe Ruth. There was no football team in Plains. There may not have been a single football in all of Yoakum County.

But all that changed in 1932 when Bill and Ida moved off the high

Clyde Turner is holding the flag. Baby sister Ilene is in the arms of a babysitter. Taken in Plains, Texas around 1930. Courtesy of Pat Turner.

plains to Sweetwater in Nolan County, 150 miles to the east. "Up there in Plains you went all the way from the first grade to graduation in the same school building," Clyde recalled, "and of course there was no such thing as a football team. I didn't know anything about football 'til after we moved to Sweetwater. In 1932 my dad went over there and traded for some property and started buying and selling cattle, and then he came back and got us."[12]

"When I was in high school," Clyde explained, "we had just moved from way out in West Texas where I was born and raised, and we moved to Sweetwater because our school out there was losing its affiliation. I had a brother just older than me and my mother wanted him and all of us to go to college. We wouldn't be able to go to college from out there so we moved to Sweetwater where he graduated from high school, and he, as far as I know, is still the youngest student to graduate from Sweetwater. He was 13."[13]

The family bought a big two-story house on the north side of town (destroyed by fire a few years later). Bill ran a gas station in Sweetwater and bought a cotton farm near the town of Dunn (Scurry County), between Sweetwater and Snyder. There is evidence that Bill Turner was a man who enjoyed competition and that his children may have learned from him a strong desire to compete. One year, in a contest sponsored by Montgomery Ward, Bill brought the first bale of cotton to gin in West Texas. Montgomery Ward bought the bale for 15 cents a pound, for a total of $75. Bill Turner was also a businessman and entrepreneur. He bought out the general mercantile store in Dunn and started a meat market. Ida and the kids lived in the big house in Sweetwater during the school year, and then worked on the cotton farm when school was out for the summer.[14]

Growing cotton was one of the few ways to make money in some parts of West Texas, but the uncertainty of rainfall made even that an "iffy" proposition. Then when the rain fell and cotton did grow, there being no mechanical harvesters in West Texas at the time, the stuff had to be picked by hand. And in a world where it is difficult to find two people who agree on anything, there is unanimous agreement among experienced cotton-pickers that picking cotton is a miserable way to make money. No one who has done it has anything good to say about it. Cotton pickers crawled across the fields on their knees in the hot sun with no shade, dragging a long sack behind them that, when full, weighed close to 100 pounds. They were paid by the number of pounds picked.

"I hated to pick cotton worse than anything I've ever done," one old-timer confessed. "Rather be whipped with barbed wire." The fear of spending a lifetime picking cotton drove many a young West Texan to use whatever talents he or she had to avoid that dreadful possibility. In desperation, men turned to gambling, swindling, wildcatting, music, bootlegging, boxing, bank robbery, and football.

Clyde Turner picked cotton when he had to, but like everyone who has done it, he despised it. When no one was looking, he put rocks in his cotton sack so it would weigh more. Even then he made only pennies a day for his misery.

Needless to say, the Turners spent their happiest times at the big house in town. Sweetwater was one of the bigger municipalities in West Texas, and as towns go it was a step up from Plains. Still, no one mistook Sweetwater for Paris, France—or Paris, Texas for that matter.

•••

In 1925 Dorothy Scarborough wrote a book called *The Wind* about a sheltered teenage girl from Virginia who came to live at her cousin's ranch in Sweetwater, Texas. To the girl from back East, Sweetwater was next door to hell. As soon as she arrived, the wind and the sand went to work on her mind. She was especially annoyed by the wind, which never stopped blowing. The isolation and the loneliness of West Texas, accompanied by the constant moan of the wind, were more than she could handle. She slowly went insane. She committed murder, then suicide, all caused by the wind and the sand.

The novel was a bestseller in New York, Chicago, and the West Coast and became a silent film starring Lillian Gish. The film, made in 1928, was one of the last silent pictures released by MGM Studios. The book even sold well in Sweetwater until people actually read it, and when they did, Sweetwater, Texas was not amused, especially when citizens discovered that the story portrayed their town as a dreary, windblown hellhole inhabited by crude, uncivilized, and narrow-minded people. One night citizens brought their copies of *The Wind* into town and had the first book burning in West Texas on the lawn of the Nolan County Courthouse. They say the flames could be seen in Roscoe, eight miles away.

At least there was football in Sweetwater. The local team, the Newman High School (later Sweetwater High School) Mustangs, was the focus of social life in the fall, and Clyde Turner quickly took notice of the attention the players were getting. There were pep rallies every Friday, and when the players traveled to Abilene, Lubbock, San Angelo, Midland, Odessa, Lamesa, Snyder, or Big Spring almost everyone in town came to the train station to see them off. Lettermen were hot stuff, with their red slip-on sweaters with a big white "S" on the front. The prettiest girls gravitated to the boys in the sweaters. In Sweetwater, a boy who didn't play football was invisible.

"The first time I got interested (in football), really, was when I saw those boys in Sweetwater wearing those sweaters," Clyde remembered. "Those guys were really the celebrities, and I kind of liked the idea."[15]

"It was my junior year when I first went to Sweetwater High. I noticed that some of the boys there had a big 'S' on a knit sweater they wore, and that those boys got all the attention. So I decided that maybe I ought to get me one of those knit sweaters. I learned that the boys wearing 'em were football players. Well, I picked cotton after school most of that fall 'cause we needed the money, but I finally told my dad, 'I'm going to quit picking cotton. I'm going out for football.' He asked why, and I said 'I want to get me a sweater.' That's all I wanted was an old slip-on knit sweater with a big 'S' on the front of it."[16]

A young athlete had to work hard to get his letterman's sweater, and when he got it, he walked with a swagger and strutted like a peacock. Girls noticed boys with sweaters. Even an ugly boy with a sweater was practically assured of a date to the prom. The entire community gave football players special treatment. The players, after all, carried the hopes and dreams of the entire town on their shoulders.

"Man, I went through many a rough hour to get that sweater," Clyde recalled. "The first day I went on the field was the roughest day I ever spent on a football field. That includes college through pro. I had cleat marks all over my shins. There were 14 on the squad, the Sweetwater Mustangs, and I was the No. 1 substitute. I played every position except quarterback, I guess."[17] Ironically he did not play center; a position at which he would earn football immortality.

He did get his name in the paper, although few people noticed the words "Clyde Turner," buried in a column on the sports page in the August 27, 1934 edition of *The Big Spring Herald*. Clyde noticed. He cut out the article and carried it around in his pocket until the paper turned brown and disintegrated. Speculating on the coming season, the reporter wrote that one of two boys, Lud Wood or Clyde Turner, would move into the starting tackle slot for the Sweetwater Mustangs that fall vacated by a graduating senior. Lud got the job. The same article described A. J. Roy as "a promising running back." Later Roy would be Clyde's teammate at Hardin-Simmons before losing his life in World War II. A. J. Roy was the first man to call Clyde Turner "Bulldog."

During the difficult times of that long football season, Clyde Turner drew inspiration from some local gridiron heroes. Sammy Baugh was already a legend and the most famous athlete from Sweetwater, but he wasn't the first young man to earn a reputation as a football player beyond Nolan County. That distinction belongs to Granville Myrick "Buster" Mitchell. Buster played end and halfback for the Sweetwater Mustangs in the 1920s. Later he became one of the first Texans to play professional football.[18] Buster Mitchell inspired scores of Sweetwater teenagers, including a young cotton-picker named Clyde Turner, to take up the game.

Buster Mitchell was born on February 16, 1906 in Irene, Texas, a prairie town southwest of Hillsboro. His family moved to Nolan County when Buster was a child. In high school Buster stood 6 feet tall, weighed 190 pounds, and had good speed. The 1923 high school yearbook, the *Yucca Glorioso*, shows him with a look of determination and a thick head of dark curly hair. He played running back and end, and he was the kicker. In 1922 he drop-kicked a 25-yard field goal that beat San Angelo. Buster liked the attention he got playing football but wasn't known for dedication or hard work. The caption under his picture in the yearbook read, "We all want to see 'Buster' train just a little more next year." After high school graduation he played football at Randolph College in Cisco for two years; then at Davis and Elkins College in Elkins, West Virginia.[19]

On November 8, 1929, Davis and Elkins College played West Virginia Wesleyan. Davis and Elkins won the game, but the West Virginia Athletic Association, acting on an anonymous tip, found that the winning side had played an ineligible player. That player, Buster Mitchell, had not passed eight hours of college credits the previous semester. Davis and Elkins forfeited the game.[20] Buster's college career was over.

Then Buster made an amazing discovery. He could play football for money—in a fledgling organization called the National Football League. In fall 1930, Buster signed on to play end for the Ironton (Ohio) Tanks coached by Earle "Greasy" Neale (Hall of Fame 1969). Later he played for the Portsmouth Spartans (and Coach Steve Owen, Hall of Fame 1966), Detroit Lions, New York Giants, and Brooklyn Dodgers. Even after his career in the NFL ended, Buster played, off and on, for several pro and semi-pro teams including the Chester, Pennsylvania Camels of the Eastern Pennsylvania Conference and as a member of an All-Star squad that took on NFL teams in exhibition games.[21]

His statistics are hardly worth mentioning when measured against today's standards. In seven seasons he caught only 13 passes for 169 yards and one touchdown. He carried the ball nine times for 52 yards (5.8 yards per carry) and one touchdown. But he was a hell of a blocker and tackler. He was All-Pro in 1934, primarily for his defensive skills, on an all-star team that included Cliff Battles, Bronko Nagurski, and Bill Hewitt. A Chicago reporter wrote of him, "He's the only wing-man the Bears haven't fooled or flanked this year."[22] Even the immortals had difficulty running his way. He once tackled Red Grange 14 times in a game at Universal Stadium in Portsmouth, Ohio.[23]

During the Depression, Buster Mitchell sometimes traveled by hopping freight trains. A hobo once robbed him as he rode in a box car on his way back to Sweetwater.[24] But when he had money in his pocket, he was something of a dandy. A reporter for the *Abilene Reporter-News* wrote, "Homefolks remember when 'Buster' came back from a successful season sporting a raccoon coat and driving an open air roadster."[25] Buster Mitchell was the envy of every teenage boy in Sweetwater, including Clyde Turner.

The other local hero was a modest man who needed no gimmicks to attract attention. His great talent thrust him into the spotlight.

Samuel Adrian Baugh was born on St. Patrick's Day in 1914 near the railroad town of Temple. His father was a freight handler for the Santa Fe Railroad, and when Sammy was in the 10th grade the company transferred his father to Sweetwater in the big country west of Abilene. Bad news for the Temple Wildcats. Good news for the Sweetwater Mustangs.

Sammy had a gift for throwing things. He dreamed of throwing baseballs in the Major Leagues, but circumstances sent him to TCU, where he was an All-American punter and single-wing tailback, and finally to the Washington Redskins of the NFL. He led the Horned Frogs to a share of the national title and the Redskins to two NFL championships.

Football was a game in transition when Sammy Baugh entered the NFL, and he was uniquely positioned to take advantage of the changes. The old game was a rough and often bloody affair. A big problem was the popularity of mass formations, like the flying wedge, in which the offense, as a tight unit, charged at full speed at a similarly arranged defense. When those formations collided, serious injuries often occurred. There were 19 deaths on American football fields in 1905. The sport was so violent that Baylor University banned football in 1906, although an outcry from students and fans led to its reinstatement, along with some significant rule changes, one year later. After Johnny Airhart, a very popular quarterback and captain of the Simmons College (later Hardin-Simmons) Cowboys, died from injuries suffered in a football game in 1909, the college banned the sport for eight years.

Throughout the early years football was primarily a running game where bulk and brute force held sway over speed and quickness. Contests were low scoring and not very exciting. Passes were as rare as honest politicians and even discouraged by the rules.

But in the 1930s some changes opened up the college and pro games. First, passing became legal from anywhere behind the line of scrimmage. Previously, the passer had to be at least five yards behind the line. Then in 1934 the shape of the football changed. The old ball was fatter around the middle and blunt on the ends, just like in rugby from which the American game descended. The new rules made the ball smaller around the middle, more pointed on the ends and a lot easier to throw.

Coach Darrell Royal always said, "When you throw the ball, three things can happen, and two of 'em are bad." Coach Royal didn't have Sammy Baugh. When Sam wrapped his long slender digits around the new football, he changed the game like no one else before or since. He lit up the passing lanes. He threw anytime, anywhere. He threw in sunshine, rain, or snow. He threw on third and short or fourth and long. It was not unusual for Sammy to throw 50 times a game. He transformed the forward pass from a seldom used trick play into a primary weapon that sparked the great offensive revolution in American football. In the process he changed the game from a low-scoring grunt-and-groan affair with limited appeal into a high scoring contest of speed and finesse that appealed to a much wider audience. Attendance went up. Teams made more money. The NFL gained popularity and respectability. Sammy Baugh did for professional football what Arnold Palmer did for golf. Both men brought excitement to their respective sport that attracted millions of new fans. Sammy Baugh set the tone for Bobby Layne, Otto Graham, Johnny Unitas, Joe Namath, Roger Staubach, Joe Montana, Troy Aikman, Tom Brady, and Peyton Manning.

Sammy Baugh and Clyde Turner did not know each other in high school, but later in life their paths crossed many times on football fields in Chicago, Washington, and New York. "Sammy Baugh was two years ahead of me at Sweetwater High," Clyde Turner recalled, "so that makes two of us from one school that made the Pro Football Hall of Fame. But Sammy had already gone when I started."[26]

Chapter 3
A Silver Lining in a Funnel Cloud

When Sammy Baugh hitched up his pants, slipped on his black dress boots, and caught the train to Fort Worth, he left a big sweater to fill. Clyde Turner wanted to fill it, but his efforts fell short. He played halfback, guard, tackle, and end for the Sweetwater Mustangs, but didn't start a single game.

The Great Depression was in full swing when Clyde Turner and his family were on the move from Plains to Sweetwater in 1932. Unemployment in the United States was 13% and climbing like mercury in a West Texas thermometer. That spring, Texas lawmen captured Bonnie Parker, a waitress from Rowena (near Ballinger), after a failed bank robbery in Kaufman. Bonnie's partner, Clyde Barrow, a refugee from the Ellis County cotton fields, killed a man in a robbery at Hillsboro. The biggest songs on the radio were "All of Me" by Louis Armstrong and "Brother, Can You Spare a Dime?" by Bing Crosby. Johnny Cash was born in Kingsland, Arkansas. The Marx brothers made the film *Horse Feathers*. Elizabeth Taylor was born in London. Bob Wills left Fort Worth for Waco. His Light Crust Doughboys became the Texas Playboys. Babe Didrikson won gold medals in the javelin throw and the 80-meter hurdles at the Olympics in Los Angeles. The Chicago Bears won the 1932 NFL Championship after defeating Buster Mitchell and the Portsmouth Spartans 9–0. The weather was so cold that December in Chicago, the game was played indoors at Chicago Stadium. The field was only 80 yards long. Bronko Nagurski threw a two-yard pass to Red Grange for the game's only touchdown. Portsmouth argued that Nagurski was not the required five yards behind the line of scrimmage when he threw the ball, but the play stood. The German Max Schmeling was the heavyweight champion. Gene Sarazen won the U.S. Open and the British Open. Lamar Hunt, one of the founders of the American Football League, was born in El Dorado, Arkansas. The price of gasoline was 10 cents a gallon. On June 3, Lou Gehrig hit four home runs in a game against Philadelphia. That fall the Yankees beat the Cubs in the 1932 World Series in Babe Ruth's 10th and final World Series appearance. In the fifth inning of game three, the Babe was seen gesturing to the outfield fence as he stood at the plate. Charlie Root's next pitch went out of the park in what is known in history as "Babe Ruth's Called Shot."

But in Sweetwater, only the keenest observers of Mustang football would have noticed Clyde Turner's brief and unremarkable experience as a high school football player. In the summer of 1934 the Turners completed the move from Plains to Sweetwater, and that fall Clyde traded his cotton sack for shoulder pads and a leather helmet. The Mustangs finished the season with a record of 2–6, beating McCamey and Colorado City but losing big to Abilene, Cisco, Lubbock (twice), Big Spring, and San Angelo. The team had a difficulty scoring that was matched by an inability to play defense. In their six losses, the Mustangs crossed the goal line twice but gave up 24 touchdowns. Running backs ran through the Sweetwater defense like wind through a barbed wire fence.

Clyde, as usual, didn't mince words. "That year we had a lousy team," he recalled. "We won maybe a game or two the whole season, but I got my sweater, and in getting it I developed something that I didn't anticipate. I found I loved to play football. So I was real fired up and looking forward to the next football season, but then they said I couldn't play anymore for the high school." Clyde was caught in the eight-semester rule.

"I was 15, see, and I was supposed to have graduated," Clyde explained. "A lot of boys down here in Texas graduated young. Why I don't know. Anyway, I should have graduated, but the move from Plains to Sweetwater was such a big jump that I failed my first year in

Sweetwater and I didn't graduate. I had to go another year. But they said I was ineligible for football."

Watching his senior year from the stands was almost more than he could take. "That nearly run me crazy. I said, 'Heck, I can't stand this.' So I ran off from home. I ran off to see if I could get me a place on a college team. At that time I had an old cow, as I recall, and cows brang about $8. I sold that cow and bought me some new gloves and a new coat, and I think I still had a good bit of money before I left."[1]

Back then it was easy to hitch a ride, and the day after he left home he thumbed his way to Dallas. It was the middle of winter—wet and cold. Big "D" was buzzing about the Texas Centennial exhibit and celebration at Fair Park just south of downtown that would be opening the following year and took no notice of his arrival.

"I hitchhiked around for a while," Clyde said, "and then I went to Fort Worth and checked into a hotel. In those days you could get a room for $1.50 a week, so I stayed there and went around to colleges within hitchhiking distance and told them 'I want to be an athlete.' Every one of them turned me down."[2]

Clyde Turner was bold and confident, but he was not wise in the ways of the world. "I thought I could just walk into a college and persuade them to give me a scholarship," he said. He soon found out it wasn't so easy.

Clyde asked directions to the campus at SMU in Dallas. He found the campus, walked into the coach's office and said, "I want to play football." The answer he got was not what he expected. "We have enough football players. We don't need anymore," and they sent him on his way. He got the same cool reception at TCU in Ft. Worth. No one wanted to waste a scholarship on a skinny kid from Sweetwater who had never started a single game in high school. If a coach hadn't read your name in the paper, he wasn't interested.

Clyde knew the problem. "The trouble was," he explained, "I had no reputation as a football player."[3]

Now Clyde Turner was an optimist by nature, the kind who could see the silver lining in a funnel cloud, but after every college football team in Dallas and Fort Worth turned him down, his resolve and resources were running low. He really thought he would have a scholarship by then. If he didn't get a scholarship soon, he would have to go back to Sweetwater and pick cotton. That bleak prospect haunted him and kept him going.

Out on the highway, with a cold wind blowing in his face, he headed north. He didn't know the name of many colleges, but he knew that the University of Oklahoma was somewhere north of the Red River—if only he could find it. When he left Sweetwater he had his heart set on playing football at SMU or TCU. Now he was tired and hungry and willing to try his luck at any junior college or business school that fielded a football team.

"I had a dime and a candy bar in my pocket when I got out on the highway," said Clyde. "A guy came by in a great big ol' yellow roadster-type car, and he said, 'You got any money to help me buy some gas?' I said, 'No sir, 10 cents is all I've got left.' He said, 'Oh, well, I'll give you a ride anyway.' So we didn't drive but about 40 or 50 miles till he pulled into a gas station and says, 'Well, if you ain't got any money for gas, I believe I'll let you buy me a cigar.' I told him, 'I ain't got but that one dime, and if you want it, I'll buy you that much worth of gas.' Then he said, 'No, I believe I will let you buy me a cigar.' And that fellow spent my last dime for a cigar. My candy bar was the last bite I had to eat for five days and five nights."[4]

The cigar smoker in the yellow roadster took Clyde to Lawton, near Fort Sill, in southern Oklahoma. Clyde walked around Lawton for awhile, and then he saw the lights of a football field. He walked towards the lights until he found the field house at Cameron State Agricultural College. Clyde knew it by reputation. "I had heard they kind of took tramp athletes," he said. This, he sensed, was his last chance. He walked into the coach's office and announced, "I want to play football."

Even in that gridiron backwater the coaches had to snicker at a kid who was built like a fence post and whose name they had never seen in print. They had no place for him, and no scholarship. But the boy had a gaunt, hungry look about him, and out of kindness, or pity, and the time being near noon, the coaches invited the starving cowboy to go with them to the cafeteria before sending him down the road on a cold winter afternoon. Even though he was starved, Clyde passed on the opportunity.

"I'll tell you how country I was," Clyde remembered. "I got up to

Lawton, and I went in to meet the athletic director and the coach and all. I had been better than two days getting there. It was wintertime, and I was half frozen. The coach looked me over and said, 'Son, why don't you come over to the cafeteria with us and have lunch?'"

"Well, that word cafeteria scared me to death. Never heard of it. Didn't know what a cafeteria was. So rather than expose my ignorance, I said, 'No thank you. I just ate before I came in.' Which was a lie because I hadn't eaten in two days. I felt so ignorant that I got out of there and headed for Wichita Falls."

Now there was nothing left for Clyde to do but try to get back to Sweetwater before he starved to death. "I was two days getting to Wichita Falls," Clyde recalled, "which made five days and five nights without a meal. In the morning I hitchhiked down as far as Throckmorton, and I was starving to death. I walked into a filling station, which also was kind of a grocery store, and I asked, 'How much are them apples?' The man had some green apples there and, as I told you, I had bought me some new gloves when I left home and I wanted to find out what I could get most for my gloves. I said, 'I want to trade my gloves for something to eat.'

"The man said, 'I'll trade you a sack of them apples for your gloves. They're 25 cents a sack.'

"That was a big old sack—I'd say half a bushel in there. Well, I was so hungry that I traded him the gloves and I tied into them apples. But I ate only about half an apple and I'm full. I hadn't eaten anything in so long that my stomach just drawed up. And there I got the whole sack. So I was out there hitchhiking and carrying that sack of apples with me and I thought, 'I could have traded for something a lot easier to carry.'

"Finally a guy stopped and said, 'Where are you trying to get to?'

"'I'm trying to get to Sweetwater,' I said. I wanted to get home. 'Well, I'm going to Sweetwater,' he said. And he took me home. I had been gone three weeks. I walked in the house and mamma started crying.

"I guess I looked real bad. I had lost a lot of weight and my eyes were sunk back. My dad laughed and said, 'Well, it wasn't so great out there, you seeking your fortune.' But I had been out there trying to get myself a scholarship because I wanted to play football. I didn't care about no fortune."[5]

Just when it looked like Clyde Turner would never play football again, Frank Kimbrough, the coach at Hardin-Simmons University invited Clyde to a tryout. Hardin-Simmons is a small Baptist school in Abilene, 40 miles east of Sweetwater. In the late 1930s enrollment was about 1,000. Hardin-Simmons wasn't TCU or SMU, but that didn't matter to Clyde. It was the chance he had been looking for. He wouldn't have been happier if Knute Rockne was in the parlor with a full scholarship to Notre Dame.

Coach Kimbrough recalled the first time he heard Clyde Turner's name. "Ed Henning, the Sweetwater High School coach, was a good friend of mine," Kimbrough said. "I went over in the spring to see if he had anyone I could use.

"Henning didn't, but said there was a boy in school who might make a great player. He said the boy's name was Turner, but hadn't played football because his parents moved around a lot on a railroad job and wasn't eligible under the one-year transfer rule.

"We looked for the boy but couldn't find him. I told Henning to have the boy come to see me at Abilene. Turner came over and wanted a tryout. He was just a big rawboned kid who weighed about 170 and stood about six-two."[6]

That spring, Clyde said, "[I] trained like you wouldn't believe. I ran something like 15 miles a day getting ready for that camp."[7] A. J. Roy, Clyde's Newman High School teammate, was also invited to try out at Hardin-Simmons. The two boys trained together under the hot West Texas sun, and they discussed their chances of making the team. They were nervous about the tryout and wanted to give themselves every possible advantage, even to the extreme of inventing tough-sounding nicknames for themselves that might catch the attention of the coaches.

"I've forgotten just exactly how it all came about but we were both goin' to get a tryout down at Hardin-Simmons and we worked out during the summer before we went down there—we worked out together. Of course we would do a lot of running up and down the highway," Clyde explained, "and we came up with an idea if neither of one of us was looking very good in the scrimmage down there the other would cheer him on."[8]

This is the plan they concocted that summer. If A. J. was having a bad practice, Clyde would yell, "Hey Tiger, you need to get your butt in gear." If Clyde wasn't having a good day, A. J. would say, "Hey Bulldog, you ain't cracking these boys like you did back home." Clyde picked the name "Bulldog" himself. He thought it created an aura of fierceness. Well, both men made the team, so their plan wasn't fully implemented, but when Roy told the story in the locker room, Clyde Turner's nickname stuck like a dried Rice Krispy to a cereal bowl— probably because it fit so well the way he attacked the game. From that moment on, he was Bulldog. His given name became an answer to a sports trivia question. No one but his mother called him Clyde again. There are only two professional football players who nicknames are inscribed in the Pro Football Hall of Fame: Elroy "Crazylegs" Hirsch and Clyde "Bulldog" Turner.

"Yeah. The hard part has been shucking the name," Bulldog admitted. "It didn't bother me while I was playing, but after I've gotten to be 95 years old, it's embarrassing. You know even the telephone company called me and asked me if I'd list my name as 'Bulldog Turner' because they have so many calls from people looking for Bulldog Turner because nobody knows your first name. So I'm listed in the phone book as Clyde Douglas 'Bulldog' Turner. I still can't get rid of it."[9]

"I've got teammates and classmates I went to school with for four years who don't know my name is Clyde."[10]

"I've got first cousins that don't even know my name."[11]

"You can call me whatever you want, young man," he once told a reporter, "but *nobody* calls me Clyde."[12]

Still, no one can deny he got a lot of mileage out of that name. It gave him notoriety and more than his share of headlines. He might not admit it, but that handle gave him a psychological advantage and helped build the legend. It was like he was two different people. Clyde Turner was an ordinary guy, but Bulldog Turner, the person he invented, struck fear in the hearts of opponents and made rookies quiver in their cleats.

Then an oversight almost torpedoed his college plans. When he registered for classes that summer, Bulldog discovered that he had forgotten one small detail. He left high school before graduation and had forgotten to go back. He never graduated. Then his mother bailed him out. Ida Turner went to J. H. Williams, the Newman High School principal, and talked him into letting Bulldog do some extra school work over the summer. In August 1936, Bulldog got his high school diploma and entered Hardin-Simmons to study journalism and play football.

Bulldog had made the cut, but he still faced an uncertain future. There were no guarantees. "Back then almost the entire football team was on a full scholarship," Bulldog said. "Nobody had any money—this was during the '30s.

"Now what you have to remember is that a scholarship wasn't like it is today. It was more a day-to-day thing, and Hardin-Simmons was pretty good in those days. They had two groups come in—110 the first week and 38 the second. I went in the second week, and there was only one other boy from that group that made it. We got room, board and tuition, but we had to buy our own books, and we were supposed to take care of two jobs. I had to sweep out the gym and wait tables, but I kind of farmed out the sweeping after a while. It was tough, but I loved it. And the more I played, the more I liked the game."[13]

He felt at home on the field and in the locker room, but Bulldog had some trouble fitting in socially in Abilene. College students whose parents had enough money to send their children to a private college could be hard on a poor country boy who craved acceptance. He wanted attention and sometimes tried too hard to get it.

The Brand, the student newspaper at Hardin-Simmons, was some-times vicious and haughty in reporting his social life. A campus poll named him the student with the "poorest table manners."[14] Bulldog took it quietly, but the cruelty probably angered him and made him even more determined to make something of himself. So he worked harder than ever on the football field—the place where talent, not wealth or social status, was paramount. And one day he would show them all. When he became a star, no one would make fun of him again.

In the meantime Bulldog had to watch his P's and Q's because even after a player made the team, his scholarship could be revoked at any time for bad grades, misconduct, or poor performance on the field. There was a cruel ritual at Hardin-Simmons for players whose services were no longer needed. "If you fouled up they would 'break your plate,'" he said. "If you went to dinner one night and your plate was broken, that meant you were gone."[15]

Players who managed to keep their plates in one piece not only got scholarships, but also received privileges and special treatment not available to regular college students, especially when it came to highly prized summer jobs. A group of Abilene businessmen always took care of athletes in exchange for premium seats at Parramore Field. Most of the players worked in the oil patch. Bulldog worked on a pipeline. Gordon Wood, Bulldog's friend and teammate, worked as a lifeguard at the country club swimming pool. But summers were short for football players. By early August, everyone was back in Abilene for practice.

On a hot August day in 1936, Frank Kimbrough stared in disbelief at a lineup of the latest crop of freshmen cow punchers and cotton pickers he would have to mold into a football team. As usual, he was not impressed. To turn this mess into a team, he said to himself, would take great effort. Perhaps divine intervention. He made a mental note to ask the chaplain for prayers. With a look of disgust on his face, he blew his whistle and said, "Anybody who thinks he's tough, step forward." A skinny kid from Sweetwater, who never learned to hide his candle under a bushel, took a step to the front. Afterwards Bulldog realized he was the only one to step up.

"Naïve wasn't the word," Bulldog said. "I was just country—and dumb."[16]

But stepping up when others held back was vintage Bulldog Turner. And that kind of bravado made an impression on Frank Kimbrough. Bulldog brought a swagger to the field house that fit perfectly with Kimbrough's brand of football. Kimbrough was a rough man, and he expected his players to be the same. His team might occasionally be outscored, but these Baptist boys never backed down and never lost a brawl. In the 1937 Sun Bowl game in El Paso, the Cowboys racked up over 100 yards in penalties in a game marred by several fist fights.[17] Bulldog Turner was always ready to "throw the dukes" when the situation called for it.[18] Playing for Kimbrough would serve Bulldog well when he moved to his next assignment in Chicago.

Meanwhile, that September Bulldog watched from the sidelines as the starting center on the freshman team went down with an injury. Coach Kimbrough asked Turner to try out for that spot. "Right then and there," Turner recalled, "I knew I found my place."

It wasn't long before Frank Kimbrough learned that this Turner kid was no ordinary football player. "He was a natural-born athlete," Kimbrough recalled years later, "and could play any position. We played him at center but made him run with the backs. He weighed 235 by the time he was a senior."[19]

"Ah, I just kept filling out." That's the way Bulldog explained it.[20]

God had given Bulldog Turner a great talent but kept it hidden for a while. Then in college he blossomed as an athlete. By his sophomore year the skinny kid from Sweetwater weighed 190. And he was still growing. By the second game of his sophomore season he was crowding Eddie Bigelow, a popular player from Amarillo and the man everyone assumed had a lock on the starting center job. A reporter for the student newspaper wrote that Bulldog "played end and tackle at Sweetwater, and lacks experience at center, but may qualify for the position before the season ends, some sideline observers believe."[21] By the third game of the season, Bulldog's brilliance had relegated Bigelow to the ranks of a non-playing co-captain.[22]

By his senior year Bulldog stood 6'2" and weighed 235. He had a barrel chest, thick arms and legs, and was solid as a slab of granite. He was football's version of a perfect storm. He had the size of a lineman with the speed of a running back. And he was a natural at any sport he tried. He was an excellent calf roper and a talented golfer. He played intramural basketball, scoring 48 points in a single game. Every year he would register for the Golden Gloves heavyweight division. Some years, no one else would enter.[23]

But football was the game he loved. By his junior year he completely dominated all the small college linemen he played against. He had a combination of the two physical attributes that separate most great football players from the rest of us—he was big *and* fast. He was, and this is no great exaggeration, a man among boys. J. D. "Jakey" Sandefer III heard the following story from his grandfather who was the president of Hardin-Simmons in the 1930s. "I'll tell you how mean Bulldog was. Sometimes in the spring Hardin-Simmons would scrimmage the other colleges in Abilene. One year the Abilene Christian coaches told their linemen if they didn't play well, they would have to play across from Bulldog Turner. Nobody wanted to do that."[24] And his team was a powerhouse. The Hardin-Simmons Cowboys won 23 games, lost 3, and tied 2 during Bulldog's three varsity seasons (1937, 1938, and 1939).

Thanks to Frank Kimbrough and an assortment of top-flight athletes, the Hardin-Simmons football program was formidable, even if it was not well known beyond West Texas. In 1936, while Bulldog played on the freshmen squad, the varsity team won 9 of 11 games, losing only to Baylor and Texas A&M of the mighty Southwest Conference. Baylor beat the Cowboys 13–0 on a muddy field at Municipal Stadium in Waco and was the only team to score in double digits against the Cowboy defense that season. Hardin-Simmons played A&M in Wichita Falls in a game that almost ended in a scoreless tie. When the final Aggie drive stalled inside the Cowboy 10-yard line, A&M kicked a field goal with three seconds on the clock to beat the Cowboys 3–0. In the other nine games Hardin-Simmons barely broke a sweat. The defense posted five shutouts and gave up just 25 points. The offense averaged 34 points a game. The Cowboys beat Texas A&I 39–6 and Fresno State 28–6. They ran wild beating Oklahoma Baptist 52–0. They drubbed West Texas rival Howard Payne 31–0 and rose to number 16 in the nation after defeating Creighton 13–7. On January 1, 1937 the Cowboys defeated El Paso Mines (today The University of Texas at El Paso) 34–6 in the Sun Bowl.

"He [Bulldog Turner] was just a freshman in 1936 and couldn't play on the varsity," remembered Si Addington, quarterback for the Cowboys. "We would love to have had him, but he wasn't eligible yet. Since it was a team made up of mostly seniors, he really took a lot of hazing and teasing from the older players, but we could see he was going to be good."[25]

And yet the extent of his talent was not obvious to everyone. A reporter for the school newspaper wrote, "The pivot [center] position has been a constant source of worry for Cowhand mentors for many seasons, and this year [1937] the problem is more acute that ever. . . . The only man with varsity experience at center is Edgar Bigelow, and he saw only slight action in '36. Unless either Bulldog Turner or R. E. Campbell, sophomores, come through with sensational developments, the very heart of the '37 club will be susceptible to failure."[26]

A quote from the 1937 *Illustrated Football Annual* contained perhaps the first mention of Bulldog Turner in the national press. While discussing the Cowboys' coming season the magazine stated, "The ends and guards are on par with the best but center looks like a danger spot. If Turner, a big, likely looking youngster, comes through at center, the Cowboy first string will leave little to be desired." Bulldog delivered, but not without some drama.

In 1937, Bulldog's first varsity season, the Cowboys won 8 games and tied 1. The star of the team was T. Burns McKinney, a little All-American running back from Wichita Falls. That year Hardin-Simmons beat Fresno State 14–7, walloped Kansas State 66–6, and destroyed West Texas State 40–0. The only blemish on an otherwise perfect record was a 7–7 tie with Howard Payne—the other West Texas Baptist school.

In those days there was a fierce competition between Hardin-Simmons and Howard Payne, exceeded in intensity only by the rivalry between Hardin-Simmons and Texas Tech. Between 1926 and 1935, Tech (called the Matadors until adopting the Red Raider mascot in 1935) and Hardin-Simmons played 10 football games. Tech won five games, Hardin-Simmons won four, and one game ended in a scoreless tie. At stake in many of those games was the unofficial college football championship of West Texas. But Bulldog Turner never experienced the Cowboy/Red Raider rivalry because the two schools broke relations in 1935 after a group of Hardin-Simmons students threw eggs at buses carrying the Texas Tech band back to Lubbock after a game in Abilene. Eventually the schools made up, and competition resumed as intense as ever in 1940, but too late for Bulldog to take part in it.

In the meantime, other rivalries developed with schools far beyond West Texas, made possible by the railroad. "We used to travel by train in those times, you know," Cowboy quarterback Si Addington recalled. "The team, the yell leaders, all the students, our parents, teachers and girl friends would all load on a special train for a road trip. We used to have a ball on those trips."[27]

In 1937 the Cowboys rode the train all the way to Los Angeles to play Loyola Marymount. The trip itself was a remarkable feat for a small, frugal college during the Depression, and some citizens in Abilene questioned the necessity of a trip to the West Coast when there were plenty of football teams to play a lot closer to home. Then Texas Tech one-upped the Cowboys by taking a train to Fort Worth and boarding an American Airlines flight to Michigan (the first such flight in the school's history) for a game against the University of Detroit. The expense of the Hardin-Simmons trip was forgotten in light of Tech's extravagance.

Still, the journey to sunny Southern California was the experience of a lifetime for the country boys from Abilene. The trip began with a rousing sendoff at the train station. Two hundred fans cheered the cowboys as Dr. R. N. Richardson, vice-president of Hardin-Simmons, spoke to the team. Then 29 players, Coach Kimbrough, Gib Sandefer—graduate student manager—and 57 fans boarded the Sunshine Special for California. Three days later the group arrived in Los Angeles. Between practices the team took a tour of Hollywood and visited MGM studios in Culver City where the film *Mannequin*, starring Joan Crawford was shooting on the back lot. The other star of the movie, Spencer Tracy, visited with the team and posed for pictures with the players.[28] Layne "Shotgun" Britton, a quarterback for Hardin-Simmons in the 1920s who worked as Joan Crawford's makeup man, arranged the whole affair.[29]

Even the vast expanse of West Texas was not big enough to contain a character like Shotgun Britton. He was born and raised in Stephenville before graduating from Abilene High School. He picked up the name Shotgun at an early age. He played quarterback at Hardin-Simmons in the 1920s, when he was eligible, which apparently was about half the time.[30] He was known for fast talk and outrageous behavior. He liked to be noticed and talked about. He was one of a long line of colorful characters that West Texas produces more than its share of.

In 1930 Shotgun took his rugged good looks and smooth-talking ways to Hollywood where his craziness was not only tolerated but admired. He landed a small part in a silent film called *The Forward Pass* that starred Douglas Fairbanks and Loretta Young.[31]

Shotgun's style never achieved full expression on the silent screen, so in 1932 he schmoozed his way into a job at MGM studios as a makeup artist because he liked to be around pretty girls. As it turned out his skills with a powder-puff were good—so good that the studio ensured his right hand for $50,000 and his left hand for $40,000, but it was his wicked sense of humor and wild and crazy personality that endeared him to everyone he met, including just about every major star in Hollywood.

Then in 1938, Shotgun was implicated in a scheme to pass phony promissory notes. George Smart, an obscure sound man at MGM, forged the names of celebrities, including Louis B. Mayer, Jeanette McDonald, Nelson Eddy, and Charles Laughton, to notes totaling $100,000. When an officer at the Santa Monica Commercial Savings Bank called MGM studios to see if the notes were good, Shotgun intercepted the call, impersonated Mayer, and covered for Smart. The Los Angeles police arrested Britton and Smart and charged them with forgery and grand theft.[32] But Smart claimed Shotgun was an unwilling participant, and Shotgun said he thought the whole thing was a joke.[33] On August 4, 1938, a California court cleared Shotgun of all charges.[34] Even while accused of a felony, he never wanted for work. If anything the notoriety made him even more popular in the crazy world of Hollywood.

Shotgun did makeup for Greta Garbo, Gloria Swanson, Joan Crawford, Jean Simmons, Robert Taylor, Walter Pidgeon, Ava Gardner, Clark Gable, Lucille Ball, Jane Russell, Bob Hope, Bing Crosby, Robert Young, Marilyn Monroe, Elizabeth Taylor, Robert Mitchum, Frank Sinatra, Sammy Davis Jr., John Belushi, and John Candy. He did makeup for the Frank Capra movie *It's a Wonderful Life* and for Orson Wells in the movie *Citizen Kane*. He was Henry Fonda's makeup man in Fonda's last film, *On Golden Pond*. Robert Mitchum once threw firecrackers into Shotgun's dressing room to wake him up.[35] Sinatra got Shotgun a few scenes in *Tony Rome*, and after that Shotgun played small roles in films. In 1989 he played Grandpa in *Meet the Hollowheads*. He was the "Cheeze Whiz guy" in *The Blues Brothers* in 1990. He appeared on television in *Starsky and Hutch*, *Room 222*, *Felony Squad*, *The Groucho Marx Show*, and *You Bet Your Life*. When Shotgun traveled to New York, he always reported with great fanfare to Toots Shor's the minute he got to town. His name was a regular feature in Hedda Hopper's column.

In his younger days, Shotgun liked to make a splash in his hometown and occasionally returned to Abilene driving a shiny new car and carrying a set of $500 custom-made golf clubs. On one of those jaunts he met Bulldog Turner at the Wooten Hotel in downtown

Abilene. After Bulldog turned pro, he and Shotgun liked to practice the art of "recreational drinking" whenever Bulldog was in Los Angeles.

Meanwhile, the Hardin-Simmons–Loyola football game, watched by 18,500 fans, was a defensive struggle between two excellent football teams. The winning score came on a trick play from the Hardin-Simmons 35-yard line that caught the Lions completely by surprise. The Cowboys broke the huddle and hurried to the line. Bulldog Turner snapped the ball to quarterback Si Addington before the Loyola defense was set. Addington then pitched the ball to Burns McKinney who went 65 yards untouched for the game's only touchdown.

In the meantime, Bulldog proved time and again that he had a flair for the dramatic and a knack for spectacular play in big games against the biggest stars. On October 1, 1938, Hardin-Simmons played Centenary College of Shreveport, Louisiana in a game that drew a lot of attention. It was homecoming at Hardin-Simmons. Alumni filled the stands at Parramore Field to watch the Cowboys take on a football powerhouse. Although Centenary had a small enrollment, the Gents returned 19 lettermen from a team that had shellacked the TCU Horned Frogs and the SMU Mustangs the year before. In the 1930s the Centenary Gents posted victories over Louisiana State University, the University of Texas, and Notre Dame. Led by Winfred "Weenie" Bynum, the great Centenary running back, the Gents beat the Cowboys 26–13 that day in 1938. But the play everyone remembered, and talked about years later, was a pass from Bynum to Birkelbach who tore past Cowboy safetyman Luke Railey. Birkelbach ran untouched for 56 yards, only to be run down in the open field and horse-collared by Bulldog Turner at the three-yard line. One of players watching from the sideline thought the scene resembled a grizzly bear chasing a chipmunk. Hardin-Simmons fans were used to such things, but Centenary players and fans were in shock. No one could believe a man that big could run that fast.[36] That play was a big part in building the legend of Bulldog Turner. Even the usually stoic Frank Kimbrough told a reporter, "With the exception of Weenie Bynum, he [Bulldog] was the best man on the field in the Centenary game."[37]

Bulldog was the only 60-minute man for the Cowboys that afternoon, but it was his defensive play that made people sit up and take notice. Bulldog played linebacker like no one had ever played it before.

A linebacker crouches just behind the line of scrimmage, in a two-point stance with his head up. His job is to quickly analyze the development of every offensive play and be prepared to stop it, be it run or pass. He has to be big enough and tough enough to take on the fullback at the line of scrimmage and fast enough to cover a receiver downfield. His job is all the more complicated because many offensive plays are designed to fool the linebacker with motion going in one direction while the ball carrier goes the other. Quarterbacks and halfbacks use fakes, trickery, and deception to make the linebacker think run when the play is really a pass. A linebacker has to be smart enough to read the play in progress and instantly take the correct action. If he reads it wrong, touchdowns happen.

Bulldog was a natural at linebacker, or "backerup" as it was called back then. A reporter for the *Abilene Reporter-News* wrote, "An outstanding example of line backing as it should be done was given by Bulldog Turner of Hardin-Simmons in the San Francisco, Centenary and West Texas games. He was so keen at diagnosing plays that he often crashed through the line of scrimmage to drop ball carriers for a loss. Then, many times, he backed deep to knock down passes thrown by such experts as Centenary's Weenie Bynum and Canyon's Foster Watkins."[38]

Led by Bulldog Turner at center, the Cowboy offensive unit was just as impressive. Martin "Pug" Marich, a football player at Arizona State who later coached the Phoenix College baseball team to two national championships in the 1960s, described the Cowboys' furious style of gridiron play. "They were in a single wing, and I was told to get in there at defensive end," Marich said about a football game against Hardin-Simmons in Abilene. "On one play, everyone pulled, even Bulldog Turner, and the whole stadium seemed to come at me. I stopped the interference, but it cost me my two front teeth."[39]

The success of the Cowboys on both sides of the ball made fans of West Texans who had never seen a football game in their lives. A seat at Parramore Field became the hottest ticket in town. "Cowboy Fever" became an epidemic and even extended to out-of-town games. A herd of loyal fans followed the Cowboys wherever they played—even to the West Coast. Loyola Marymount, who lost to Hardin-Simmons by a score of 7–0 in 1937, hoped to even the score when the Cowboys returned to Southern California the following year. In November

1938, 90 football players, band members, and an entourage of fans, including Hardin-Simmons president Jefferson Davis Sandefer and two horses—"Bear" and "Silver"—boarded the train in Abilene for the three-day trip to Los Angeles.

A round-trip ticket from Abilene to Los Angeles and back cost $38 coach and $48 tourist Pullman. Gib Sandefer, by then the business manager for the Hardin-Simmons athletic department, secured the special rates from railway officials in Dallas. The train left Abilene on November 16 and reached Los Angeles on November 19, with a stop-over of a few hours in El Paso. When the train arrived in Los Angeles, two special chartered Pageway Buses transported the entire group to "Cowboy headquarters," also known as the Hotel Hayward on Spring Street in downtown Los Angeles.

The football team played perhaps its best game of the season against Loyola, but it was the halftime show that really captured the mood of the day with a mixture of West Texas and Hollywood. The Cowboy Band, directed by Marion McClure, played "The Eyes of Texas" and "The Last Roundup" while trick ropers Rex Felker (riding Bear) and Phil Cadenhead (riding Silver) performed stunts. And the game attracted an unusual number of Hollywood heavyweights, all arranged by Shotgun Britton, who seemed to know everybody in Tinsel Town. Spencer Tracy and actor George O'Brien received commissions as honorary Texas Rangers on the 50-yard line while Bing Crosby and George Raft watched from the press box. Thanks to Shotgun Britton, Crosby already had a relationship with Abilene and Hardin-Simmons. He had ridden Bear, the Cowboy mascot, in his 1936 movie *Rhythm on the Range*, one of only two westerns Crosby ever made.[40]

The show business atmosphere was a perfect backdrop for Bull-dog's flashy performance on the field. At center he was flawless, me-chanical perfection, and he was a demon on defense. The Cowboys beat the Lions 19–0, shutting them out for the second year in a row.

The team returned to Abilene on November 22 as conquering he-roes. A large crowd, led by Abilene Mayor W. W. Hair and Judge J. P. Stinson, a Hardin-Simmons trustee, met the Cowboys at the Texas and Pacific Depot. There was a downtown parade and a welcoming ceremony at the courthouse, all broadcast over KRBC radio. "We're just getting started," Judge Stinson told the boisterous crowd of supporters. "We'll keep right on going till we wind up in the Rose Bowl."[41]

The Cowboys never played Pasadena, but even the doubters were amazed at their success on the field. Over the next two seasons the Cowboys won 15 games, lost 3, and tied 1. Hardin-Simmons beat Howard Payne both years, including a 7–6 win in 1938. When Howard Payne scored its only touchdown that year the Yellow Jackets lined up to kick the extra point that would tie the game. Bulldog Turner broke through the line and blocked the kick.[42]

The Cowboys played Loyola Marymount again on October 28, 1939 in California. Although Hardin-Simmons lost the game 6–0, Bulldog's performance was generally considered to be the pinnacle of his college career. He had 26 tackles and two interceptions. By then his reputation had preceded him. The stands were loaded with West Coast reporters. "I never had a chance to play before any big-time newspapermen before that," Bulldog explained. "I made a lot of tackles that night, and it led to my pro contract with the Bears."[43]

That same year Loyola Marymount played Santa Clara. The center for Santa Clara was John Schiechl, the first team All-American, and the man generally considered to be the best college center in the country. But the Loyola Marymount coaches, players, and fans knew better. John Schiechl was good, but he couldn't hold a candle to that West Texas cowboy from Hardin-Simmons.

Chapter 4
Young Hercules

"**P**ro ball didn't get into my mind 'til my senior year at Hardin-Simmons," Bulldog said. "Then I got to thinking 'maybe I can play pro ball.'"[1]

At the time few others thought much of his chances. The prevailing belief among NFL coaches and scouts was that small colleges just didn't produce NFL-caliber athletes. The Ivy League was known for its football back then. Notre Dame was a national power. But pro coaches paid little mind to small college athletes, particularly from schools west of the Mississippi. Bulldog might have had no professional career at all had it not been for a little luck, a Jersey calf, an apology, and an industrious and resourceful journalism teacher at Hardin-Simmons named Clarence Herschel Schooley who doubled as the sports information director for the Cowboy athletic program. Bulldog needed exposure, and Schooley was the man to help him get it.

Bulldog listed his major as journalism (later changed to physical education and economics), so he and Schooley spent a lot of time together in the field house and in the classroom. The two men became great friends. Schooley watched Bulldog's NFL chances dying on the vine and hatched a plan to do something about it. Schooley became Bulldog Turner's personal publicist, promoter, and press agent. Bulldog taught Schooley's journalism classes while Schooley spun yarns about Bulldog and sent them to newspapers and coaches all over the country. Bulldog was fortunate to fall in with a man like Schooley who knew how to generate media exposure. Schooley turned Bulldog's humble West Texas roots into a publicity bonanza and rescued Bulldog's dream of professional football from the ashes.

But just as Herschel Schooley was turning Bulldog Turner into something of a Western folk hero, Bulldog got into trouble and almost got himself booted from the team. It was no secret that Bulldog's evening activities, which included honky-tonk music, dancing, and bootleg alcohol, were not in accord with the strict Baptist code at Hardin-Simmons. The school administration admired Bulldog's athletic prowess but seemed uncomfortable with this West Texas cowboy who was a little too wild and free for the straight-laced Baptists in Abilene.

Taylor County and Abilene, the county seat, were officially "dry" and had been since abolishing saloons in 1903, but there were plenty of ways to get around prohibition, as college students quickly learned. Alcohol flowed just to the west in Sweetwater and Nolan County and to the east in Baird and Callahan County. Even in Abilene there were plenty of bootleggers, particularly around the college campuses, and there were even several private "recreational clubs" in Abilene authorized to sell beer to patrons who purchased memberships.[2] The newspaper reported that illegal beer traffic was steady in the "Mexican section of Abilene." Some cafes even sold "near beer"—a drink that looked like the real thing but with an alcohol content of only one-half of one percent. But sipping suds at full strength could be risky in Abilene and Taylor County. Possession of alcohol could get a man 30 days in jail and selling it could get him 60 days.[3] Of course Abilene society had no such worries. While ordinary beer drinkers risked jail time, socialites could drink without fear at the Abilene Country Club. Bulldog Turner must have been struck by the hypocrisy of it all.

Whether Bulldog's trouble involved strong drink is not known, but in the spring before his junior year school administrators charged Bulldog with violating the athletic code. According to one source he was about to be removed from the team when a publicity stunt orchestrated by Herschel Schooley saved his career.

That spring Schooley hired a Dallas-based sports photographer named Jimmy Laughead to take publicity shots of the team. Laughead's style of sports photography was unique and attracted a lot of

Jimmy Laughead took this picture of Bulldog Turner, second from left. To Bulldog's left, wearing a cowboy hat, is Owen Goodnight. The player on the far right is Joe Pee. Courtesy of Brad Bradley.

attention. He was the first photojournalist to pose athletes to appear as if they were in action. His photos of the Hardin-Simmons Cowboys, especially a center from Sweetwater, caused a sensation.

Since most of the players were real West Texas cowboys, Laughead took their pictures in a natural setting. He shot pictures of players in hats and chaps. He took their pictures riding horses and roping. Later that afternoon Laughead turned to the group of players gathered around him and asked of no one in particular, "Who's the star around here?" Bulldog, who had been in some group pictures but as usual was angling for a close-up, stepped forward, just as he had that first day of football practice at Hardin-Simmons. "I guess you mean me," he said.[4]

Laughead photographed Bulldog Turner in full cowboy regalia—chaps, boots, and hat—riding a white stallion. Then on a whim Herschel Schooley brought a 350-pound Jersey calf into Parramore Field. The calf belonged to Spanish professor Modrel Moffett Ballard of the Hardin-Simmons faculty (who was also the tennis coach). Laughead

The picture that launched the legend. Jimmy Laughead took this shot of Bulldog Turner carrying Professor Ballard's calf. Courtesy of Brad Bradley.

asked if anyone on the squad was strong enough to pick it up. What happened next is part of football legend.[5]

"A kid named Clyde Turner, who was about to be kicked off the team for disciplinary reasons, yanked that calf up off the ground and took off running around the field with it," said Laughead. "He must have lapped the field six times with that calf on his back. I went back to Dallas and wrote about how Bulldog Turner was a little All-American. I made that up of course. Nobody had even heard of him. But the picture got on the wires and Hardin-Simmons got 6,000 clippings of it from newspapers. The clips cost a penny apiece and nearly busted the school's budget. They couldn't kick Turner off the team after that."[6]

"You know how photographers are," Bulldog recalled years later. "They always say 'Just one more. Just one more.' That very day he

took some pictures of us riding horses and stuff. He took some pictures of me running at the camera with a calf over my shoulder.

"I carried that little ol' calf and we'd run at the camera, about 10
times, 'til he got what he wanted. And when we were done, me and
that calf, both, was give out."[7]

No one knows why certain stories grab the attention of the American public, but this one did. Perhaps the story caught on because the
country had a fascination with cowboys and the West. Harry Cary,
Tom Mix, Johnny Mack Brown, Gene Autry, and Randolph Scott were
big at the box office. Zane Grey's Western novels were popular. The
movie *Stagecoach*, directed by John Ford and starring a young John
Wayne, would become one of the biggest films of 1939. Amid the
uncertainty of the Industrial Age, the Great Depression, and a world
inching closer to war, America was nostalgic for the Wild West.

For whatever reason, the picture of Bulldog Turner carrying a calf
on his shoulders made Bulldog a celebrity all across America. As luck
would have it, someone at Associated Press liked the picture and for-
warded it by wire photo to all newspapers using the AP picture service.
Within a week the article, along with the picture of Bulldog and the
calf, appeared in newspapers in New York, Los Angeles, Pittsburgh,
Chicago, Washington, Billings, Greeley, and Portsmouth. People all
over the country could identify with this loveable cowboy from the
tiny West Texas college. Fan mail poured in to the Abilene post office.
The sensation caused by all the publicity even brought Lee Orr of
Fox Movietone to town. Orr spent two hours shooting film of football
practice at Parramore Field. At least 15 million viewers saw the film
at movie houses all across America.[8] Bulldog Turner had put Abilene,
Texas and Hardin-Simmons on the map. Before Bulldog came along,
most people outside West Texas thought Abilene was a Kansas cow
town and Hardin-Simmons was some kind of firm mattress.

Bulldog liked the attention. That's why he started playing football
in the first place. A reporter from the *Abilene Reporter-News* wrote,
"Turner has received letters from football fans from practically every
state in the union. Most of the letters were in the scrawling hands
of youngsters who admired Bulldog's gridiron feats. Sprawled out on
his bed in a Hardin-Simmons dormitory, Turner thumbed through his
more recent correspondence pointing out to us some of the choicer
bits of humor from the stack.

A Jimmy Laughead photo of Bulldog in hat and chaps. From the Bulldog Turner file in the Texas Sports Hall of Fame. Courtesy of Brad Bradley.

"The remarks were from Baltimore, Maryland, Wilmington, Delaware, Carmel, New York, West Los Angeles, California, Pasadena, California, and Brownsville (Texas)."

"From the Drew Seminary for young women in Carmel, New York, came a perfumed epistle addressed to Mr. Bulldog Turner. She thumbed through *Illustrated Football* and must have been fascinated either by Bulldog or the starry-eyed look in the calf's eyes."

An admirer from North Berwick, Maine wrote, "I saw your picture in the annual football magazine with a calf slung over your shoulders and thought if you could do that you could sling some ink as far as Maine. Please send me your autograph."[9]

For the moment, Bulldog was out of the doghouse, and all talk of his removal from the team stopped. Suddenly he was the biggest thing to hit West Texas since the rotary cone drill bit. Around campus he was known as "that man with the face," referring to his picture that appeared in newspapers all over the country. He was the center of attention wherever he went, and he reveled in the spotlight. A reporter wrote of "[f]reshmen girls rushing Bulldog down at the train Sunday evening" after the University of San Francisco (USF) game.[10] He and a classmate named Larry Jack Cunningham of McLean formed a musical duet that performed at events around campus. They billed themselves as "The Smith Hall Ramblers." Cunningham played guitar, and Bulldog played the fiddle and sang. That winter Bulldog was a finalist in the "Beauty and the Beast" Contest. He lost. He was never in the running in the "Beauty" category, and the title of "Beast" went to Long John Treadway, an unsightly tackle from Nacogdoches, who won a date with Beauty (Nell Gee) that included a chauffeured limousine complete with a footman, a show at the Paramount, dinner, and incidentals.[11]

Bulldog took it all in stride. All his life he craved attention, and now he was getting it. He was having the time of his life. The country boy shyness he had when he first came to Abilene was long gone, replaced by a level of self-confidence that sometimes approached arrogance. Bulldog was feeling his oats. On Saturday nights he polished his boots, slipped on his letterman's sweater, and turned into a party animal. An article in *The Brand* (the Hardin-Simmons student newspaper) noted the Bulldog "swings a mean jitterbug for a man his size."[12] When a *Brand* reporter asked Bulldog what he would do if he suddenly had a million dollars, Bulldog replied, "I would find me a good-looking blonde and throw a party."[13]

There is a good chance that all the attention and the nationwide publicity went to Bulldog's head, because in the spring he was in trouble again, this time of a more serious nature. The March 16, 1939 edition of the *Abilene Reporter-News* broke the story to the world that Bulldog Turner had "bumped into trouble with the administration and will not return to school."[14] The paper would later describe him as "boisterous" and "rambunctious" but gave no further details except to say that "Turner left school earlier in the semester after running into trouble with the administration over breaking of campus rules."[15] On March 19, the day before spring football practice began, Bulldog left Abilene and went home to Sweetwater.[16]

What Bulldog did to get himself suspended from school is a mystery, although he had probably been on the administration's radar for some time. Too many of the sordid details of his evening activities appeared in print for all to see. In 1937 the school newspaper reported that Bulldog and teammates Odis Crowell, Ed Cherry, Sam "Nig"

Kirk McKinnon and Bulldog Turner. Courtesy of Brad Bradley.

Oatman, and Kirk McKinnon raised such a ruckus at a California night spot after the Loyola game that Los Angeles police chased them from the scene.[17] *The Brand* also reported that after the Centenary game, Bulldog and Owen "Dimples" Goodnight "had a huge time" prowling the streets of Shreveport long after the bars closed at midnight.[18] That Bulldog was a frequent visitor to beer joints and honky-tonks was widely accepted by students at Hardin-Simmons. In early December 1937, *The Brand* reported that "[t]he Christmas rush is on. Ties are on sale at Abilene's leading night club for only 30 cents. Ask Bulldog Turner for details."[19] Bulldog enjoyed himself so much that his school work suffered. Despite his great feats of athleticism on the football field, he failed to meet the scholastic requirements for the fall semester of 1938 and did not receive his varsity letter after his junior season.[20]

The episode that sent Bulldog packing may have taken place in the Corral Cafe, a campus eatery attached to the gymnasium, but details are fuzzy. The following story appeared in a tabloid called *Cut-Throat*—a special edition of the school newspaper published each year on April Fools Day. *Cut-Throat,* a much anticipated campus tradition, was known for savage personal attacks, filth, dirt, smut, and spoofs of legitimate news stories. It was vicious but entertaining, and most students were honored to be parodied on its pages.

Under the front-page headline TURNER SUBDUED AFTER RAMPAGE, a reporter with tongue in cheek wrote, "General excitement and terror rose from the Corral the other day when Bulldog Turner, discipline problem of the faculty and special hobby of Fay Nell Spears, suddenly reverted to his true nature. It occurred when the nickelodeon broke loose with 'Jungle Drums,' during which time Bulldog tore off his clothes, pounded his chest and broke a chair in half with his teeth.

"Several women fainted, and when he flashed a purposeful look at the coeds, they all rushed for the nearest exit. He was subdued by Football Men [Lewis] McCaleb, [Lloyd] Guy, and [Harold] Russell after a struggle that demolished the cigarette machine and all the front windows. Gordon Shelton, manager of the café, made no comment."[21]

Whatever happened that day in the Corral, it was serious enough that Bulldog got the boot, and everyone assumed his days at

Hardin-Simmons were finished. There were rumors that Mose Simms, coach of St. Mary's, was in town to try and lure the Bulldog to San Antonio. *The Brand* reported that "[a]pparently Simms is seeking some way in which he can get Bulldog enrolled in his school in the Alamo City. It is also hinted that scholastic standing wouldn't cut so much ice at that school."[22]

Meanwhile in Abilene, managers cleaned out Bulldog's locker, and Leslie "Red" Lewis, a 190-pound transfer from Decatur Junior College, moved into the starting center position. (Lewis would later become head track coach at Hardin-Simmons.) But Lewis was no Bulldog Turner. Newspapers suggested that Coach Kimbrough's number-one problem that spring would be replacing Turner, the big center "who is no longer in school." The coach tried to gloss over the situation by suggesting that the Cowboys were bigger than one man. Kimbrough assured fans that "[w]e'll have a center on the field—contrary to the belief of many—and he'll be a good one."[23] But alone in his office, Kimbrough certainly knew that replacing the Bulldog with someone of equal talent was impossible.

Fans of Cowboy football did not give up hope that some kind of arrangement could be made to bring Bulldog back into the bunkhouse. In fact by the middle of March, Bulldog had communicated a desire to return, but school administrators were slow in responding. A reporter for *The Brand* wrote, "Clyde 'Bulldog' Turner has not been admitted to the ranks as of this writing (Thursday Night). The Bulldog has not been granted enrollment. After many postponements and delays, the administrative council is reported ready to take action on the unusual case."[24]

Then on March 27, after an absence of several weeks, Bulldog was back at Hardin-Simmons, hat in hand, asking for reinstatement.[25] Coach Kimbrough, whom Bulldog admired and respected, may have made a trip to Sweetwater. It has also been suggested that Bill Turner, whose advice Bulldog valued, convinced his son to return to school and make amends. "My daddy always taught us that if we start something, we need to finish it," sister Ilene recalled.[26] No one knows for sure what brought him back. A sanitized explanation came from a story in the *Abilene Reporter-News*, although the paper was vague about the particulars. A reporter wrote, "Turner was dropped from the University for infringement of campus regulations a few weeks ago. His reinstatement was announced Monday by Dr. R. N. Richardson, executive vice-president of the school, with the promise of Turner that he would cooperate with the University in its disciplinary regulations in the future."[27]

Whatever Bulldog had done, the University was willing to forgive and forget. His punishment came through the athletic department, not through the school administration. Bulldog was back in good graces, for the present, and most important for sports fans, he was ready to play football. He reported to spring practice that afternoon. He ran plays with the third string for a while, and then moved back into his familiar spot in the starting lineup.

While some people felt he got off light because he was a football star, West Texas sports fans in general seemed happy that Bulldog was back, even though he was overweight and out of shape. One reporter wrote, "At last the final decree was issued in the Bulldog Turner case. A week ago today the Bulldog received his reinstatement, thus sending the purple and gold soaring to new heights. The rugged center reported in harness Monday and went through a stiff workout. In a pair of practice sessions during the chilly week, Turner dropped ten pounds of the excess twenty."[28]

Although he was the center of attention at spring practice, Bulldog kept his head low and his mouth shut. He appeared remorseful and genuinely happy to be back at Hardin-Simmons. A school reporter wrote, "Bulldog Turner came through [spring football] in remarkable fashion during the practice period. Turner was on the proverbial spot by starting the training grind late. By hustling every minute of the lengthy sessions, the Bulldog made good and regained lost prestige."[29]

There is a chance that Bulldog Turner would have been nothing more than a footnote to history had he not returned to Hardin-Simmons that spring. Although injuries prevented him from playing in several games, the 1939 season only added luster to his reputation as a football player and propelled him to immortality in the National Football League. That fall the Cowboys traveled to California again to play the University of San Francisco (USF). For Bulldog it was a coming-out party. California was in the business of making celebrities, and this time it chose to anoint the kid from West Texas with the calf on his shoulders. That picture made Bulldog Turner famous, and all eyes were on him. Even USF fans chanted his name from the stands, and mobbed him for autographs. And Bulldog did not disappoint. He ran wild against the USF Dons. On offense he blocked like a Sherman tank, and on defense he made 22 unassisted tackles. After watching Bulldog's performance, the San Francisco coach said he would trade his entire second string for "that Turner kid." That quote made news in sports pages all over the country.

The press heaped praises on his Herculean performance in California. A reporter for the *San Francisco Foghorn* wrote that "Johnny Schiechl of Santa Clara might make all-American, but he won't make the USF Dons' all-opponent team. Bulldog Turner, the bad-man from Hardin-Simmons, is rated by the USF players as a better pivot man than Bronco Schiechl. The Dons aver that Turner may not receive the press notices that Schiechl does, because Hardin-Simmons is an obscure college in the wilds of Texas. However he is a better center, because his tackles are more deadly and he covers more territory than Santa Clara's Johnny."[30] In a later edition, the *Foghorn* added that "Los Angeles sports writers were unanimous in saying that Bulldog Turner of Hardin-Simmons is the greatest center ever to perform in Southern California."[31]

Other journalists described him in Homeric prose as "Young Hercules, he looks like, the pride of Hardin-Simmons campus, Clyde 'Bulldog' Turner, 218-pound senior center. This son of the wide open spaces prepared for his athletic career by wrestling with steers, and when he walked into college he was almost too rough for the other lads to associate with. Not mean, just playful."[32] Another article quoted an opposing coach as saying that "after we played the Abilene Cowboys last fall, all anyone had to do was to walk into my boy's dormitory, yell 'Bulldog,' and the whole squad would scramble under their beds."[33]

Clearly the Golden State was smitten with Bulldog Turner. If one believed *The Oakland Tribune*, Bulldog could heal the sick and walk on water. "He tore the USF line to ribbons. It was no exaggeration to say he made 73 percent of the tackles for his club and whenever he hit an opponent, the opponent stopped. He spent a good deal of time in the Dons' backfield disrupting interference and hurling ball carriers on their backs."[34]

Bulldog made a lasting impression on all who saw him that day.

When the football season ended, Lee Dunbar, lead sportswriter for *The Oakland Tribune*, picked his All West Coast college team. At center Dunbar chose Rudy Mucha of Washington, but made clear that he yielded to geography in making his selection.

"If I'd been picking an all-star team from all the many clubs I've seen in action this year, Rudy Mucha would not have landed the plane. Bulldog Turner of Hardin-Simmons is the best center I've seen this year or any other year for a long time back.

"But this kid isn't a Pacific Coaster, hence he can't go on an All-Coast team. He's cursed by the fact that he works for a little school in a bush league in Texas, [and] hence won't get much All-American play, although I notice he's made a couple of them. But he's the best center I've seen in years and that goes for everything produced on this coast for a long time."[35]

West Coast newspapers made Bulldog Turner a star in California. In fact, at that stage in his career he was better known in California than in his home state of Texas where Ki Aldrich from TCU got most of the ink. But Bulldog was not so well known in the Midwest or on the East Coast, and all the NFL franchises were located in that section of the country. Bulldog wanted to play professional football, but he needed a little luck and some Hershel Schooley magic to escape the bush league.

Pro football was certainly a lofty goal for a poor boy from West Texas, but the sport was not the glitzy game of millionaires that it is today. In fact pro ball was a poor stepchild to the college game back then. Tens of thousands watched the big college rivalries, while hundreds watched NFL games. Thirteen thousand fans watched the first televised NFL game between the Philadelphia Eagles and Brooklyn Dodgers played at Ebbets Field on October 22, 1939. The day before, 70,000 spectators packed Yankee Stadium for a college game. Michigan versus Michigan State might draw 100,000 fans. Ninety-two thousand spectators saw the 1940 Rose Bowl Game in Pasadena, California, while fewer than 37,000 watched the Bears and the Redskins in the NFL championship game held in Washington, D.C. later that year.

"In those days the life of a professional football player wasn't very glamorous," J. R. Boone, Bulldog's teammate in Chicago, recalled. "We lived in a motel and traveled by bus or train. Football was simpler then. Nothing fancy or expensive. We lived on a shoestring. Everybody had a roommate to save money. Even the Chicago Bears were a bare-bones organization. There were only four coaches for the whole team. There was a head coach, an offensive coordinator, a defensive coordinator, and a special teams coach. We practiced at Wrigley Field, and we had another practice facility there in Chicago. Monday was a day to watch some film and review the game we played the day before. We usually got Tuesdays off. Wednesday was defense, Thursday was offense, and Friday was special teams. We did a run-through on Saturday and played on Sunday. We did some live practice but not much, especially after the season started. We couldn't afford to get anyone hurt."[36]

Professional football was a different game back then and in some ways it did not even resemble the modern contest. In the old days no players wore face guards. A few players didn't even wear helmets. Unlike the specialists of today, the players in 1940 played both ways. In 1942 Sammy Baugh did something unheard of in the modern era of two-platoon football. He played every minute of every game for the entire season. There was no artificial turf. Players actually got dirty. The coaches did not send in the plays, but the quarterback called all plays in the huddle. The goal posts were on the goal line, not at the back of the end zone. Lou Groza, the great kicker for the Cleveland Browns, would regularly split the uprights on kickoffs. The position of the goal posts sometimes produced strange and comedic situations. It was not unusual for a receiver running a slant pattern at full tilt to turn his head for the ball and be stopped dead in his tracks, not by a defensive back, but by colliding with the goal post. In the 1945 NFL Championship game, Sammy Baugh uncorked a pass in his own end zone that struck the goal post and fell incomplete. The crazy rules of the time gave the other team a safety. As a result, the Redskins lost the game 15–14 to the Cleveland Rams. The Redskins' owner, George Preston Marshall, was so mad at the outcome that he forced a change in the rules. In 1946, in what became known as the Baugh/Marshall rule, a pass striking the goal post was ruled incomplete.

But the greatest difference between modern corporate football and the old days is the money, or more accurately the lack of it. In 1940, Bulldog Turner's rookie season, there were no radio or TV contracts.

The only way a professional football team generated money was from gate receipts. It was a week-to-week proposition with no guaranteed income. Two straight weeks of bad weather and small crowds could drive a franchise into bankruptcy. In 1953 a premium grandstand seat at Wrigley Field in Chicago cost $2.75, so an owner had to fill a lot of seats to turn a profit. And unlike Major League Baseball, whose teams played over 160 games a year, a football season lasted only 10 or 11 games, plus two or three preseason contests. The owners charged admission to exhibition and preseason games, even though such games were considered practice and paid nothing to players except three dollars a day meal money and per diem if the game was out of town. Oftentimes the money made from exhibition games represented the difference between a money-making season and insolvency.

Major League Baseball could be a stable business on gate receipts alone, but professional football needed television. Before television, the highest-paid stars in the NFL made only a few hundred dollars a game. All professional football players had second jobs. No family could live all year on a pro football salary.

Ed Sprinkle, Bulldog's teammate with the Bears, had a good off-season job at a steel plant in Chicago. Lou Creekmur, a Hall of Famer who played for Detroit in the 1950s, worked at a shipping company in Detroit while he played for the Lions.

"I would play a game on Sunday," Creekmur said, "then be at work Monday morning. I'd work from 7 a.m. to 9:30 a.m. on weekdays, go to practice, and then come back to work at 2:30 in the afternoon. I thought nothing of it. I didn't know any better."

Even road trips gave him no relief from his day job. "If we went to say, San Francisco, for a game, my company expected me to keep working. I'd have to go knocking on doors of clients in that city on Friday and Saturday."[37]

Creekmur missed the 1958 Pro Bowl because his boss needed him to work that day. For Creekmur, it was a no-brainer. He made more money as the manager of the Saginaw Transfer Terminal than as a pro football player.[38]

Saul Sherman was a third string quarterback for the Chicago Bears in 1939 and 1940. He loved the game but had to face reality. "I was making $150 a game and Halas didn't pay us for exhibition games.

By the end of the season I managed to save a quarter." Sherman quit after the 1940 NFL championship game to work in a business. "I had gotten married," he said, "and had to earn a living."[39]

Even many owners were strapped for cash. There was no significant radio coverage for regular season professional football games until after World War II and no television contracts until much later. Fans stayed away in such large numbers that most franchises, including the mighty Chicago Bears, were on very shaky financial ground. Owners dared not look too far ahead. Their goal was to make payroll, their biggest expense, and cover the current year's costs. George Halas, owner and coach of the Chicago Bears, regularly borrowed startup money every summer against season ticket sales.

Halas and the other owners fought for financial survival by every means possible. They even colluded to keep player salaries low. When the NFL ratified its first constitution on June 18, 1921, that document contained a reserve clause that became a standard part of every player contract. The reserve clause, modeled after a similar one in baseball, bound a player to his team forever. A player whose contract had expired could renegotiate only with the team that owned his contract. If a good player and the owner could not agree to terms, the team put the player on a reserve list, and no other team was allowed to negotiate with him. Unlike workers in other professions, a first-rate professional football player was not free to shop around for higher pay from another team even after the term of his contract expired. The bargaining power of players improved when in 1947 the NFL adopted the "one-year option" rule that allowed a team to exercise its renewal option only one time for each player. Still, the owners had the advantage in bargaining for salaries, and their actions, based on gentlemen's agreements, kept player salaries low. A handful of backfield stars had the power to negotiate a good salary, but linemen, even the great ones, played for peanuts.

Pro football, for many reasons, was not the spectacle it is today. Many Americans in the 1930s did not even know pro football existed. In the deepest recesses of far West Texas, every school boy knew of Babe Ruth and Lou Gehrig. There was no Little League, but Golden Gloves boxing was big. Most people could name the current heavyweight champion. But almost no one could name the top NFL quarterback. Pro football scores were not even mentioned in newspapers outside New York, Washington, Philadelphia, Pittsburgh, and Chicago, and even then the stories were buried deep in the sports section.

To make things worse there were many people in America, including some big-time college coaches, who thought pro football was "low rent," even sinful. Some college coaches actually discouraged their young players from turning pro. There was a segment of American society in the 1930s that didn't like the commercialism represented by pro football. There was, some believed, just something dirty about the game. Many Americans believed that the pros were too rough. There were too many injuries. There was a lack of good sportsmanship. The games were fixed. Pro coaches would do anything to win. Because of the rift between the college coaches and the pros, the media was afraid to publicize pro football for fear of offending their bread and butter—the big universities and their coaching staffs. There was an unwritten rule in the college ranks that said if a player turned pro, he could never get a job coaching a college team.

Amos Alonzo Stagg of the University of Chicago was one of the best college coaches of the early twentieth century. He loved the purity of college football and was a bitter opponent of the pro game. He hated the pros because they played on Sundays and because he believed the pros were too chummy with gamblers and the mob. Professional football, he believed, forced dishonesty on some players who played under assumed names in order to keep their amateur status. If a University of Chicago graduate turned pro, Stagg would recall that player's letter.

"To cooperate with Sunday professional football games," Stagg said, "is to cooperate with forces which are destructive of the finest elements of interscholastic and intercollegiate football and to add to the heavy burden of the schools and colleges in preserving it in its ennobling work."[40]

Once the University of Chicago football team traveled on the same train with the Chicago Cardinals of the NFL. Coach Stagg locked the doors between the two teams to keep the pros from contaminating his players. The great Cardinal running back Ernie Nevers tried to speak to the coach one day on the platform at a train station. "How are you, Mr. Stagg?" Nevers repeated the greeting eight or ten times, but Stagg looked the other way and never responded.[41]

The scouting and drafting sides of the pro game were certainly in their infancy when Bulldog Turner was a senior at Hardin-Simmons. Pro coaches usually compiled their draft lists by reading newspapers and perusing football magazines containing the annual predictions of All-America teams for the coming season. Scouts were expensive. Some teams couldn't afford them. Consequently many draft choices were made sight unseen. Players from small and little-known colleges, like Hardin-Simmons, received little ink and were not usually included in the draft.

But people outside West Texas were beginning to notice Bulldog Turner from Hardin-Simmons. After the calf picture, business picked up. With the help of his journalism friend and personal press agent, and some spectacular performances in the big media market on the West Coast, Bulldog made the Associated Press Little All-America team and the *New York Sun* All-America Team his senior year.

Bulldog also caught the attention of Frank Korch, a scout for the Chicago Bears who always kept an ear to the ground for rumors of promising young talent. Korch saw the picture of Bulldog Turner and the calf, along with just about everyone else in the country who read a newspaper. Korch also heard the hoopla surrounding the big center from Hardin-Simmons through Herschel Schooley's press releases and from West Coast newspapers. Korch had the job of helping George Halas compile the Bears' draft list, and after watching Bulldog play in California, Korch was confident that Turner was the man the Bears were looking for to round out a team that would dominate the world of professional football in the 1940s. The Bears had the number seven pick in the 1940 draft, and they intended to take Bulldog Turner as their top choice, if he was available.

The problem was that Herschel Schooley had done his job well, and by draft time Bulldog Turner was no secret. The Bears' great rivals, the Detroit Lions, had also heard the stories coming out of the Texas plains. The Lions wanted Bulldog too and would go to great lengths to get him. The Lions wanted Bulldog so much that their owner, George A. Richards, broke NFL rules and several federal laws in an attempt to secure Bulldog's services. The courting of Bulldog Turner was intense and sleazy, and the shenanigans surrounding the 1940 draft and Bulldog's entry into professional football produced the biggest scandal in the history of the NFL draft.

"I guess you could say my pro career really started one day in 1939 when I was a senior at Hardin-Simmons," Bulldog recalled. "We rode out to play Loyola of Los Angeles in Gilmore Stadium, Los Angeles, and it held about 20,000 people. Well, we had a sell-out crowd. I mean, I never saw so many people in my life. Anyway, I had a super game against those Loyola guys, and boy, we smoked 'em. Now at the time George Richards, who owned the Detroit Lions, had a house in Los Angeles, and what happened, a guy phoned him at halftime and said, 'George, you better come out here to the game. There's a guy you ought to be here watching.' When the game was over, George Richards was right there, and he said, 'Would you be interested in playing pro football?' I said, 'You bet.' And so George Richards said, 'Well, I'd like to have you on my team, the Detroit Lions.' I'd never heard of the Detroit Lions or anybody else, except I had seen a film of the Green Bay Packers. 'We're going to see that you get to play with the Lions,' George Richards told me."[42]

Richards knew how to make an impression on a poor boy from West Texas. Richards took Bulldog to Hollywood. They ate at the best restaurants, and they visited several high-class drinking establishments. Bulldog had tasted the high life, and he never forgot it. Richards also gave Bulldog some "walking-around" money and some money to "get his teeth fixed" (a euphemism for "what we are doing is illegal so take this money and keep quiet about it"). Some sources claimed Bulldog really did visit Richard's Beverly Hills dentist, although Bulldog denied it. One reporter wrote that when the dentist asked Bulldog which teeth he wanted fixed, Bulldog winked at the dentist and said, "Fix them all and spare no expense."[43]

Keep in mind that George Richards was a businessman. In addition to owning the Detroit Lions, he owned radio stations in Detroit and California. When he spent money, he expected a return on his investment, and for this investment, the return he expected was Bulldog Turner in a Lions' uniform. Along with the money he gave Bulldog was a verbal agreement to keep quiet about the Hollywood trip and to turn down overtures from any other professional team. The Lions assumed Bulldog was their secret and wanted to keep it that way. They had the number-six pick in the first round, just in front of Chicago. Lions head coach Gus Henderson went into the 1940 draft with orders from Richards to make Bulldog Turner the Lions' number-one pick.

Bulldog played along. In December 1939, days before the draft, he publicly announced his decision not to play professional football in 1940. "I lack about a year's worth of work before I can take my degree," he said, "and I plan to complete that first."[44] Earlier he told a reporter for the Hardin-Simmons student newspaper that pro football "sounds okay, talking about it, but I intend to get my fill in college."[45] But sportswriters knew something was up. Several newspapers around the country reported that "some clubs are telling Bulldog Turner, Hardin-Simmons' All Center, 'Tell everybody but us you're not interested in pro football so we can put you on our draft list. Haw!'"[46]

Frank Korch and George Halas knew nothing of George Richards's courting of Bulldog Turner, and they pursued Bulldog along normal channels. As a part of their recruitment process the Bears mailed a questionnaire to every college player they wanted to draft, and they sent one to Bulldog down in Sweetwater. Remembering the gentlemen's agreement with George Richards, Bulldog wrote on his questionnaire, "I do not want to play professional football" and mailed it back to the Bears. That statement made Halas suspicious. Halas knew that if a player truly wasn't interested in playing pro ball, that player never even bothered to fill out the form, so when Halas read Bulldog's written statement, he smelled a rat.

Still, Halas couldn't believe his luck on draft day when six teams, including the Lions, passed on Bulldog in the first round. Why didn't the Lions select Bulldog as planned? There were at least two reasons. Gus Henderson felt safe in not taking Bulldog in round one because the coach did not believe that any NFL team would select a lineman in the first round. It just wasn't done. Only high-profile quarterbacks and running backs from big universities were first-round selections. Furthermore, Henderson believed that Bulldog Turner was the Lions' secret and could be taken "in stride." That assumption turned out to be a colossal mistake—like putting Bulldog Turner in charge of curfew. Coach Henderson was so certain that Bulldog was in the bag that he passed on one of the greatest football players who ever lived and instead made Doyle Nave, a second-string quarterback from USC, his first-round pick, intending to take Bulldog in a later round. (In Coach Henderson's defense the Lions desperately needed a quarterback.) He never got the chance. As soon as Henderson announced his first-round pick, George Halas leaped from his chair and shouted, "Clyde

Turner of Hardin-Simmons," before Henderson could reconsider. A young sportscaster for the Detroit Lions named Harry Wismer, who later owned the New York Titans of the American Football League, ran to the phone to tell George Richards that Bulldog Turner was a Chicago Bear. The news did not sit well with Richards.

"Meantime, Richards didn't give up on me," Bulldog recalled. "He said, 'You're still going to be with the Lions. You just tell the Bears you're not going to play pro football. I'll make you a coach at a high school out here in California for the first year, and after George Halas gives up on you, you can come with the Lions.'

"So I went along with that, but then Halas invited me to fly up to Chicago on an expense-paid trip. Being the country boy I was, I had never been on an airplane before, so I couldn't say no. It took all day to fly to Chicago then. George and his wife met me at the airport, which George Halas didn't do normally. But I didn't sign a contract. I was grateful for the trip, but I kind of strung Halas along, you might say. However, Richards found out I went up there, and he was mad."[47]

"He came down to Abilene, Mr. Richards himself did, and registered incognito," Bulldog remembered. "Now I had a friend on the newspaper, Herschel Schooley, and I told Herschel, 'George Richards is in town and he wants to talk to me tonight.' Well, you can't tell a newspaperman secrets. Herschel said, 'I'm going with you,' and carried a pad and pencil. We went up there to the room, and Mr. Richards came out of the shower with a towel wrapped around him and he said, 'Who is this?' I said, 'This is Herschel Schooley, a reporter.' Richards said, 'A reporter!' And man he hit the ceiling. He said, 'I've come all the way from California incognito, and you bring a newspaperman here?' Herschel said, 'Why you old s. o. b.,' and I had to step in and cool the smoke down. Anyway we finally worked it out that Mr. Richards was going to send me $100 a month until something happened on the high school coaching job. But real soon after that I asked him to quit sending the $100. Mr. Richards promised me the world, and I'm sure he would have kept his promise, but I signed with the Bears. I didn't want to lay out a year."[48]

Meanwhile, the fallout from the 1940 draft day debacle caused a shakeup in the Lions organization. George Richards never forgave Gus Henderson for disobeying orders and letting Bulldog Turner get

away, and he fired the coach before the start of the season. The owner also voided the remaining years on the coach's contract. Coach
Henderson got his revenge by telling NFL Commissioner Carl Storch
how Richards illegally used money, booze, and a trip to Hollywood to
influence a player who had not yet completed his college eligibility.
Far worse for the league, Henderson let the commissioner know that
he (Henderson) had letters in his possession that proved Richards bet
on his own team. After an investigation, the NFL executive committee
fined George Richards $5,000 for tampering with the draft by attempt-
ing to influence a player in his choice of employers. The executive
committee also ordered Richards to pay $8,000 to Gus Henderson in
settlement of his two-year contract. Richards tried to dodge the fine
by selling the Lions to Frederick Mandel Jr., a Chicago department
store owner, but the League held up the deal until the money was paid
in full. The sale was actually orchestrated by George Halas who feared
that the League would be destroyed if Richards's gambling practices
became known to the general public. But even after paying the fine
Richards came out smelling like a rose. He bought the franchise in
1934 for $20,000 and sold it to Mandel in 1940 for $200,000—an indication that pro football was finally becoming big business.

The whole ugly story could have ended there, but George Richards
was not a man to go away quietly. A year later, with Chicago poised
to make another haul in the draft, George Richards got his revenge for
losing Bulldog Turner. No one saw it coming.

In the 1941 draft it looked as if Chicago, already the best team in
the NFL, might get the two best running backs in the country: Tom
Harmon, the Heisman Trophy winner from the University of Michigan
(and actor Mark Harmon's father) and Jarrin' John Kimbrough, a West
Texan from Haskell and Texas A&M (and Frank Kimbrough's brother). In a deal made twelve months earlier, lowly Philadelphia (with
the number-one pick) and last-finishing division Pittsburgh (number
three) dealt their opening round selections to Chicago. In addition to
the first and third picks, the Bears had their own number-nine pick
giving the defending champions an unprecedented three first round
selections in 1941.

Then, as now, League rules gave teams with the worst records
the top draft choices as a way of promoting parity. Each team could

select a total of 20 players. Teams, of course, could sell or trade their picks, and that's how Chicago acquired two additional first round draft choices that year. George Halas could hardly wait for draft day, but the rest of the owners were so unhappy with the champions getting two additional first round selections that they passed a rule prohibiting any team in the future from selling its first or second-round draft picks without consent of all other team owners.

But for the present, the Bears were on a roll. They got Harmon but missed Kimbrough when the cross-town Cardinals drafted the Haskell Hurricane number two. Still Halas was happy with his number-one pick and prepared to sign Harmon to a hefty salary. But Harmon wanted to be a sportscaster as well as a football player, and in that desire George Richards found a way to stick it to the Bears. When Richards got wind of Harmon's radio ambitions, he offered Harmon a big contract to do a radio show at the station Richards owned in Michigan—as long as Harmon agreed to play for any team but the Bears. Harmon wanted the radio show and turned down the Bears to sign with the New York Americans of the American Football League. The AFL defaulted after one year, and Tom Harmon became a pilot in the Army Air Corps. His plane went down over China during the war, and he suffered injuries that ended his athletic career.

The Bears picked Norm Standlee, a fullback from Stanford, number three in the 1941 draft. Standlee was a power runner, standing 6'2" and weighing 240 pounds. He played one year with the Bears, finishing fourth in the league in rushing (414 yards, 5.1 yards per carry, 5 touchdowns). After the 1941 Championship game, Standlee joined the armed forces fighting in Europe. At the conclusion of the war, the Bears traded him to San Francisco.

The Bears' final first-round pick in 1941 was Don Scott, a brilliant passer and ball carrier and a two-time All-American quarterback from Ohio State. Like so many young athletes of his day, Scott never got the chance to strut his stuff in the NFL. In college he participated in the Civilian Pilot Training Program sponsored by the Civil Aeronautics Administration. When he volunteered for the Army Air Corps right after Pearl Harbor, he was already a commissioned pilot. On October 1, 1943, Don Scott died when his bomber crashed during a training run.

•••

Bulldog Turner was untainted by the scandal that rocked the NFL, and back in Abilene he savored his role as a celebrity. A reporter for the *Abilene Reporter-News* wrote, "Turner doesn't keep a scrapbook but he treasures the recent letter he received from Dana X. Bible, University of Texas coach."

Coach Bible wrote, "I want to congratulate you on being selected as a member of the West team in connection with the East-West Shrine game to be played in San Francisco on New Year's Day. I am sorry that I will not be able to be with you this year, but I want to extend my best wishes for a Western year.

"The team will be in charge of Percy Locey, manager, Babe Hollingbery and Biff Jones, coaches. You will find these men thoroughbreds, and I am sure you will enjoy your association with them to the fullest extent."[49]

The East-West Shrine game was the biggest event of the year for college football players not involved in a bowl game. Only big stars from important universities made the team so the invitation to play in the game was recognition that Bulldog was finally accepted by the college football establishment.

He celebrated his selection with a prank before leaving for California. The school newspaper reported that "All American Bulldog Turner was having himself a batch of fun whirling an antique ambulance with sirens screaming, around the gridiron during the Feud Bowl (an intramural football game) this week. . . . We hope he will be having as much fun on New Year's Day . . ."[50]

Bulldog spent an early Christmas that year with his family on the cotton farm at Dunn. Two days later he boarded the Sunshine Special at Buffalo Gap. When he arrived in San Francisco, he stared at the tall buildings and felt the excitement of the city. San Francisco never slept, and the energy was intoxicating to this young country boy. From the train station he hailed a cab that took him to the Sir Francis Drake Hotel at 450 Powell Street, less than a block from Union Square in the heart of downtown. From his window he could see San Francisco Bay. It was great to be back in California, a place that helped build his reputation.

And yet some sportswriters wished he had stayed at home. Bulldog came to San Francisco for fun and to play football, and was unaware that his very presence in the city by the bay caused consternation in the sports world. He made the sportswriters especially nervous. They had, after all, named John Schiechl of Santa Clara, not Bulldog Turner, to the All-America team. If Bulldog outplayed Schiechl, sportswriters would have a lot to explain.

Elucidation and back-tracking began almost immediately. When practice commenced at Kezar Stadium (made famous by Dirty Harry Callahan in the 1970s), everyone assumed Schiechl would be the starter for the West squad, but by the second day of practice, everyone was talking about Bulldog Turner. Bulldog outplayed Schiechl and beat him three to five yards in every 50-yard wind sprint. Then 48 hours before kickoff, as the West squad went through a light workout, Bulldog tangled with a tackling dummy and hurt his leg. His coaches were unsure if he could play at all. Sportswriters breathed a collective sigh of relief.

But by game time Bulldog was ready. He was the first small college player to start in the East-West Shrine Game, and his 26-minute performance there created a buzz, and a bit of embarrassment, in the sports world. Fifty thousand fans watched Bulldog dominate the middle part of the line of scrimmage. The East, led by Duke All-American George McAfee, was the odds maker's choice to win the game, but the West beat the East 28–11.

Everyone who watched Bulldog was impressed with his performance. Coach Babe Hollingbery, head coach at Washington State (where he coached Mel Hein) and for decades a close observer of the game, believed Bulldog may have been the best center he had ever seen. The coach also saw something unusual in Bulldog's technique that gave the Texan an edge over other centers. "He's the only center I ever saw who doesn't put the ball out in front of him," the coach recalled. "He grounds it between his legs and uses powerful wrist action to snap it. It's a neat trick and enables him to charge faster than if he were using the usual method."[51]

No less than the most recent Heisman Trophy winner, sang Bulldog's praises. "That Turner is the fastest and hardest tackler that ever roamed across anybody's gridiron," said Nile Kinnick of Iowa, Bulldog's teammate on the West squad.

There was no shortage of talent to watch that New Year's Day in California. In fact, the greatest collection of college centers ever gathered in one place was at that game. In addition to Bulldog Turner and John Schiechl were John Haman of Northwestern, Archie Kodros of Michigan, and Mike Kopcha of Chattanooga. But the best of them all was a West Texas, Dust Bowl cowboy from tiny Hardin-Simmons University. He was something special.

By the time he returned to Abilene in the middle of January, Bulldog had lost interest in school, but Hardin-Simmons embraced him as it never had before. Bulldog was a star. When he first came to Abilene in the fall of 1936, some of his classmates ridiculed him and made fun of his country ways. There were some cruel comments in the school newspaper. "Bulldog Turner, you came to the city too late to get the country out of you, but you could at least TRY," a reporter wrote. "People are tired of your 'hick from the sticks' ways. You might play second string on the football team but you don't rate that well on campus."[52] But Bulldog showed them all. Now he was famous and too big for a little place like Abilene. His classmates who had once ridiculed him now picked him as one of the Outstanding Personalities in 1939—right behind Hitler and Eleanor Roosevelt. Then in the spring of 1940, *The Brand* held a mock presidential election. Bulldog got quite a few write-in votes, but those ballots were tossed out, handing the election to Franklin Roosevelt.

Chapter 5

The Roughest Team on the Planet

he first NFL draft in 1936 was an unpretentious affair. Franchise owners crowded into Commissioner Bert Bell's hotel room at the Ritz-Carlton Hotel in Philadelphia, shucked their jackets, passed around the bottle, and divvied up the best college talent in the country. In later years Jimmy Conzelman, coach of the Chicago Cardinals, played the piano while George Preston Marshall, owner of the Washington Redskins, sang to pass the time while Pittsburgh and Cleveland made up their minds. The first pick in the 1936 draft, Heisman Trophy winner Jay Berwanger from the University of Chicago, skipped the NFL for a career in business. George Halas picked West Virginia tackle Joe Stydahar (Hall of Fame 1967).

Today the NFL draft is televised live in prime time on ESPN and streamed in real time on the Internet. Millions of dollars are on the line. A poor country boy can become rich beyond his wildest dreams if he is selected in the early rounds. But in early December 1939, the draft was no big deal in Abilene, Texas. Most West Texans thought the NFL draft had something to do with horses or beer. Bulldog Turner did not even know he had been drafted until he got a call from the sports editor at the *Abilene Reporter-News*, and he was surprised to learn he had been picked by the Chicago Bears, not the Detroit Lions. At first Bulldog acted as if he wasn't interested. He pledged again to remain at Hardin-Simmons and finish his degree but later changed his mind and said, "I guess I'll be up there next fall."[1]

Being a celebrity had given Bulldog an attitude. He expected people to make a fuss over him. "Being drafted in the first round didn't impress me that much," he confessed. "By that time I had gotten so much publicity, I figured that maybe I deserved to be a first-round pick."[2]

Bulldog Turner was sure of himself to the point of being cocky, but there were people in Chicago who second-guessed George Halas for passing over so many big name players to draft Bulldog Turner. Many fans in the Windy City had two burning questions that cold December day when they learned of Chicago's first-round selection: "Who is Bulldog Turner?" "Where is Hardin-Simmons?" Both of those questions would be answered in due time. And Bulldog would vindicate, with his performance, the faith Halas placed in him. Halas may have known exactly what he was doing or he may have been lucky. Either way, Bulldog Turner turned out to be the perfect center for the Bears' T-formation offense of the 1940s.

The number-one pick in the 1940 draft was a running back from Tennessee named George "Bad News" Cafego. The Chicago Cardinals picked Cafego who turned out to be no news at all. The number-two pick was a left-handed, single-wing tailback from Duke named George McAfee who could run like a deer and change directions like a scared jackrabbit. The Philadelphia Eagles drafted McAfee in the first round, and then traded him to the Bears where he had a Hall of Fame career as a running back and a kick returner. The Brooklyn (football) Dodgers drafted tackle Banks McFadden of Clemson number four. The Dodgers also drafted Nile Kinnick, an All-American running back from Iowa and the 1939 Heisman Trophy winner, but Kinnick declined a contract to play pro football.

The Philadelphia Eagles picked John Schiechl number 13 in the 1940 draft. The Cleveland Rams picked Johnny Haman number 20, and Archie Kodros went to the Green Bay Packers in round 17. Of the three only Schiechl played professionally. The other heralded center of 1940, Mike Kopcha of Chattanooga, went to med school and never entered the draft. The New York Giants drafted Weenie Bynum, the great Centenary running back, in the 21st round, but he never played a down in the NFL. He was ambitious, and he went into business to make some real money.

It is no overstatement to say that the Monsters of the Midway, as the Chicago Bears of the 1940s were known, were built on the 1940 draft. In addition to Bulldog Turner and George McAfee, Chicago took Ken Kavanaugh (round 3, number 22), Ed Kolman (round 5, number 37), Hampton Pool (round 9, number 77), Young Bussey (round 20, number 187), and Scooter McLean (round 21, number 192). The Bears' 15th-round pick was Bulldog Turner's college teammate, Owen Goodnight from Hardin-Simmons. Goodnight (born August 27, 1917 in Holland, Texas) played only one year with the Cleveland Rams and then served in the army until the end of World War II. He tried to make a comeback in 1946 with the Bears, but Chicago cut him before the first game. About all he did after that was to go back home and become a Texas coaching legend at San Marcos High School. Owen Goodnight Middle School in San Marcos is named for him.

Most of the top picks of the 1940 NFL draft signed on to play in the College All-Star Game, a prestigious preseason contest between the reigning NFL champions and a team of the best college players who had just graduated. *The Chicago Tribune* promoted the event held every summer from 1934 to 1976 at Soldier Field in Chicago. Proceeds benefitted Chicago-area charities. Sportswriters from all over the country voted for their favorite college seniors, and the players who received the most votes made the 72-man squad. Secretly George Halas hoped his new rookie center would not get enough votes to be an all-star since making the squad would delay his reporting date to the Bears and give Bulldog Turner only three weeks to learn the 350 plays in Halas's playbook before the Bears took the field against Green Bay in the first game of the regular season. But Halas didn't figure on Herschel Schooley who mounted a letter-writing campaign and media blitz to make Bulldog an all-star. Schooley circulated petitions all over the Southwest urging sportswriters to cast a vote for the big center from Hardin-Simmons. Accompanying the petitions were "background stories and raves from various newspapers about Turner."[3]

It worked. Of the 6.5 million all-star votes cast from 47 states, Bulldog received 784,993 votes, and was the first small-school player to crack the starting lineup at the College All-Star Game. Nile Kinnick, the All-American from Iowa, was the only player to poll over a million votes. On August 11, 1940, the all-stars reported to their training facility at Evanston, Indiana for 18 days of practice.

It wasn't enough. On August 29, 1940, Bulldog Turner and the College All-Stars played the Green Bay Packers before 84,567 fans at Soldier Field on the Chicago waterfront in the inaugural game of the 1940 football season. The All-Stars were good—so good that George McAfee, an All-American and later a member of the Pro Football Hall of Fame, didn't make the team. On the All-Star squad that night were nine future members of the College Football Hall of Fame including Ken Kavanaugh (LSU), Bulldog Turner, Banks McFadden (Clemson), George Cafego (Tennessee), Dr. Eddie Anderson (Head Coach—Iowa), Harry Smith (University of Southern California), Kenny Washington (University of California-Los Angeles), Tad Wieman (Princeton), and Nile Kinnick (Iowa). The All-Stars scored the first three times they touched the ball, but the Packers won the game 45–28—an indication of just how far the pros had advanced in comparison to the college game. The All-Stars could not contain Don Hutson, who caught three touchdown passes and whose threat to catch more opened up the Packer running game. The All-Stars tried everything to stop Hutson—zones, man to man, double coverage, and triple coverage. Nothing worked.

The Packers and the All-Stars played on Friday night. On Saturday morning, Bulldog Turner, Ed Kolman, Lee Artoe, and Ken Kavanaugh traveled in style to their new place of employment. They hopped a milk train from Chicago to training camp in Erie, Pennsylvania. That night they played for the Bears in an exhibition game against the Pittsburgh Steelers.[4] Even before he played his first game in a Bears uniform, some sportswriters touted Bulldog as successor to the great Mel Hein. And Coach Halas soon discovered that he had no need to worry about his rookie center learning the plays. Bulldog devoured the voluminous playbook like a Zane Grey novel.

Off the field the naïve young man from the wilds of West Texas was exposed to the full force of American popular culture in the twentieth century. In 1940 young Americans listened to the music of Rosemary Clooney, Count Basie, Dizzy Gillespie, Artie Shaw, Glen Miller, and Bing Crosby. (Bulldog preferred Bob Wills.) John Lennon was born that year in Liverpool, England. The big movie stars were Cary Grant, Katherine Hepburn, Spencer Tracy, Vivian Leigh, and Clark Gable. Al Pacino was born in Manhattan. Joe DiMaggio was the best hitter for average in the major leagues. Hank Greenberg of the

Tigers and Johnny Mize of the Cardinals were the home-run kings. Bob Feller of the Indians used his 98-mph fastball to pitch a no-hitter on opening day. Josh Gibson and Cool Papa Bell, denied admission to Major League baseball because they were Black, played in the Mexican League. Joe Torre was born in Brooklyn, New York. The NBA (National Basketball Association) didn't exist. Byron Nelson was the PGA (Professional Golfers Association) Champion, and Jimmy Demaret won the Masters. Ben Hogan got his first PGA tour victory in 1940. Jack Nicklaus was born in Columbus, Ohio. FDR was in the White House, and Adolph Hitler was the chancellor of Germany. Winston Churchill became prime minister of England. German bombs fell on London. France surrendered to Germany, and the Nazis goose-stepped down the Avenue des Champs Elysee.

Americans were not yet ready to formally declare war, and Nile Kinnick, the Iowa halfback who scored the touchdown that beat mighty Notre Dame, expressed in words the isolationist mentality of the country when he said during his Heisman acceptance speech at the Downtown Athletic Club in New York City that he preferred "football fields in America to the battlefields of Europe." Still, he passed on a career in the NFL to enlist in the Navy in 1941, months before Pearl Harbor and the American entry into the war. Kinnick became a carrier pilot in Squadron 16 in the Navy Air Corps. On June 2, 1943 the engine in his F4F-4 Grumman Wildcat sputtered and lost power, and he went down in the Gulf of Paria off the coast of Venezuela. He and his plane slid beneath the surface and disappeared forever.

But war was no certainty when Bulldog Turner moved to Chicago in 1940, and his main interests were football and fun. Bulldog liked Chicago from the start. It was a rough and rowdy town—the kind of place to make a Sweetwater cowboy feel right at home. It was a noisy, blue-collar town that admired tough guys and easily overlooked their glaring imperfections. In the 1920s the Boys Scouts cheered Al Capone at Wrigley Field. In Chicago there were more bookies than insurance salesmen, more prostitutes than secretaries. There was a saloon on every corner, and people carried guns. After the years Bulldog spent in Abilene, the openness and honesty of sinful Chicago must have been refreshing.

They tell me you are wicked and I believe them, for I have seen your
painted women under the gas lamps luring the farm boys.
And they tell me you are crooked and I answer: Yes, it is true. I have
seen the gunman kill and go free to kill again.

From the poem "Chicago" by Carl Sandburg

In contrast to the dullness and monotony of his home in West
Texas, Bulldog Turner found the excitement of Chicago stimulating,
intoxicating, and irresistible. He loved Chicago and its wicked ways,
and the Chicago city slickers loved his cowboy swagger. The big problems of the world were still distant. In the summer and fall of 1940,
Bulldog and the citizens of Chicago were focused on their own lives.
Bulldog was no idealist, and he didn't want to change the world. He
wanted to play ball, and he wanted to party.

The mob still ruled Chicago in 1940, but most mobsters kept a
low profile. Capone, eaten alive by syphilis, was in retirement in Florida, but otherwise it was business as usual in the Windy City. Mafia
bosses and corrupt local politicians quietly ran Chicago like the well-
oiled political machine it was. People migrated to Chicago, especially
from the South, looking for work. Black musicians brought the blues
to Chicago from the Mississippi Delta. Chicago was the kind of place
that embraced its heroes, whether they were musicians, athletes, or
gangsters.

Occasionally a special bond develops between a city and its
hero—Joe DiMaggio and New York, Ted Williams and Boston, Johnny Unitas and Baltimore. Bulldog Turner bonded with Chicago and
soon earned a special place in its heart. The only other athlete in
Chicago that came close to Bulldog in popularity with people on the
street was Dizzy Dean of the Cubs, but by 1940 Diz was washed up.
His earned run average (ERA) that year was 5.17. Bulldog, by contrast, was young and at the dawn of a brilliant career. He worked
hard when the sun was up and played hard when the sun went down,
just like the blue-collar beer drinkers who came to watch him every
Sunday afternoon. Bulldog connected with Chicago, and Chicagoans
accepted him as one of their own. Within a year of his arrival the
people of Chicago would yell out his name when he walked down the
street. They smiled at him and shook his hand. They gave him privi-

leges and asked for his autograph. They gave him free drinks and the best tables. He didn't have to wait in line. Chicagoans treated him like royalty. It was not unusual for fan mail, simply addressed to "Bulldog Turner—Chicago Illinois," to find its way into his mail box.[5]

His legions of fans worshipped him. Suddenly young Bears fans who had never heard of Hardin-Simmons or Abilene before Bulldog came to town dreamed of playing for the Cowboys, and at least two Illinois high school football stars signed letters of intent with Hardin-Simmons, sight unseen, simply because Bulldog Turner played there. But Abilene was not the cowboy Camelot they read about in the newspaper, and the West Texas climate, especially in the summer, had more in common with Death Valley than with Chicago. The wind, the sand, and the August heat were too much for them, and they quit after a few days. "We'll just have to watch Turner play this year," one of them said as they boarded the train in the triple-digit heat for the cooler temperatures in Chicago.[6]

Even casual sports fans wanted to know more about Bulldog Turner, but the information that came out was not always accurate. Some newspapers described him as the only player in the NFL with a degree in journalism, when in fact he never finished his degree. There was another story, widely circulated in newspapers across the country, that he was the only player in the NFL too young to register for the draft. (He was 21 in March 1940, months before he first reported to the Bears in Chicago.) Some reporters wrote that he was a bachelor: a surprise, no doubt, to a young lady back in West Texas.

Bulldog met Helen Waultina Herman, the daughter of Marvin Herman of Lamesa and Annie Herman of Abilene, in 1939. Tina graduated from Abilene High School and attended St. Joseph's Academy.[7] After a whirlwind courtship, Clyde Douglas Turner and Helen Waultina Herman married on March 1, 1940. The groom was 20. The bride was 19. J. W. Parmer, the justice of the peace in Baird, performed the private ceremony. Tina wore a blue teal dress. There is no record of the groom's attire. Katherine Crook and Van Burnette, Bulldog's teammate at Hardin-Simmons, attended the ceremony in Baird.[7]

The young couple was happy for a time—until Bulldog went off to Chicago that summer. Daughter Sandra was born later that year, and daughter Pat was born in 1943. Bulldog cared for his family and supported them financially. His earnings from professional football made it possible to send daughter Sandra, who was hearing impaired, to a special school.[8] But the marriage didn't last. Circumstances made Bulldog a part-time husband. While he was a Chicago celebrity during football season, Tina and the girls spent most of their time back in Texas. Sandra and Pat only saw their dad play football a couple of times. Bulldog and Tina lived apart for much of their married life. Apparently the relationship between them was never strong, and the months apart took a toll and eroded an already shaky foundation.

When Bulldog and Tina divorced in 1943, no one was surprised, but not much was said about it. Whatever went wrong in the marriage was never talked about outside the family. West Texans do not air their dirty laundry in public. Still it was a sad affair. Then several years after the divorce, Tina had a seizure, followed by a time of declining health. She died in an El Paso hospital in 1950. She was 28 years old.[9]

But in the spring of 1940, Bulldog Turner was walking in high cotton. He had a new bride and a date with destiny. He flew in to Chicago on April 26, 1940 and met with George Halas the next day.[10] When time came to discuss a contract, Bulldog acted as his own negotiator. He had no agent. No one had agents in those days.

"There's a funny story," Bulldog said, "you've probably heard it, about the first guy who hired an agent. Some guy was having a contract problem with the Green Bay Packers. He was in talking to the coach about his contract. He told the coach, 'You'll have to contact my agent and we'll work through him.'

"That coach said, 'Well, you may work through your agent but you tell him to call Cleveland 'cause you're not going to be in Green Bay anymore.'"[11]

George Halas as usual wanted to close the deal immediately, but Bulldog pocketed the contract and flew back to Texas to consult with his father and with a Sweetwater legend who had some knowledge on the subject.

"Sammy Baugh was the only guy I knew that knew anything about pro football," Bulldog explained. "So, being fairly close where I could get ahold of him, I went out to see him."

Bulldog borrowed a truck and drove out to the Double Mountain Ranch. "I showed him what kind of contract I had been offered and I asked him, 'What do you think about this?' He said, 'I think it's a pretty good deal. I think you'd better sign it.' I was signing for $2,000 and he, at that time, was making $18,000. So, sure he thought it was a great deal for me."[12]

On the advice of Sammy Baugh and with his father's consent, Bulldog signed on the dotted line and mailed the contract back to Halas in Chicago. The agreement was a three-year deal that reportedly made Bulldog the highest paid rookie-lineman in the NFL. His actual salary was $2,000 the first year, $2,250 for the second, and $2,500 for the third. The salary figure that appeared in *The Chicago Tribune* was $5,150 for three years, but that misinformation was surely the work of George Stanley Halas. Coach Halas, the cantankerous coach and owner of the Chicago Bears, was a notorious tightwad and was fiercely secretive about salaries. Halas made certain that the smallest salary figure came out in the papers so that he would have a more advantageous negotiating position with the other players.

To be fair to George Halas he had little money back then, and for decades he ran the Bears on a tight budget before big crowds and multimillion dollar television contracts began to pay off in big dollars. In the early days he had to juggle the books, creatively manage the cash flow, pinch pennies, and post-date checks just to stay in business.

George Halas began his career in professional sports as a baseball player. He played right field for the New York Yankees but lost his place in the starting lineup when the Yankees traded for a pudgy left-handed pitcher turned outfielder from Boston named George Herman Ruth. The Babe turned out to be an adequate replacement. Then Halas switched to football. He played for and coached the Decatur Staleys—later to become the Chicago Bears. He was also a co-owner of the team until he purchased the franchise outright.

Halas could squeeze a nickel as tight as anyone, but it still took a series of fortuitous events to keep the Bears afloat. The first savior was Red Grange when he signed with Chicago in 1925. Already known as "The Galloping Ghost" for his college exploits at the University of Illinois, Grange played his first game as a Chicago Bear on Thanksgiving Day 1925. The financial impact was immediate. Wrigley Field had 36,000 seats, and the game was a sell-out. "If there had been room, we could have put in another 30,000," Halas recalled.

Then came the Great Depression and the Bears almost went into bankruptcy. "In 1932 we lost $30,000 and couldn't borrow from anybody," Halas recalled. "We had to write promissory notes of $1,000 each to pay off Nagurski, Grange, and Coach Ralph Jones, and I believe (Bill) Hewitt took a note for $500."

Most people would have gotten out and found a more profitable business, but Halas did the unthinkable. He bought out his partner, Dutch Sternaman. "I scraped together $40,000 and bought Dutch out," said Halas. "George Trafton's mother put up $20,000 and $5,000 each was put up by my mother, Jim McMillan, Charley Bidwell's nephew and Ralph Brizzolara." Now Halas controlled it all, both the assets and the liabilities.[13]

In those years George Halas did everything for the Bears except play and drive the bus. He was the owner, the coach, the bookkeeper, the general manager, and the father figure. He negotiated the contracts, arranged travel, paid the bills, and sometimes did the laundry. When his players got in trouble, he bailed them out of jail.

In the early days in the NFL, all transactions were in cash. As soon as a game ended Halas met with the owner of the opposing team in a smoke-filled room to divide the gate receipts. Then he stuffed the cash in his pocket and hurried out to catch the team bus.

Coach Halas was one of the great characters in all of sports. He was a part of professional football almost from the beginning. Halas was there on September 20, 1920, in the showroom of Ralph Hay's Hupmobile dealership in Canton, Ohio, when representatives from 14 professional teams sat on the running boards of the cars and formed what would become the National Football League. He paid $100 for a franchise that is now worth $1.1 billion. How important is George Halas to professional football? The address of the Pro Football Hall of Fame is 2121 George Halas Drive.

His personality was larger than life. No organization personified its leader more so than the Chicago Bears personified George Halas. "Oh, I heard all the stories," Bulldog said. "I guess old George must have been a little bit of a Jekyll and Hyde. He was always great to me. I used to tell people that when I got in trouble, I prayed to the Lord and then called George Halas. Halas usually answered first."[14]

During a football game Coach Halas prowled the sideline like a bipolar grizzly bear. He screamed and he cussed. He patted guys on the back and kicked them in the butt. Coach Halas was a spitfire. When Halas chewed someone out, he left teeth marks. His tirades are football legend and could bring a 250-pound lineman to tears. His sideline behavior made Woody Hayes look like a Boy Scout.

Nobody intimidated George Halas. He was tough, and he expected the same of his players. He thought face guards and arm pads made players soft. "Halas hated those face guards," Bulldog said. "Only let you wear one if you had broken bones in your face."[15]

"Halas was tough," Bulldog recalled. "He had rules. If you broke the rules you were fined. You always had to allow time for the drawbridges on the way to practice. He ran the show. You didn't question what he did. If you were late for the train home, you were fined and you paid your own fare. Also, you weren't supposed to have sex after Thursday night until after the game."[16]

"Mr. Halas was a very dynamic person," remembered Bill Bishop, a West Texan from Borger and Bulldog Turner's teammate in Chicago. "When you were playing for him you called him cheap. After you played for him you called him frugal. He hated yes men, he liked to kibbitz and he took losses as hard as anyone."[17]

Halas was also hard on referees, and the refs never missed a chance to return the favor. Once when Halas was riding a referee pretty hard, the ref penalized him five yards for coaching from the sideline, which really was illegal in those days.

"Well," screamed Halas, "that just proves how dumb you are. That's fifteen yards not five yards."

"Yeah," answered the ref, "but the penalty for your kind of coaching is only five yards."

At another game a referee penalized the Bears right in front of the bench. The coach cupped his hands and yelled, "You stink."

The ref walked off another 15 yards, turned to Halas and shouted, "How do I smell from here?"[18]

The play-calling system George Halas used in Chicago would confuse Einstein. The playbook was a bulky, cryptic mass of lines, circles, and arrows containing hundreds of plays and formations. Bulldog studied the system and understood it, but other players wilted under the pressure. One of the guys who had great difficulty deciphering the complicated Chicago system was a young quarterback named

George Blanda. In college, Blanda played blocking back in the old Notre Dame box formation used by Bear Bryant at the University of Kentucky.

"Everything was color-coded," Blanda recalled about his time in Chicago. "Halas had a passion for secrecy and I'd go into the huddle with my head full of chartreuses and burnt ochres, and then I'd have to remember the letter designations, A, U, M, B, or Z and whether we would use a Jack or Jill formation and so on."

Still, it seemed that Blanda had bigger worries than an inability to comprehend the playbook. At training camp his rookie season the coaches listed him a distant third on the depth chart, which meant he would see action only if a Chicago skyscraper fell on the first two quarterbacks. Most of the coaches didn't even know his name. The trainers hadn't even gone to the trouble of putting his name on his locker. They didn't want to waste time or resources on a player whose days with the team were numbered. But sometimes the football takes a funny bounce.

"As things worked out," Blanda remembered, "Sid (Luckman) was slow to recover from a thyroid operation and Lujack had a bad leg, so I played in most of the scrimmages in the training season. After a while I began to look far better that I was. I still hadn't been able to digest all those plays, and good old Bulldog Turner, unbeknown to the coaching staff, was feeding me the plays in the huddle. I'd come back to the huddle and I'd say, 'O.K., Bull, whattya got?' and he'd outline some terrific play and I'd look good calling it and executing it. The Bull would go to the sidelines and say to the coaches, 'Say, that Blanda's really a pip, isn't he? He must really be studying that playbook.'"

Still, the time in Chicago was frustrating for Blanda. The system was complicated, and he had a cool relationship with Coach Halas. "My only satisfaction in those Bear years," Blanda recalled, "came from hobnobbing with the likes of Luckman and Lujack and Bulldog Turner and Ed Sprinkle."[19]

Secrecy wasn't Coach Halas's only obsession. He was fussy about a player's weight. Players who reported to camp overweight had to sit at the fat man's table that served no starches, sweets, or deserts. George Halas's formula for weight loss was simple and based on the only system that really worked—"The energy output must exceed the caloric intake."[20]

And players had to maintain a certain weight throughout the season. "Mr. Halas weighed you in (every Tuesday in season)," Bulldog said, "and fined you $50 a pound for every pound you were over what he told you to weigh."[21] But Bulldog knew how to play the game.

"Bulldog liked to play about 240," his friend and teammate Ed Sprinkle remembered, "but for some reason Coach Halas decided that Bulldog's ideal playing weight was 232. I think Coach Halas may have picked 232 because that's what Bulldog weighed in 1940 when he came up from Hardin-Simmons. Well, Bulldog had to be real careful what he ate on Sunday night and Monday so he wasn't too heavy for the weigh-in. Then later on in the week he'd have a big steak and three or four beers and he'd be back at his playing weight."[22]

Bulldog never missed a meal or turned down a beer, and as he got older, he had a much tougher time maintaining the weight Coach Halas set for him. So he developed some tricks to fool the scales. He claimed he could knock off a few pounds by standing with his long toes curled around the edge of the step-plate. He would hang his t-shirt on the balance arm when the coaches weren't looking. When all other methods failed he would get his teammate just behind him in line to boost up his rear end with one finger under each butt cheek. "The finger" technique could be dangerous, for Bulldog and the finger man, and Bulldog cautioned anyone who used it to be sure the man behind was "a good friend."[23]

He was caught overweight only once. In 1944 he reported to training camp at 258 pounds and took a chair at the fat man's table. He paid the fine, but "Coach Halas gave it back to me as a bonus at the end of the season."

Bulldog had nothing but good things to say about Coach Halas. "He treated me top shelf," Bulldog said. "I don't have a complaint about him. I know others have ridiculed him, but I think, in most cases, it came from players who were cut or traded. I never had that problem. He would always give me the bonus I thought I should get at the end of each season, and as for signing a contract, I wouldn't sign one until I was happy and got what I wanted. And in other dealings he treated me real fine. I think the only people who really talked badly about him were people that weren't helping him. And I can understand that."[24]

Halas and Turner were like father and son. They loved each other but fought like cats and dogs—usually over money. At the end of his rookie year, Bulldog was an All-Pro with an NFL Championship ring. Two hundred dollars a game wasn't enough. Bulldog demanded a new contract.

"I knew, or found out through the grapevine, you know, who the highest-paid lineman was, and I went to see Mr. Halas about renewing or tearing up the old contract and getting a new one. I wanted one just like Danny Fortmann, and he was the highest-paid lineman. After three weeks of arguing, I got it. And then I didn't have any more problems with Mr. Halas the rest of the year. But every year when it came to contract time we had lots of conferences."[25]

George Halas was tight with a dollar, but he knew how to treat his best players. At the end of that first season Halas raised Bulldog's salary to $4,500 a year—the same as Danny Fortmann. Halas didn't give in easily, but he wasn't about to lose the greatest lineman of the era in a contract dispute.

Whatever else might be said about George Halas, the man knew football talent, and Bulldog Turner joined a Bears team poised for greatness—maybe the greatest collection of football talent in history. In the 1940s the Chicago Bears played the roughest and toughest football on the planet.

Five outstanding rookies joined the Bears that year including Bulldog Turner, George McAfee, Ken Kavanaugh, tackle Ed Kolman from Temple, and tackle Lee Artoe from the University of California. When McAfee arrived at training camp, he commented that he "never saw so many big men in all my life." Of course everybody looked big next to McAfee, who was only 6 feet tall and weighed just 175 pounds. Every time he carried the ball it looked as if his life was in danger. But his speed and shiftiness made it difficult for a tackler to get a good shot at him. He was a dancing, spinning, rhythmic runner, and one of the most dangerous kick returners in the history of the NFL. With that core of rookies, Chicago would win four NFL championships in seven years. The 1940 squad may be the best one-platoon football team ever assembled.

There were eight future Hall of Famers with the Chicago Bears of the 1940s: Bulldog Turner, George Halas, George McAfee, guard Danny Fortmann, quarterback Sid Luckman, tackle George Musso, and tackle Joe Stydahar. Bronko Nagurski, another future Hall of Famer, retired after the 1937 season, but would return for one last curtain call to help the Bears win the NFL championship in 1943. A lot of people still believe that Bulldog and Red Grange played together with the old Chicago Bears, but Grange retired in 1934—six years before Bulldog came to Chicago. Still, Grange usually showed up at training camp. "I never did play with him," Bulldog said. "But he was always there, seems like. He wasn't listed as a coach, but he was always there."[26]

One reason for the mistaken belief that Bulldog and Grange were teammates can be traced to Darrell K. Royal of Hollis, Oklahoma. Royal was just 33 years old when he took the head coaching job at the University of Texas at Austin in 1957. In those early years he spoke to more booster clubs, Lions Clubs, and other civic organizations, and ate more chicken-fried steaks with cream gravy, than he cared to remember. Coach Royal knew how to warm up an audience of Texas football fans. He began many of those speeches with a tall tale about Bulldog Turner. The story went this way: Bulldog Turner and Red Grange were teammates on the old Chicago Bears and roommates on road trips. One of the favorite pastimes of bored athletes on the road was staring out hotel windows at the scenery below.

Turner and Grange were "inspecting the sights" from a fourth-story window one day when a particularly pretty girl walked by. In an effort to get a better view, Bulldog leaned out too far, lost his balance and fell to the sidewalk with a resounding crash.

The incident threw passing traffic into chaos and caused a minor earthquake. A policeman rushed over to Turner who was by then on his feet and casually brushing himself off.

"What's going on here?" the officer asked.

"Damned if I know," Bulldog remarked. "I just got here myself."[27]

Navigating the streets of Chicago could be confusing to a West Texas cowboy who hadn't been to town too often, but Bulldog learned his way around his new home, sometimes by trial and error. "I found an apartment," he said, "and I took the L (elevated train) to Wrigley Field for practice every day. I learned that my stop was about eight blocks from my apartment, and I changed to a local each time so I could get that close. What I didn't know was that if I stayed on the express, I could have gotten off about a block from my house. I found that out at the end of the season."[28]

Bulldog may have had some problems getting around in the big city, but once he arrived on the football field, he had all the confidence of a man who knew exactly what he was doing. In fact, he got off the train in Chicago with a smart-ass attitude that rubbed some of the veterans the wrong way—at least in the beginning. He wasn't shy, and he wasn't going to ride the bench. He made his intentions known the first day at camp.

"Here was George Halas's method of operation on practice," Bulldog said. "First he'd say, 'Give me a center!' Then he'd say, 'Bausch!' He'd say, 'Give me two guards!' Then he'd say, 'Fortmann and Musso!' Well, the first time I heard Halas say, 'Give me a center!' I didn't wait for nothing more and ran out and got over the ball. I noticed he looked kinda funny at me, but I didn't think anything about it. I found out later that Pete Bausch was the center—a big, broad mean ol' ballplayer, a real nice German from Kansas. But all I knew was George Halas drafted me No. 1 and I had signed a contract to play center, and I thought when it came time to line up I should be at center. From the beginning I was overendowed with self-confidence. I feared no man. So I just went out there and got over the ball, and I was there ever since. They didn't need Pete no more.

"I was such a good blocker that the men they put in front of me—some of them were stars that were supposed to be making a lot of tackles—they would have their coaches saying, 'Why ain't you making any tackles?' They'd say. 'That bum Turner is holding!' Well, that wasn't true. I held a few, but I was blocking them, too. I used to think I could handle anybody that they put in front of me."[29]

The Bears' first game of the 1940 season was against the defending champion Green Bay Packers. Chicago rookie George McAfee, the fastest man in the NFL, ran for three touchdowns—including a dazzling 93-yard kickoff return—and threw for a fourth as the Bears won the game 41–10. The rout at Green Bay foreshadowed things to come for Bulldog and the Bears that season. Bulldog started the game at center and right outside linebacker. For the next 13 seasons, except for his time in the army, he rarely left the field with time on the clock.

"The only time when I'd come out," Bulldog remembered, "would be maybe with two minutes to go in either half. I'd come out when nothing was going to happen. Of course if something's happenin' out there I wouldn't come out."[30]

Even as a rookie his speed, toughness, and exceptional play caused the rest of the League to sit up and take notice. After the Bears beat the Brooklyn Dodgers 16–7 on October 29, 1940, *The New York Sunday News*, described him as a one-man wrecking crew. "Another of the big bad Bears who are wrecking the pro leagues is Turner, the 230-pound center from Hardin-Simmons," the New York reporter wrote. "He has been good enough to replace Pete Bausch, formerly regular pivot of the club. The Bulldog is the toughest man to take out of a play."

"'You just bounce off him' is the way Ralph Kercheval, veteran Brooklyn back, put it. 'He's never off his feet, and he can't be hurt. Blocking assignments just can't be carried out against him. He's too big and tough.'"[31]

Through seven games the big bad Bears were 6–1, losing only to the Chicago Cardinals at Comiskey Park on September 25. Then came a mid-season slump. On November 10, in a less than sterling performance, the Bears lost to the Lions 17–10 in Detroit. (Even in defeat a Detroit newspaper called Bulldog a "one-man riot.") The next game was against the Washington Redskins in what was billed as a preview of the 1940 NFL championship game, but preparations for Washington hit a snag when the Great Armistice Day Blizzard slammed into Chicago on Monday, blowing out windows all over town and dropping temperatures from a high of 63 to a low of 16. Wind gusts hit 65 mph at Wrigley Field. Five ships sank on Lake Michigan.

Even with good weather, adequate practice time, and a sound game plan most teams would have a tough time beating a Redskins squad that included four future Hall of Famers: the incomparable Sammy Baugh, tackle Turk Edwards, end Wayne Millner, and Coach Ray Flaherty. On November 17, 1940, a sell-out crowd of 36,000 packed old Griffith Stadium in the nation's capital to watch the Redskins beat the Bears 7–3 in a slugfest. Chicago had 16 first downs and moved the ball inside the Redskins' 15-yard line four times in the second half but could not get in the end zone. The weak offensive performance prompted a frustrated George Halas to make some innovative and historic changes. Still, the Bears and the Redskins each won their divisions, and the stage was set for one of the most famous games in football history.

Chapter 6
The Worst Thrashing in History

On December 8, 1940, three weeks after their 7–3 loss to the Redskins, the Bears played the Redskins again in the 1940 NFL Championship Game. The Bears' record was 8–3, and they were the West Division Champions. The Redskins were 9–2, and they were champions of the East.

Most games of that era were forgotten long ago. There was no ESPN. Very little film of that time exists, and not many people who watched pro football in 1940 are still around to tell us about it. But the 1940 NFL Championship Game is a part of football legend. People will talk about that game as long as football is played.

Going in to the game the elements did not favor the Bears. The weather in Chicago was awful the week of the championship game. Snow and freezing weather forced the Bears to work inside the entire time. By contrast, the weather in Washington was balmy and beautiful. The Redskins worked out every day in perfect football weather—cloudy to partly cloudy skies and cool temperatures.

There was a lot of trash talk leading up to the game, most of it coming out of Washington, and every unkind comment made headlines. When some of the Chicago players complained to the press about a controversial no call on pass interference on a play at the end of their regular season game, the owner of the Redskins, George Preston Marshall, called the Bears "crybabies." He told reporters, "They

The Chicago Bears starting lineup for the 1940 NFL Championship Game. In front from left: George Wilson, Lee Artoe, George Musso, Bulldog Turner, Danny Fortmann, Joe Stydahar and Bob Nowaskey. In the backfield, from left, George McAfee, Bill Osmanski, Sid Luckman, and Ray Nolting. Turner, Luckman, Musso, Stydahar, McAfee, and Fortmann are in the Hall of Fame. Reprinted by permission of the Associated Press.

are a bunch of quitters. They fold up when the going gets tough. They are a first half club. They don't know how to win a close game."

George Preston Marshall was a loose cannon, but he was no fool. And in some ways he was ahead of his time. He was one of the first owners to realize the NFL was show business. He was the first to bring in marching bands to perform at intermission. In the old days, halftime was just a break in the action. Marshall gave football the halftime show. He also understood the power of the media. He knew that controversy generated publicity and sold tickets.

Early that week Marshall sent George Halas a telegram that read: "Congratulations. You got me in this thing and I hope I have the pleasure of beating your ears off next Sunday and every year to come. Justice is triumphant. We should play for the championship every year. Game will be sold out by Thursday. Right Regards, George."

The Chicago players heard all the talk coming out of Washington.

George Halas made sure of that. He posted the press clippings containing Marshall's words in the clubhouse. And Halas turned the hype into a huge psychological advantage for his team. When the Bears arrived in Washington, they were not just looking for a championship: They wanted redemption. Angered by Marshall's words, the Bears gave the Redskins the worst thrashing in NFL history.

The Bears' coaches knew something was up by the demeanor of the team on the train ride from Chicago to Washington. Most trips were noisy with players milling around laughing and joking. This trip was quiet. The players actually studied their playbooks.

The Bears arrived in Washington and went about their business with little fanfare. George Halas had little to say to his team or the press. He knew his players were ready. Then, just before kickoff, Coach Halas walked into the Bears' locker room beneath the grandstands at Griffith Stadium. In his pregame talk to his team, he read aloud every unkind remark made by the ownership in Washington. Then, holding up a handbill containing George Preston Marshall's comments, Halas turned to his players and said, "Gentlemen, this is what George Preston Marshall thinks of you. Well, I think you're a great football team— the greatest ever assembled. Now go out and prove it."

A sell-out crowd of 36,034, including many high government officials, watched the massacre. So did 150 reporters—a record number for an NFL contest at that time. The Mutual Radio Network paid a hefty $2,500 for the rights to broadcast the game to 250 radio stations across the country. Red Barber was poised behind the microphone to describe the action to radio listeners from New York to California. Outside the stadium was a prickly situation that had never occurred before at an NFL game. Police arrested eight people for scalping tickets. Professional football was big time at last.[1]

The Bears won the toss—a bad start for the Redskins that was about to get much worse. Still the game was close for a few seconds. George McAfee went up the middle for eight yards on the first play of the game. As the play unfolded, Sid Luckman looked over the defense and saw nothing new or unexpected. On the next play, Luckman flanked Ken Kavanaugh wide left and sent McAfee in motion in that direction. Luckman then gave the ball to fullback Bill "Thunder" Osmanski who, when the off-tackle hole was closed, slipped outside the right end and darted into the open field. At the Washington 35-yard line, two Redskins closed in, but George Wilson of the Bears came from nowhere, plastered the first Redskin, and knocked him into the other. Both went down in what has to be the most famous block in NFL history. Osmanski breezed into the end zone. With 55 seconds gone, the score was Bears 7 Redskins 0.

The Bears' assistant coach Clark Shaughnessy drew up the touch-down play just before kickoff, but Osmanski added his own twist. "Clark Shaughnessy was one of our coaches, see, and Clark Shaugh-nessy to me is the most brilliant football man that ever lived," Bull-dog Turner said. "Anyway, Washington had just beaten us a couple of weeks before, so when it came time to play the championship game, Shaughnessy gave us a little lecture. He drew up a play and said, 'This play's gonna work.' He told us the reasons why. 'And I'll give you an-other play that will work.' Well, by the time he was finished, all you had to do was open the door. We were ready, 'cause, really, he had us convinced that the first play was gonna do it and if it didn't the other would. It was an off-tackle play, the first one, and you know, the funny thing about it, the play didn't work at all. At least, not the first time we used it.

"Bill Osmanski was carrying the ball, and there wasn't no hole any-where. So he started backing up, and he slipped way around the end and headed down the sideline. That was our first play of the game, and it went 68 yards for a touchdown and we went on to kill those guys. We got so much publicity from that game that later all Bill Os-manski wanted to do was run up into the line and then slide out and go around end. I got where I was disgusted with him because he wouldn't run Clark Shaughnessy's play the way it was supposed to be run."[2]

The Redskins tried to answer on their first possession and almost pulled it off. Max Krause returned the kickoff 62 yards to the Bears' 32, but the drive stalled when Redskins receiver Charley Malone, looking back into the sun, dropped a Sammy Baugh pass in the end zone. That was as close as the Redskins would get. After that the barn door opened wide, and all the cows got out. Osmanski's score trig-gered an avalanche of touchdowns.

The Bears could do no wrong against a Redskin's defense that had more holes than Swiss cheese. On the Bears' second possession, quar-

Bear on the loose. 1940 NFL Championship game. Halfback George McAfee (#5) on a sweep left in the first quarter. Bulldog Turner (#66) is rising from the ground after throwing a block. The massacre has only begun. Reprinted by permission of the Associated Press.

terback Sid Luckman scored on a one-yard run. On their third possession, the Bears' Joe Maniaci scored on a 42-yard run. The score was 21–0 before the water got hot. In the second quarter, the Redskins got a brief shot of confidence when they held the Bears scoreless for few minutes. Then, just before halftime, Luckman tossed a 30-yard touchdown pass to Ken Kavanaugh giving Chicago a 28–0 lead. The Bears cruised into intermission feeling seven feet tall and bulletproof.

At halftime, Coach Halas warned his team against being overconfident. "We can't let up," he said. "The Redskins are too good a team. They can come back."

There was no need for concern. The rout was about to turn into a travesty. As the second half started the Redskins were looking to get back into the game, but they were looking in all the wrong places. Meanwhile, the Bears didn't let up for a minute. Just 53 seconds into the third quarter the Bears scored when Hampton Pool intercepted a pass and returned it 15 yards for a touchdown. On the Bears' next possession, halfback Ray Nolting broke through the line and scored on a 23-yard run. George McAfee picked off yet another pass and returned it 35 yards for a touchdown. By the end of the third quarter, the score was 54–0 and climbing. The Bears' ninth touchdown came on a double reverse—an indication that Chicago wasn't just trying to run out the clock.

The Redskins threw 49 passes that afternoon, completing 21. Three passes went for touchdowns—for Chicago. The Bears intercepted eight passes in all. Sid Luckman, by contrast, threw just six passes, completing four, for 102 yards. There was no need to throw because the running game was unstoppable. All day long, Bulldog Turner, Lee Artoe, Danny Fortmann, George Musso, and Joe Stydahar blew holes the size of Oklahoma in the Redskins' defense. The Bears had 382 yards rushing, and the offense scored every time it touched the ball. The defense scored five times (three interceptions and two fumble recoveries). Ten different Bears scored touchdowns.

On the other side of the ball, the Bears' defense kept the Redskins' offense off balance and ineffective. Bulldog intercepted a Sammy Baugh pass, the first interception of his career, and went 24 yards for a touchdown. The play was a thrill for a lineman who had never carried the ball across the goal line. "It was my first score in pro ball, in my years at Hardin-Simmons, or my play at Sweetwater High, and it was great," Bulldog explained. "Any lineman always gets a big buzz from a chance to score, and I got an extra big one because it was in a championship game."[3] Later he crashed through the line and caused a fumble at the two-yard line that led to another score.

While the Bears streaked for the end zone, Redskins' fans streaked for the exits. Only a few diehard drunks were left when the fourth quarter started, and they only stuck around to hurl cuss words and whiskey bottles at the Bears as they dashed for the safety of the locker room when the game was over. Late in the game some boisterous and probably intoxicated fans seated near George Preston Marshall's box began taunting the owner and pelting him with trash. Then a heckler directed some very unkind remarks at Marshall. The owner, already angry and humiliated, climbed the rail and went after the heckler. The police had to restore order. Marshall left the stadium, with a police escort, and slipped quietly away like a white-tail deer in the cedar brakes. He could hardly complain about running up the score after bad-mouthing the Bears before the game.[4]

"Oh my God," a Washington reporter said when the gun sounded that ended the game. "Marshall just shot himself."

The Bears scored 11 touchdowns, a record that still stands. Statisticians in the press box wrote with both hands just trying to keep up. Chicago scored so often and kicked so many balls into the stands that officials ran short of footballs. (There was no end zone net in those days, and balls that sailed into the stands were rarely returned.) The referees met with Halas in the third quarter and asked him not to kick any more PATs (points after touchdown) as they were running low on game balls. Besides, the balls cost $18 apiece, and the loss cut into profits for the teams and the League. When the Bears scored again, Halas sent Bob Snyder into the game with orders for Bulldog to make a bad snap, but Bulldog had too much pride for that.

"Bob Snyder comes in from the bench and says to me, 'Coach said to make a bad pass from center. He said we don't want to kick any more points because we're losing too many footballs.' I think it was Snyder who was going to hold for that next extra point, but anyway, I said to him, 'I'm going to put that ball right back in your hands, and if you don't want it drop it. But I'm not going to make a bad pass.' So I centered it back there, and he just turned it loose and let it lay on the ground. I don't remember who was kicking—we had lots of guys kicking extra points that day—but whoever it was, damn if he didn't kick it up through there and lose another ball."[5]

In a classic case of bad timing, the Redskins announcer chose that moment to make a pitch for next year's Redskins season tickets. Whiskey bottles flew and the stadium rocked with boos. Moments later in the Chicago dressing room, the Bears hoisted the Ed Thorp

Trophy, awarded to the champions of professional football. Outside the Redskins band played "Auld Lang Syne." Washington fans were in a state of shock.

"The next day in the paper they say that point was missed due to a bad snap from center," Bulldog remembered in an interview 50 years later. "Hell, I never made a bad pass in my life."[6]

He was still mad at that reporter.

The final score was Bears 73 Redskins 0—still the most lopsided score in NFL history. Sixteen different Bears scored touchdowns or PATs in what is arguably the most fearsome performance ever seen on the gridiron. When the score came out in the papers the next day, many readers across the country thought it was a misprint. The Redskins hoped it was all a bad dream. It wasn't. On the bright side the Redskins had over 200 return yards, which seems like a lot except that all the return yardage came from kick returns after giving up 11 touchdowns. The weirdest statistic of all was the number of first downs. The Bears had 17 first downs. The Redskins had 18.

The gate grossed $112,508, the biggest payoff thus far in NFL history. Chicago's share was $32,137.68, while the Redskins' organization pocketed $21,825.17. The players' pool amounted to $54,362.80. The win at Washington also gave the Bears the right to play in the NFL All-Star Game in Los Angeles on December 29, 1940 and in the College All-Star Game in Chicago the following August. And most important to the Bears was the guaranteed $25,000 share from each of those contests. George Halas could rest easy. He could pay his bills for another year.

Every Chicago player pocketed a record payout of $873 for winning the world championship of professional football. Each Redskin received $606.25. Some of the players put their money in the bank or invested it in the stock market. Bulldog Turner had never heard of Wall Street, and when it came to banks, he was a lot better at withdrawing than depositing. In a move reminiscent of his old Sweetwater hero Buster Mitchell, Bulldog spent his winnings on a new Olds 88 convertible, tromped on the accelerator, and headed for Sweetwater in a cloud of dust.[7]

"I've got my own ideas about what happened in that championship game," Sammy Baugh remembered, "and I don't know whether they'd be right or not, but I think it starts with the fact that we had played the Bears three weeks earlier and had beat them 7–3. Boy, it hurt 'em. Leaving the field, both teams had to go down the same steps, and I remember some of those Bears were crying. Oh, they were cut to pieces. Their pride was hurt bad. I remember Bulldog Turner coming down those steps and saying, "You just remember one thing—we'll be back in three weeks."[8]

Bulldog had a simpler explanation for the massacre of the Redskins. "It just seemed like everything we did was right and everything they did was wrong."[9]

At a press conference George Preston Marshall, as usual, said whatever was on his mind. "Some of our boys have been playing on their reputations," he said. "We've got to make a few changes." The owner went on to say, "It looked as if some of our lads had fountain pens in their pockets trying to figure out who was going to get that share of the play-off money."[10]

After the game a reporter interviewed some of the players in the quiet Redskins locker room. The reporter asked Slingin' Sammy if the game would have been different if Malone had caught the touchdown pass in the first quarter. "Hell yes!" Sammy drawled. "The score would have been 73 to 7."

Saul Sherman, the Bears' third-string quarterback, recalled: "On the train back from Washington after that game we had quite a celebration. It was all something to remember."[11]

Only with the passage of time did the Bears begin to understand just what they had accomplished. "I didn't realize it at the time," Bulldog Turner said, "but the 73–0 victory by the Bears over Washington in the 1940 pro championship game is the biggest thing that ever happened. That night we kept hearing about it on the radio—and I still get a kick out of hearing about it."[12]

The day after the game the NFL owners held their annual meeting. A lot of people expected trouble between George Marshall and George Halas, but Marshall stunned everyone by walking up to Halas and saying, "George you misunderstood me. I said 7–3 not 73."[13] Halas laughed it off. The two men really did like each other. On another occasion when Marshall's wife, the actress Corrine Griffith, criticized Halas, Marshall was furious. "Don't you dare say anything against Halas," Marshall fumed. "He's my best friend."[14]

On December 29, 1940, three weeks after the championship game in Washington, the Bears played a group of NFL all-stars at Gilmore Stadium in Los Angeles. Bulldog Turner was familiar with the old field on Curson Avenue. He had some of his greatest college games there. This game, won by the Bears 28–14, was an early version of the Pro Bowl.

On his way from Chicago to the all-star game in Los Angeles, Bulldog stopped in Abilene to see his family and revel in the limelight at Hardin-Simmons. He made a surprise visit to the field house and to Hershel Schooley's journalism class. A *Brand* reporter wrote that "Mrs. Turner, the former Waltina (sic) Herman, will accompany him to the West Coast. They will stay over for the Rose Bowl game to see Nebraska, coached by Major Biff Jones, Bulldog's East-West game coach last year, and meet Clark Shaughnessy's Stanford team that he (Bulldog) calls the 'Little Bears.'"

The Brand also reported that Bulldog was delighted to see his little daughter, Sandra, born a few weeks earlier. Sandra only weighed five pounds at birth. "She's not much bigger than a football," Bulldog said, "but she's cute."[15]

To that same reporter Bulldog announced his plans to return to Hardin-Simmons in the spring to finish his degree. His mother wanted it that way, and for Bulldog a degree would mean a measure of acceptance. "All 33 members of the Bears are college men," he told students in Hershel Schooley's journalism news class. "Almost all have their college degrees, and I'm going to get mine as fast as possible.

"We have three doctors on the Bear team," he said. "Others studying to be. Several are businessmen and everybody has a serious purpose in life."[16]

The 1940 NFL Championship game was a landmark for reasons other than the lopsided score. It was during that game that a player for the last time in NFL history played without a helmet. Chicago Bears end Dick Plasman, a 6'3" 210-pound end from Vanderbilt, played the entire game bareheaded. The NFL made helmets mandatory in 1943, but they were in universal use by then anyway. (The NFL mandated socks in 1945.) The 1940 Championship Game was the first to be broadcast by network radio to fans across the country.

But the biggest and most important feature of that game was an offensive innovation used by the winning side. The Bears scored all those points using the T formation with a man in motion rather than a variation of the single wing used by the Redskins and most football teams. The T formation was not new. The Bears used it in the 1930s, but defenses caught on. In the old days opponents stopped the T by jamming the middle.

Then prior to the 1940 Championship Game, after the 7–3 regular season loss to the Redskins, George Halas hired Clark Shaughnessy to put in an updated version of the T. Shaughnessy was a football innovator who had been tinkering with the T for years. He had just finished an undefeated season as head coach at Stanford. On New Year's Day his Cardinals would dismantle the Nebraska Cornhuskers in the Rose Bowl.

In the hands of a talented team, Shaughnessy's offense was practically unstoppable. The quarterback was under center in the T formation. He touched the ball every play and could do many things with it. A good quarterback was the key to making the T work. He could give it to the fullback up the middle or off tackle, pitch it to the halfback going wide, sprint out and pass, or drop back and pass. Plays developed faster because the backs were closer to the line of scrimmage. Even the center became a better blocker because his head was up at the snap. He didn't have to look between his legs to center the ball to the wingback who was four yards behind the line of scrimmage.

In the old days the game belonged to the left halfback—men like Thorpe, Grange, Nagurski and Nevers. The T formation changed all that. With the rise of the T, offenses now used the halfback to draw in defenses to open up the passing lanes. Before the T, a team might throw 10 times a game. With the T in full bloom, teams sometimes threw 10 times a quarter.

The T revolutionized football, and it took defenses a few years to catch up. Clark Shaughnessy added the man in motion and the counterplay to keep defenses from jamming the middle. As a result, teams accustomed to playing against the single wing had neither the defensive schemes nor the personnel to combat the T. In the old days almost all teams used a six-man defensive front with two linebackers. After 1940, some coaches began experimenting with a five-man line and an extra linebacker as a way to defense the T.

As much as anything else, the T formation made possible an exciting brand of football that emphasized speed and quickness over muscle and mass. Teams scored more, attendance went up, and more money came in. Within four years over half of the college and professional teams were using a variation of the T, and those that weren't were considering it. By 1949 the Pittsburgh Steelers were the only NFL team still using the single wing.

"When I went up there we were already playing to sold-out stadiums everywhere we went," Bulldog recalled. "Because, you know, we had just put in what they call the new T formation where it was hand to hand from the center to the quarterback and then we sent a man in motion.

"So we put on a good show regardless who was winning the game because our offense was fun to watch.[17]

"We were so far ahead of everyone else that it got out of hand. It was so bad we would have to give the other team a break just to keep it entertaining—after all we were in the entertainment business. So sometimes in exhibition games, we'd tell them what play to run and we'd let them score with it, just so fans wouldn't leave early."[18]

"It (the 1940 NFL Championship Game) made the entire country 'T' conscious," George Halas said, "and I believe it was the biggest reason for the influx of the T formation in college and pro ball."[19]

Another reason for the T's popularity was Bulldog Turner. He took the T back to Abilene and taught it to coaches all over West Texas. Within a few years the single wing was a relic from a bygone era. No one did more to spread the word than Bulldog.

In 1941 Frank Kimbrough left Hardin-Simmons to coach the Baylor Bears in Waco, and Hardin-Simmons hired Warren Woodson to take Kimbrough's place. Coach Woodson, from Fort Worth and a Baylor graduate, had won a string of championships at Arkansas State Teachers College in Conway, where he used an offense that was a variation of what was commonly called the Notre Dame Box (a version of the single wing with the back who normally lined up outside the end was brought in tight so that the positions of the backs in the backfield resembled the four corners of a box). In the early 1940s Bulldog Turner would go back to Abilene every spring to help Coach Kimbrough, and later Coach Woodson, with spring training. Bulldog taught the Chicago T offense to Coach Woodson.

Coach Woodson embraced the T formation and added a twist of his own. He moved a halfback from the normal full-house backfield to the "wing," a place outside the end. That player, called a wingback, was in a position be a receiver, to block on the sweep or to carry the ball on a reverse. The impact was immediate. That first year using the wing T the Cowboys finished 8–0–1 and were Border Conference champions. While Coach Woodson was at Hardin-Simmons, the Cowboys compiled a record of 58 wins, 23 losses, and 6 ties. During the 1940s the Cowboys had the 10th winningest college football program in the nation. Later in his career Warren Woodson took his wing T to the University of Arizona and New Mexico State.[20]

The same year that Bulldog taught the T to Warren Woodson, a young West Texas coach had just taken his first head coaching job. Gordon Lenear Wood grew up picking cotton near Abilene and was Bulldog Turner's teammate and friend at Hardin-Simmons. In college Wood played football and basketball, and he was a Golden Glove boxer (light heavyweight). Bulldog and Coach Wood spent a lot of time talking football, and soon Bulldog convinced the coach to abandon the single wing and put in the T. Coach Wood used a variation of the Woodson wing T in his high school programs at Rule, Roscoe, Seminole, Winters, Stamford, Victoria, and Brownwood. By the time Gordon Wood retired after 46 years, he was a true West Texas legend. His teams won 496 games, and they won or shared 25 district championships and 9 state football titles.

Wilford Moore from Littlefield played guard next to Bulldog Turner at Hardin-Simmons. Moore learned the T from Warren Woodson who learned it from Bulldog. Moore used a version of the wing T when he became the head football coach at McMurray. He taught the T to Grant Teaff, one of his players, who became head coach at Baylor.

Bulldog taught the T offense to his friend Eck Curtis who in turn took it to the one of the legendary programs in college football. As a young man in the 1920s, Curtis played at Vernon High School and Abilene Christian College. He coached at Anson, Ranger, and Electra before following Pete Shotwell at Breckenridge—a West Texas high school powerhouse.

Eck Curtis met Bulldog Turner sometime in the early 1940s. They corresponded, and Coach Curtis made several trips to Abilene and Chicago to watch Bulldog and the Bears play—and to learn the T.

With Bulldog's help and encouragement, Coach Curtis installed the T at Breckenridge.[21] The Buckaroos made the state semifinals in 1942.

In 1945 Coach Curtis took the T to Highland Park High School. That first year the Scotties tied Waco High for the state championship in a game played at the Cotton Bowl in Dallas before 45,000 fans. In 1946 Coach Blair Cherry, who had succeeded Dana X. Bible at the University of Texas, hired Curtis as an assistant coach. Coach Curtis introduced the T to Texas Longhorn football just in time for Bobby Layne, one of its greatest practitioners. The revolution was complete.

Chapter 7

Bombs and Blitzes

Thanks to radio, a medium that drew in the masses in ways that newspapers never could, the 1940 NFL Championship Game had a nationwide audience for the first time. The Chicago Bears and some of the more successful teams were beginning to build a fan base beyond the city they called home. The owners were optimistic about the coming season and with good reason. The League was making strides, not yet by leaps and bounds but with slow and steady growth. The 55 NFL games played in 1940 drew 1,245,217 paying customers—up about 15,000 from the previous year. The New York Giants led the League in attendance drawing 247,642 in seven home games.

But just when pro football was starting to catch on with sports fans, two men reminded Americans that baseball was still our national pastime. In 1941 Joe DiMaggio hit safely in 56 straight games and Ted Williams batted .406—the last .400 hitter in the Major Leagues. In September the St. Louis Cardinals called up a kid named Stan (not yet "The Man") Musial for the last two weeks of the season. He hit .426 for the final 12 games. Pro football could not yet compete with the Yankees and Red Sox. Even a horse got more press than the NFL. Whirlaway won the 1941 Triple Crown, and became a national hero.

Boxing had a huge following in America and around the world in the pre-war years. On September 29, 1941, Joe Louis, the Brown Bomber, made the cover of *Time Magazine*. Another popular fighter, for a brief moment, was Lew Jenkins, Bulldog Turner's friend from Sweetwater.

Lew Jenkins was the only West Texan to win a world boxing championship. He was born in Milburn, a wide spot in the road between Brownwood and Brady, and raised in Sweetwater. As a teenager he picked cotton for a dollar a day. He first fought for money in carnivals in a desperate attempt to escape the West Texas cotton fields. He was a wild, bony kid, just 5'7" and 135 pounds, but he was one of the most feared punchers of his day. In 1938 he hooked up with Fred Browning, a Fort Worth gambler and boxing promoter (who tried to sign Jay Turner in 1941), and Hymie Caplin, a manager who had trouble staying out of jail. Jenkins trained at Top O' Hill, Browning's restaurant, tea room, casino, and brothel in Arlington (now a part of Arlington Baptist College). On May 10, 1940, Jenkins, dubbed "The Sweet Swatter from Sweetwater," stood alone in the spotlight. He knocked out Lou Ambers in the third round and became the light heavyweight champion of the world.[1] He was the Rocky Balboa of West Texas.

After he won the championship, he was on top of the mountain. He was famous, and he had lots of money. "I was big in New York in those days," he said. "I used to go ice skating with Mayor LaGuardia. Tuffy Leemans, Mel Hein, Bulldog Turner, Steve Owen—were my best buddies. They loved to see me fight, and I loved to see them play."[2]

Lew Jenkins and Bulldog Turner spent time together whenever Bulldog was in New York. The two men had a lot in common. Both were poor boys from West Texas who were famous sports figures. Both men found the nightlife irresistible.

But fame and money are dangerous things for a man prone to excess. Jenkins liked whiskey, motorcycles, fast cars, and loose women more than he liked to train and take care of himself. He started losing fights he could have easily won with a little preparation. His personal life was a mess. Jack Dempsey and Lew Jenkins almost came to blows outside the ring when Dempsey accused Jenkins of having an affair with Dempsey's wife.[3]

Jenkins spent money like he had an endless supply and soon spent it all. As his personal life unraveled, he hit the bottle even harder; sometimes crawling into the ring so drunk he could barely stand. At age 23 he was a world champion. At age 25 he fell off the mountain and rolled all the way to the bottom. His rowdy fans once filled Madison Square Garden and the Polo Grounds, but now no one recognized him on the street or came to his fights. By 1950 he was a dead-broke alcoholic. When he hit rock bottom he had exactly what he started with—nothing.[4]

Bulldog Turner watched his pal self-destruct. Some of Bulldog's friends suggested the experience made him work harder at his craft and temper some of his own bad habits.

Although other sports overshadowed pro football in popularity, the 1941 NFL season was a great show for fans who paid attention. The Packers' Don Hutson, "The Alabama Antelope," was the League MVP. Sammy Baugh won the triple-crown, leading the NFL in passing, punting, and interceptions. The Bears of the Western Conference finished the regular season with a record of 10–1. The Packers, also members of the Western Conference, finished with an identical record of 10–1 (using the box offense Coach Curly Lambeau learned when he played for Knute Rockne at Notre Dame). To complicate matters, the Bears and the Packers voided the official tiebreaker by splitting the two games they played during the regular season. The League decided that a playoff game between the Bears and the Packers would determine which team would play the New York Giants in the 1941 NFL Championship game.

Then one week before that historic playoff game came the news that changed the world, and by the second week of December even baseball had trouble grabbing a headline. Bombs and blitzes—having nothing to do with football—dominated the news. War had raged in Europe since 1939, but so far the United States had stayed out of it. That situation was about to change. An event was about to occur on a tiny island in the Pacific that would rattle windows all across America.

There were three NFL games on the schedule for Sunday afternoon, December 7, 1941. The Brooklyn Dodgers and the New York Giants played at the Polo Grounds located on the corner of 155th Street and Eighth Avenue in Manhattan. It was Alphonse "Tuffy" Leemans Day, honoring the great Giants running back. In a 10-minute pregame ceremony, just before all hell broke loose, Tuffy got a silver tray and $1,500 in defense bonds (soon to be renamed war bonds). In the other games the Redskins and the Eagles did battle at Griffith Stadium on Georgia Avenue in Washington D.C., and Bulldog Turner and the Bears played their south-side rivals, the Chicago Cardinals, at Comiskey Park on West 35th Street in Chicago.

In Washington and New York, sportswriters watched the Associated Press ticker for the score in Chicago. At the end of the first quarter the score was Cardinals 7 Bears 0. Then without warning the ticker interrupted its report with the words "cut football running." Something big was up. Suddenly the game didn't matter.

It was early afternoon in the Eastern Time Zone when the first wave of zeros came in low over Diamondhead and bombs fell on Battleship Row. The games in New York and Washington had already started when the *Arizona* went to the bottom with a thousand sailors. In Washington, George Preston Marshall ordered his staff to make no public announcement to the stadium crowd, stating that he did not wish to divert the fans' attention away from the game. Still, rumors flew when the public address announcer at Griffith Stadium began paging government officials. Stern announcements at all three games ordered military personnel to report immediately to their bases. When reporters started asking questions, NFL and stadium officials told them to contact their offices. The fans in Washington who cheered when Sammy Baugh threw two fourth-quarter touchdown passes to beat Philadelphia would soon learn that thousands of American soldiers were dead or dying at a place called Pearl Harbor.

Sports lost its luster in light of the day's events. The NFL season went on, but the passion was gone. Attendance fell off. The Western Conference playoff game took place on December 14, 1941 on a cold day at Wrigley Field before a smaller than usual crowd. With snow flurries blowing in off Lake Michigan and a high temperature of 14 degrees, the Packers and the Bears squared off in the first playoff game in NFL history. Before the game both teams agreed to play on, past regulation, to a sudden death finish, to avoid a tie—an agreement that wasn't necessary.

The Packers had a 14–3 lead until Chicago scored 30 unanswered points, including 24 points in the second quarter. Six of those points came when the Bears' Hugh Gallarneau returned a punt 81 yards for a touchdown. Don Hutson of the Packers had just one catch for 19 yards. The Bears won the game 33–14 and earned the right to play the New York Giants in the 1941 NFL Championship Game.

On December 21, 1941, exactly two weeks after the attack on Pearl Harbor, the Bears attacked the Giants at Wrigley Field in Chicago. Only 13,341 fans were in the stands, the smallest crowd ever to see a title game since the NFL came into existence. Two rookies, Young Bussey of the Bears and Jack Lummus of the Giants, played their last football game that day. Bussey, a quarterback from Timpson, Texas and Louisiana State University, joined the army at the end of the season and died on the beach in the Philippines in 1945. Jack Lummus of Ellis County, Texas and Baylor University was in the first wave of Marines to land at Iwo Jima. He lost both legs from a hand grenade and later died of his wounds. He received the Congressional Medal of Honor for bravery after his death, becoming the second NFL player to receive the country's highest military award. Maurice "Footsie" Britt of the Detroit Lions also received the Congressional Medal of Honor in 1946.

The Bears were in control of the championship game from the start. Bob Snyder kicked three field goals and George McAfee scored on a five-yard run. Then on the final play of the game the Giants muffed a lateral. Ken Kavanaugh scooped it up and ran 43 yards for a touchdown. On offense, Bulldog Turner whipped every player in front of him, and on defense he shut down the pass and the run to his side, but he still couldn't get his name in the paper. The Bears beat the Giants 37–9 and became the first team in NFL history to win back-to-back titles. After Kavanaugh's touchdown, Ray "Scooter" Mc-Lean of the Bears drop-kicked the extra point, just to see if he could. Drop-kicking was a common thing in the early days of the NFL (Jim Thorpe was especially proficient at it), but by the 1940s it was a dying art, perhaps because the post-1932 football made dropkicking more difficult. The old ball was blunt on the ends and gave a truer bounce. Six decades would pass before a player attempted another dropkick in an NFL game. In 2006, 43-year-old Doug Flutie of the New England Patriots drop-kicked an extra point against the Miami Dolphins, just to see if he could do it.

Considering the small gate, the financial report, as expected, was a disappointment. The game grossed only $46,108.45 with a net of $41,985.50. Radio receipts brought in an additional $9,000, but the NFL paid $6,297.83 for stadium use. The players' share of the gate was $31,281.37. Of that amount, the Bears received $16,891.94, split 38 and 1/2 ways, for a total of $430.94 per man—considerably less than the loser's share the previous year. The Giants received $11,261.30, split 39 ways, for a total of $288.70 per man. The Green Bay Packers, the second-place team in the Western Conference, split $1,564.07, while the Brooklyn Dodgers, runners-up in the Eastern Conference, split the same amount.[5]

After a short trip to Sweetwater for Christmas, Bulldog Turner arrived in New York City on January 2, 1942 for the NFL All-Star game. The contest was supposed to be played in the Los Angeles Coliseum, but the League moved the game to the East Coast citing security concerns. The fear of Japanese attack also moved the Rose Bowl from its home in Pasadena, California to Durham, North Carolina.

In preparation for the All-Star game, George Halas scheduled practice at the Polo Grounds on the afternoon of January 2, but rain and snow left the playing surface a muddy mess. So the team donned sneakers and practiced in the middle of 8th Avenue. For two hours Bulldog and the Bears ran through their drills ducking L-train pillars and dodging taxi cabs.[6] Then on January 4, 1942, before just 17,725 fans, the Chicago Bears beat the NFL all-stars 35–24 in the snow. The NFL gave 50% of the gross profits to benefit the Navy Relief fund.

The 1942 NFL All-Star game marked a grand farewell to the Bears as a unit. The next day at least eight Chicago players—Norm Standlee, George McAfee, Hugh Gallarneau, Joe Maniaci, Young Bussey, Bill Hughes, Ken Kavanaugh, and Dick Plasman—left for military service, not knowing when or if they would return.

By the following spring a large number of NFL players were in military uniform. Some joined and some were drafted. In those days professional athletes got no preferential treatment, nor did they ask for any. Congress instituted the first peacetime draft in October 1940 and renewed it (though only by a single vote) in 1941. Even as bombs fell on London and the Nazis did an end run through Belgium and France, a majority of Americans wanted to remain neutral. Then came the military sucker punch that changed everything. The Japanese attacked

Pearl Harbor and most opposition to the war and the draft vanished. By the start of the 1943 season, 376 NFL players were in uniform somewhere in Europe or the Pacific. Two had already been killed. By the time the atomic bomb fell on Hiroshima in August 1945, a total of 638 active NFL players had served in the armed forces somewhere in the world. Sixty-nine earned decorations; 21were killed, and of these, three died on the microscopic island of Iwo Jima.

With depleted rosters and small crowds, the NFL carried on as best it could. Most teams had no hope of making money. They treaded financial water and aspired to break even. They just wanted to survive in the hope for better times.

In spite of the hardships, the Bears finished the 1942 regular season undefeated, including a 14–0 win over the East Army All-Stars in a game played on September 20, 1942 in Boston. The NFL donated the proceeds from that game and 14 similar exhibition contests to service charities. The games produced a total contribution of over $680,000.

The unblemished record posted by the Bears was only the second perfect regular season in NFL history—the first being the 1934 Bears who went 13–0 before losing in the championship game. This time Chicago looked unstoppable. The defense allowed just two touchdowns in the final six games. Four of those games were shutouts.

Going into the final game of the 1942 regular season, Bulldog Turner and Don Hutson of the Packers were tied for the lead in interceptions with seven. On that day the Bears played the Chicago Cardinals at Comiskey Park. Late in the game Cardinal quarterback Bud Schwenk tried to force a pass across the middle. Bulldog Turner stepped up and made his eighth interception. Don Hutson was the MVP for the year, but Bulldog Turner remains the only linebacker to lead the NFL outright in interceptions.

Pass defense was a skill Bulldog perfected in the pros. "Used to be," explained Jimmy Conzelman, coach of the Chicago Cardinals, "when he (Bulldog) first came around from Texas, he wasn't too hot on pass defense. That is, you could throw a pitch two or three yards away from him and could click. Now you're afraid to throw it when he's in the same ball park. He just reaches out and gets his hooks on it."[7]

On December 13, 1942, the Bears took their unblemished record into the NFL Championship Game in Washington. Only Sammy Baugh and the Redskins stood in the way of a perfect season and a third straight championship. On paper the Bears had the edge. They had won 24 games in a row and had not been beaten since mid-season 1941. Some bookies offered 20 points against Washington's chances.

But football is not always about X's and O's. The 1940 championship game was on everyone's mind, and the Bears had a strange feeling that this time wouldn't be so easy. Over in the Redskins' locker room there was no need for Coach Ray Flaherty to give his team a pep talk before the game. The Redskins needed no reminder of the whipping they took back in 1940. Embarrassment is its own motivator. Without saying a word, Coach Flaherty walked into the quiet dressing room, wrote 73–0 on the chalkboard, and then kicked open the door. The Bears, sitting in their locker room, heard the roar from the Redskins' dressing room. This time psychology favored the Redskins.

Still, the game could have belonged to the Bears. With the Redskins up by only eight in the second half, the Bears drove the ball to the Redskins' 12-yard line, but Sammy Baugh killed the drive with an interception in the end zone. Then late in the game Chicago took possession of the ball on its own 20 and drove the ball 79 yards to the Redskins' 1. On the next play the Bears scored but were penalized for backfield in motion. Two plays later the Bears surrendered the ball on downs. The Redskins ran out the clock and won the game 14–6.

Bulldog was scheduled to play with a team of NFL All-Stars in a game against the champion Redskins on December 27, 1942 at Shibe Park in Philadelphia, but just before Christmas he came down with a throat infection. On Christmas Day he wired game officials from Abilene that his illness would prevent him from "togging up" against the Redskins.

"I feel much better," he said, "but I don't think I could play up to par—especially after a long train ride back east."[8] Still, he was well enough to ride the train to El Paso to watch the Hardin-Simmons Cowboys in the Sun Bowl on New Year's Day.[9]

That spring Bulldog stayed in West Texas where he landed temporary work as a lab assistant at the United States Armed Forces Recruiting and Induction Station in Abilene.[10] The job was uneventful, but it paid the bills between seasons. Then a few weeks after reporting to the Bears' training camp that summer, Bulldog received notice that he was under investigation by the War Manpower Commission (WMC), an agency of the United States government charged with balancing the labor needs of agriculture, industry, and the armed forces. The investigation came on the heels of public complaints following a publicity release by the Bears' front office that indicated five players had left "essential" war jobs to rejoin the team. The other players included Hampton Pool, a mechanic in a Sunnydale, California shipyard, Dante Magnani, a pipefitter at the Mare Island Navy Yard; Al Hoptowit, a farmer in Yakima Valley, Washington; and Harry Clark, a pipefitter in Morgantown, West Virginia. Those five players may have violated the Stabilization Act, a law that barred shifts from job to job during wartime without a certificate of availability.[11]

After an investigation, with full support of the National Football League, the WMC rendered its opinion in October. The report stated that Bulldog was under contract to the Chicago Bears and was subject to recall at the start of the football season. Moreover, Bulldog's principal occupation was professional football. Therefore, any job accepted by him in the off-season constituted supplemental employment and was not subject to WMC regulations. And finally, the employer did not complain when Bulldog returned to Chicago, indicating that the employer understood that Bulldog's services were only temporary.[12] Bulldog Turner, Dante Magnani, Al Hoptowit, Harry Clark, and Hampton Pool were cleared of the charges.

During the war years the manpower shortage was critical, even in the National Football League. Because so many players were serving in the military, the Cleveland Rams did not have enough players to fill a roster in 1943 and ceased operations for the season. The two Pennsylvania teams, the Pittsburgh Steelers and the Philadelphia Eagles, temporarily folded into a single team—the Steagles. Then in 1944 Pittsburgh merged with the Chicago Cardinals. Sportswriters referred to the team as "Card-Pitt," but fans dubbed them the "carpets" after every team in the League walked all over them and they failed to win a game all season. To fill out their rosters, many teams brought some of the old guys out of retirement. Mel Hein came back to play for the New York Giants, and the Bears hired Bronko Nagurski, retired since 1937, for one final season.

In his prime Bronislau "Bronko" Nagurski was the most punishing runner in the history of football. He stood 6'2" and weighed 235. He was the biggest back of his day, and bigger than most linemen. He had a barrel chest, square jaw, muscular arms and legs, big hands and a neck the diameter of a telephone pole. His NFL Championship ring size is 19½—the largest on record.

Off the field Bronko was a quiet, gentle man who liked nothing better than to hunt and fish around his home in northern Minnesota. In the off-season he was a professional wrestler, much to George Halas's displeasure. Bronko didn't particularly like wrestling, but it paid better than professional football.

On the field Bronko was the toughest running back who ever lived. It's a good thing he had a gentle nature—otherwise he might have killed someone. Defensive lineman tried to gang tackle Bronko at the line of scrimmage to protect the smaller guys behind them, because if Bronko got loose and built up a head of steam, defensive backs that got in his way paid a heavy price. They went to the hospital, sometimes two or three a game. Bronko wasn't much of a dipsey-doo runner. But trying to tackle him head on was like trying to bring down a charging rhinoceros. He was already a legend in 1943 when he reported to the Bears' training camp. The younger players could not take their eyes off him but were afraid to speak. Then Bulldog Turner spoke, and when he did he gave Bronko the whole load.

"Gol' dog, Mr. Nagurski," Bulldog said. "I feel like I'm shaking the right hand of God. George Halas has been talking about you since the day I got to Chicago. I was beginning to wonder if a superman such as you really existed. It's a pleasure to see you with my own eyeballs."

Bronko grinned. "Bulldog," he said, "I've had my leg pulled, but never that hard."[13]

Nobody intimidated Bulldog Turner, not even the great Nagurski.

With Bronko Nagurski playing tackle, and occasionally filling in as fullback, the Bears won their division and played the Washington Redskins on December 26, 1943 for the NFL Championship at Wrigley Field. December weather in Chicago can be tricky, but this game day brought clear skies and ideal conditions despite the late date.

Going into the game the biggest headlines hailed the play of the West Texas cowboy from Rotan, just north of Abilene. That year Sammy Baugh had one of the greatest seasons of all time. He led the

League in passing (133 of 239 for 1,754 yards and 23 touchdowns), punting (50 for 2,295 yards for a 45.9-yard average), and interceptions (11 for 112 yards). But game day belonged to Sid Luckman who completed 15 of 26 passes for 286 yards and 5 touchdowns. After the Bears' defense knocked Slingin' Sammy unconscious in the first quarter, backup quarterback George "Bad News" Cafego tried to rally the Skins. He couldn't get it done.

The partisan Chicago crowd had plenty to cheer about that afternoon, but the wildest moment came just before half-time when George Preston Marshall, all decked out in a full-length raccoon coat, wandered down from his box seat onto the field and stood near the Bears' bench—too close for Chicago General Manager Ralph Brizzolara who called the police and had the Redskins' owner escorted away. Marshall was furious and vowed never to speak to Brizzolara again. The Redskins' owner insisted he was no spy but only came down to get a better look at the halftime show. Several of the Bears said that 'ol George, "just wanted to be on the winning side."

Sammy Baugh returned to the game in the fourth quarter, but the damage was done. The Bears won the game 41–21. It was their third title in four years. The gate generated $120,500 producing a "divisible net" of $93,113.63, plus $500 from radio rights. The Bears' cut amounted to $37,086.98 for the player's pool, while the Redskins received $24,724.65. Each of the Bears received $1,135.81, while each Redskin received $724.60. Green Bay and New York finished in second place in their divisions and each team received $3,433 to divide among its players.[14]

An indication of Bulldog's stature in the League came at the end of the year when the AP sportswriters across the country made their all pro selections for the 1943 season. There were three unanimous choices: Sammy Baugh, Don Hutson, and Bulldog Turner.

> "I was playing guard opposite Bulldog Turner, and I got the hell kicked out of me."
>
> *Robert Jabbusch, Ohio State—1944 College All-Star Game*

By 1943 Bulldog was the unofficial captain of the Bears, although it was several years after taking on the role before George Halas made it official. Bulldog understood the delay, "cause to be a captain, you don't only have to be a good player and a leader of men, but your off-the-field activities had to be good too, which mine weren't too good." Bulldog practiced harder than anyone, but at night he couldn't resist the call of the wild.

But to sportswriters and fans in Chicago, Bulldog was number one. They could care less about his drinking and carousing off the field. One reporter documented the passing of an era. "Turner has taken over where Mel Hein left off in the center of the line. He doesn't make many headlines, but he sure lives up to that nickname of Bulldog."[15]

While Coach Halas and many of their stars were at war, the Bears went 6–3–1 in 1944 and 3–7 in 1945, missing the playoffs both years. Despite their failure to make the playoffs, the Bears set several NFL records. They played the entire 1944 season without attempting a field goal. That same year they set the record for number of penalties and yards penalized.

The Bears always had a reputation for rough play, but some players and coaches in the League thought Chicago went too far in 1944. There were suggestions that their failure to make the playoffs drove the Bears to extreme measures. On November 26 in a game against the Eagles, Chicago had 22 penalties for 170 yards—an NFL record that still stands.

"The Bears have always been on the everything goes side," Coach Aldo Donelli of the Cleveland Rams charged, "but their rough-house tactics have stepped up since George Halas joined the Navy. Hunk Anderson's men are especially flagrant in attempting to give a younger club such as we had what they call 'Bear Fever.'"

Coach Donelli went on to say, "It is time Commissioner (Elmer) Layden do something about the Bears and the officials who let them get away with the stuff that would not be permitted in a battle royal. Statistics tell the story plainly. The Bears broke their own National League records for number of penalties and yards assessed."

Some of the Bears suggested that Coach Donelli's complaints was just sour grapes considering that Philadelphia had never beaten the Bears and that the aforementioned 28–7 trouncing of the previously unbeaten Eagles was just another triumph in a long line of victories over a weary opponent. Bulldog Turner, the roughest and toughest man on the Chicago team, denied the charges outright.

"There should be a distinction between dirty and rough football," he said. "We have never done or have been told by our coaches to do anything dirty—by that I mean something that might hurt or injure an opponent." But then he added with a touch of arrogance, "If playing hard football is rough then the Bears are rough."

Bulldog cited the Bears' reputation as a reason for the large number of penalties. He believed that officials were so busy watching the Bears for rules infractions that they often overlooked what was happening on the other side of the ball.[16]

Despite his declaration of innocence, there is no doubt that Bulldog took liberties when the refs weren't looking. His opponents gave him credit for expertise at holding—a claim he never denied, and he was an all-pro at trash talk and inconspicuous retaliation, especially at the bottom of the pile, where by all accounts he did more than his share of gouging, goosing, poking, and biting. "If someone kicked Bulldog, tripped him, or poked him in the eye," teammate J. R. Boone remembered, "he always found a way to get even when the refs weren't looking, usually when everybody was all tangled up at the bottom of a dog pile."[17]

"Let's just say that some of the things that went on at the bottom of the pile cannot be discussed in mixed company," teammate Ed Sprinkle added, a fact he knew better than anyone.[18]

The official NFL rulebook defines "holding" as illegally restraining, tackling, grabbing with the hands, or hooking with the arms an opposing player who is not in possession of the ball. From the beginning and continuing into the modern era, the use of the hands, especially by an offensive lineman, has been a subject of great controversy. Officials admit they could call holding on any play, but there seems to be an unwritten rule that holding is called only in flagrant cases or when it significantly affects a play by eliminating a tackler and giving an unfair advantage to the blocker. Because holding is so subjective, all linemen do it, and most linemen take great pride in their ability to hold and get away with it. The argument over the best at "holding" is as old as football.

Some old-timers called Lou Creekmur of the Lions the best holder of his time. George Preston Marshall claimed that Lou Rymkus of the Redskins "could hold you with one finger." But the consensus seems to be that Bulldog Turner was the most talented (sneakiest and most successful) holder of his day. Creekmur himself said so. Bulldog was a jersey holder, and by 1943 he had developed a technique that was effective yet almost invisible. When a lineman came at him, Bulldog would grab the opponent by the front of his jersey, being careful not to extend his arms, and fall backward dragging the defensive man down with him. Defensive linemen cried foul, but rarely was Bulldog called for an infraction.

Using his many talents, Bulldog was again a unanimous all-pro selection in 1944. The other two unanimous choices that year were Don Hutson (again) and Frank "Bruiser" Kinard, a tackle for the Brooklyn Dodgers.

While many of his teammates left the NFL for military service, Bulldog was content to play football. He had not been drafted because the Selective Service Act contained a paternity deferment for married men. Then Bulldog and Tina divorced in 1943, making him eligible for the draft. In February 1944, the Scurry County draft board in Snyder, where Bulldog had registered for Selective Service, classified him 1-A.[19] On July 19, 1944, Bulldog took and passed his physical in Lubbock and notified the Bears that he was awaiting induction.[20] He was inducted into the Army on January 28, 1945 and reported to reception at Ft. Leavenworth, Kansas two days later.[21] Finally, he went to Ft. Lewis, Washington for basic training.

After boot camp Pvt. Clyde Turner joined the 2nd Army Air Force in Colorado Springs—an outfit whose mission was the organization and training of bomber crews prior to overseas deployment. The Army assigned Bulldog to the Army Air Force Superbombers, a football team that played exhibition games to entertain the troops. The quarterback was Frankie Sinkwich from Georgia—the All-American and 1942 Heisman Trophy winner. "We didn't even have a base," Bulldog remembered of his Army days. "We stayed at the college there. I didn't have any duties besides playing football."

"I played two games with the Bears that season," Bulldog said. "One of my teammates out there in Colorado Springs with the 2nd Air Force was a pilot. He had to get so many hours in the air every month to collect his check. I'd get a 3-day pass, and he'd check out a plane, and we'd fly to Chicago, and I'd play for the Bears and then drive back. Nobody in Colorado knew I was gone but me and the pilot Tom Fears.

"One day he and I flew into Chicago on Saturday, but the Bears weren't playing there the next day. They were going to play in Detroit. So we went out late partying, because I knew some people in Chicago. When we got up the next morning to fly to Detroit, Tom was going to take a little nap, and he put the plane on automatic pilot. He told me what to do. He said, 'Keep that horizon right there in that spot on the instrument,' and he went to sleep. I'm rassling that thing! I'm just pushing with all my might to keep that horizon where it's supposed to be. When he woke up, I said, 'Man, I can't hold this thing anymore.' He reached down and touched a little wheel that tilted the plane to where it was supposed to be.

"We got into Detroit. The Bears had a uniform ready for me, but it didn't have a belt. So I wore my regular army belt with my football uniform."[22]

Tom Fears, Bulldog's sleepy pilot, was an 11th-round draft choice of the Los Angeles Rams in 1944. The Rams' first-round pick that year was Elroy "Crazy Legs" Hirsch, an All-American running back from Wisconsin. Fears and Hirsch combined for 743 career catches in Los Angeles. Both are in the Pro Football Hall of Fame. Ironically, the man who filled in at center for the Chicago Bears that year was John Schiechl from Santa Clara, the first-team All-American center in 1939.

While Bulldog sat in the barracks in spring 1945, he must have thought often of his family in West Texas. Brother Dugie was missing in action in Europe, and brother Jay was ill in Sweetwater. Jay died in April. Dugie came home in May.

Chapter 8

The Master of His Trade

The war ended in 1945, and the soldiers returned home to an America far different from the one they left. The Great Depression was a distant, painful memory. People had money in their pockets and more leisure time to spend their disposable incomes. The economy boomed. The price of gasoline was 15 cents a gallon. The average price of a new car was $1,120. The University of Pennsylvania built ENIAC, the first automatic, electronic, digital computer. An unknown pediatrician named Benjamin Spock published *The Common Sense Book of Baby and Child Care*—a book that from the beginning was influential and controversial. Bikinis went on sale in Paris. This old world would never be the same.

In the National Football League, there was a supercharged level of optimism and excitement. There were more people in the stands. Reflecting the changing American demographics, the Cleveland Rams moved to Los Angeles, becoming the first franchise on the West Coast. The NFL was slowly becoming national in scope. The League experienced a surge in popularity. The average American was discovering pro football. It was about time.

In Chicago, George Halas was back on the sideline at the start of the 1946 season, and he would start seven veterans from the 1941 and 1943 championship teams. There were persistent rumors, apparently true, that the new All-American Conference offered big contracts to

Bulldog Turner, George McAfee, and Sid Luckman, but in the end all signed with the Bears.

Many of the Bears were kids when they shipped out to fight in the war in 1942, but they were men when they reported to training camp at St. Joseph's College in Rensselaer, Indiana in the summer of 1946. George Halas treated them accordingly. He put his team at ease and established a spirit of respect and trust the first day at camp.

"Some of us are in better shape than others," Halas told his players at the first team meeting, "and probably none of us can do all the things we could do back in '40 or '41—at least not right away. But we're going to stick together and go through this season as a team—so relax. Nobody will be cut because he is a little rusty."

He added, "And one more thing. You've had to take a lot of orders over the last few years and you probably have had enough discipline and regimentation to last a lifetime. I know I have.

"So, all rules are off. No curfews. No bed checks. You're on your own. It's up to you individually to get in shape and play football."[1]

That talk, as much as any other factor, created the tremendous morale that carried the Bears back to the championship in 1946.

In addition to the established stars on the roster were some little-known but excellent football players. Noah "Moon" Mullins from Kentucky was a good pass defender who would retire with 16 career interceptions. Jim Keane was a fine pass receiver who would lead the League in 1947 with 64 receptions. Fred Davis, a tackle from Alabama, was a two-time all pro.

Among the ex-soldiers that showed up at the Bears' training camp that summer was another small-school Texan who George Halas found behind a tumbleweed. Stuart Clarkson, from Corpus Christi, played college ball at Texas A&I in Kingsville. The Bears made him the last pick in the last round in the 1942 NFL draft. Before playing professional football, Clarkson served in the army from 1943 to 1945. He landed at Utah Beach in June 1944 as a part of the European invasion. After the war he played for the Bears from 1946 until 1951, where he was Bulldog Turner's good friend and understudy.[2]

Edward Alexander Sprinkle, one of the most extraordinary players who ever wore the blue and orange, might never have had a career in the NFL without the help of Bulldog Turner. Sprinkle was born in

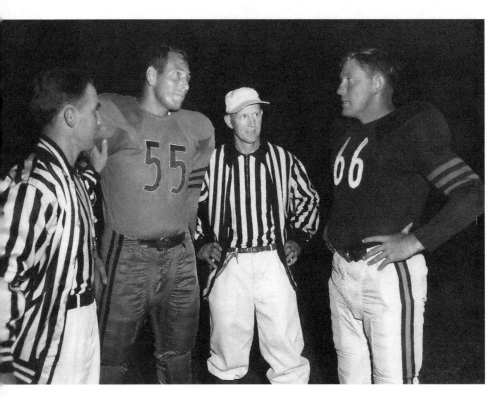

Bulldog Turner with his friend #55 Stuart Clarkson. Courtesy of Pat Turner.

Bradshaw, just south of Abilene, and raised a few miles away in Tuscola. He went to Hardin-Simmons on an academic scholarship and made the football team as a walk-on. Although he played little football in high school, Sprinkle's passion for the game and his kamikaze style of play, got noticed by the coaches at Hardin-Simmons and a rising young NFL star who returned to Abilene to help out every spring.

"After my freshman year (at Hardin-Simmons) Bulldog Turner came back to Abilene to help with the coaching during spring training," Sprinkle said. "We became great friends. Coach Kimbrough and Bulldog tried to make a center out of me, but I was not built for a center. And I didn't have the temperament for a center. My playing style was better suited to one of the other line positions."[3]

Although he only weighed 200 pounds soaking wet, Sprinkle made All-Border Conference tackle in 1942. "Then in the spring of 1943 I decided I wanted to join the Naval Air Corps," Sprinkle said. "I wanted to be a navy pilot and fight the Japanese. First I went to New Orleans for training, and then a few weeks later I got an appointment to the Naval Academy at Annapolis, Maryland. I still had a year of eligibility left so I played football at Navy. By the third game I started at tackle. We had a great team—finished number nine in the nation. We only lost one game to Notre Dame. Then I went into the Naval Reserves and asked for an early call. But by the end of that year the war was winding down. I still wanted to be a Navy pilot. I waited for the call, but it never came. Then I saw Bulldog in Abilene in 1944. He was after me to go with him to Chicago to play for the Bears. After I waited long enough on the Navy, I caught the train for Chicago."[4]

"Bulldog believed in me," said Sprinkle. "He insisted that I go with him to Chicago and try out for the Bears."[5]

If evaluated on size alone, Ed Sprinkle would never have had a career in the NFL. He was too small. In fact he almost went home that first day when the Chicago coaches came to a hasty conclusion that the team did not need a 210-pound tackle. Then Bulldog Turner stepped in and saved Sprinkle's career. After an angry meeting in the coach's office, George Halas agreed to give Sprinkle a second look, but only after Bulldog threatened to quit the team.

"When he reported to the Bears," Bulldog recalled, "I told George Halas that he couldn't be kept off the team, and I even offered to pay his salary until he made the grade. In fact, I also said 'if you don't keep him, you can't have me either.'"[6] George Halas had a sudden change of heart.

Bulldog found Sprinkle sitting in his locker packing his things. Sprinkle clearly recalled the conversation. "'Can you learn the guard position by tomorrow?' Bulldog asked. I said, 'Yes.' Coach Halas thought I was too small to play tackle, but I might make the team as a guard.

"When I finally got the chance to play the coaches saw that I was good. But I think the play that cinched it for me was one day in practice when Ray Nolting was running the ball down the sideline. I hit Ray head on at full speed and knocked him eight feet in the air. I rattled his chops. After that hit I got some respect."[7]

Sprinkle stayed and soon won a starting position. But he was more than just a player. Ed Sprinkle was a star. He played 12 seasons (1944–1955) and was first-team All NFL in 1949 and 1950. He made four Pro

#7 Ed Sprinkle and #66 Bulldog Turner with two young fans.
Courtesy of of Pat Turner.

Bowl appearances (1951, the first year of the Pro Bowl, 1952, 1953, and 1955). He was a member of the 1940s NFL All-Decade team as chosen by the Hall of Fame Selection Committee, and he played on the Chicago Bears' team that won the 1946 NFL Championship.

Off the field Ed Sprinkle was a nice man with a wife and family. In the locker room everyone liked him. Tackle George Connor called him "about the quietest guy on the team." George Halas said he was "a fine clean-cut young man." Bulldog Turner said Sprinkle was "as fine a gentleman as you could meet.[8]

But when Sprinkle took off his coat and tie and put on his shoulder pads and helmet, he turned into the lineman from hell. He enjoyed colliding with people at high speed. He wasn't the biggest man on the field or the fastest, but he had no fear. He used his hands like fly swatters and his forearms like clubs. Halas called him "the toughest player I ever coached"—an extraordinary statement from the man who tutored Dick Butkus, Bronko Nagurski, and the infamous George "The Beast" Trafton, one of the greatest barroom brawlers in the history of Chicago. Sprinkle didn't know how to take it easy. Even his buddies on the Bears hated to practice against him because Sprinkle never went half speed. Full speed was the only gear in his transmission. And his teammates learned never to play pick-up basketball with him. When Sprinkle went to the basket, someone could get hurt.

Sprinkle played end on offense. He caught Bobby Layne's first touchdown pass—a 34-yarder against Green Bay on September 26, 1948. But he sparkled on defense and sparked an NFL revolution at the same time. Thanks to Sammy Baugh, the forward pass had become the primary weapon of NFL offenses, and by the 1950s the League was filled with great passers. A strong pass rush was essential to defend against the air attacks of the T formation. Ed Sprinkle was a pass-rushing specialist—the first player to achieve fame solely on his ability to rush the passer. His job was to get the quarterback.

"I played defensive guard my first two years in the League," Sprinkle said. "Then I got my first start at defensive end in the 1946 NFL Championship Game against New York. No one paid much attention to me until I clotheslined Frank Filchock and broke his nose. The ball came loose. Dante Magnani picked it up and ran it in for a touchdown.

"I was the first in history to specialize in rushing the passer. I once had five sacks in a game up in Baltimore. There are pass rushers to-day who don't get that many sacks in their whole career."⁹

When Ed Sprinkle blocked or tackled someone, he tore into his opponent as if he were fighting for his life. A January 2, 1990 article in the *Chicago Sun Times* rated Ed Sprinkle the toughest man who ever wore a Bears uniform. Dick Butkus was a close number two. In the November 25, 1950 edition of *Colliers Magazine*, writer Bill Fay called Sprinkle "The Meanest Man in Football." When Sprinkle retired in 1955, other teams sent donations to his retirement fund. One team sent a wad of cash with a note that read "It's worth this and more if we don't have to worry about playing Ed again."¹⁰

Sprinkle was a skinny guy with long arms and elbows made of steel. He had the reflexes of a starving lion. He may have been the quickest man off the snap in the history of the National Football League. And when he played football, or anything else for that matter, he went all out. Arms and legs flew in all directions. Not only did the blocker have all he could handle, anyone in the vicinity was at risk. Innocent bystanders, even teammates, got punched, stepped on, kicked, slapped, scratched, or hit in the face—all of it apparently unintentional. That's just the way Ed Sprinkle played the game. "Finesse" was not in his vocabulary. He was a master of the head slap, the forearm to the chin, the head tackle, and the blind-side hit. He developed a technique called the "clothesline" tackle whereby he would swing his fully extended arm at the ball carrier's head. It was a vicious blow that only a karate expert could appreciate. Most of those moves are illegal today, and they are illegal because Ed Sprinkle was so adept at using them. Once in a game in 1950, Sprinkle's flailing left hand broke Bulldog Turner's nose, accidently of course.

Outside Chicago Sprinkle was the most hated man in the NFL for the havoc he created on the field. But inside the loop, Sprinkle was a hero. His legions of fans called him "The Claw." "If a running back was running by you and you couldn't get to him because a guy was blocking, I would reach out and hook him under the chin. That's where they came up with it," Sprinkle said about his nickname.¹¹

Just the thought of playing against Ed Sprinkle could raise a player's level of anxiety. On October 10, 1954, the Baltimore Colts played the Chicago Bears at Wrigley Field. The quarterback for the Colts was a rookie from Baylor named Cotton Davidson. As he warmed up before the game, Cotton was loose and confident. Then he had a conversation with a teammate that gave him concern. "Just before the kickoff in Chicago," Cotton recalled, "Buddy Young, the smallest man in the NFL, gave me some advice. 'Cotton,' he said, 'Whatever you do, don't watch your passes after you throw the ball. If you do, Ed Sprinkle will take your head off.' It was good advice."[12]

It didn't take a genius to see the problems Sprinkle presented to opposing offenses; especially with Bulldog Turner behind him at out-side linebacker and George McAfee, the fastest man in the NFL, at right defensive halfback.

"Well, he made it in a big way," Bulldog recalled, "being tried at tackle, then guard and finally wound up at end because he lacks weight. In one scrimmage he was so fired up that he just about murdered me on one play. I had to remind him I was his teammate and friend."[13]

Ed Sprinkle and Stu Clarkson learned their craft at the feet of the man generally recognized as the master of his trade. Bulldog Turner had become the standard by which future centers would be judged. As recognition of his extraordinary skill, a poll of sportswriters and coaches from all over the country named Bulldog Turner the All-Time All-American center. The formal announcement of the All-Time All-American team at Wrigley Field in Chicago on September 1, 1946 turned into a gathering of gridiron immortals.

Frank Korch, the man who scouted Bulldog Turner for the Bears, described the occasion for the Hardin-Simmons student newspaper. "The Bulldog is playing a terrific game this year," Korch said. "No doubt you are aware that he was named the All-Time All-American center in a nation-wide poll of sportswriters, radio experts, coaches, and observers. On September 1 at the half-time of the Chicago Bears-New York Giants services benefit game, Turner took his place alongside the All-Time Greats of the Gridiron—Heffelfinger, Heston, Thorpe, Grange, Hutson, Nagurski, Cannon, et al."[14] The photograph of that gathering is one of the most famous pictures of football's early days.

Inspired by the leadership of George Halas and the play of Sid

A gathering of gridiron immortals, September 1, 1946, at Wrigley Field in Chicago. Left to right: Jim Thorpe, Don Hutson, Wilbur "Fats" Henry, William "Pudge" Heffelfinger, the actor Joe E. Brown, Bulldog Turner, Jack Cannon, Bronko Nagurski, Duke Slater, General J. R. Kilpatrick, Willie Heston, Harold "Red" Grange, Bob Zuppke, Governor Green of Illinois and Admiral Murray, U.S. Navy. Courtesy of Wheaton College, Special Collections.

Luckman, George McAfee and Bulldog Turner, the Bears finished the 1946 season with a record of 8–2–1, winning the NFL's Western Division. On December 15, 1946, the Bears played the Giants at the Polo Grounds in New York for the NFL Championship. Harry Wismer called the game for ABC radio. A crowd of 58,346 watched the game—the largest crowd in NFL history up to that time. George Halas's dream for a quarter century was about to come true. The NFL was on the brink of unprecedented popularity and profitability. Bulldog Turner had helped to get it there.

Then on game day the teams were having breakfast and making their way to the Polo Grounds in Manhattan when a story broke that rocked the sports world and suggested that maybe Amos Alonzo Stagg was right about pro football after all. A bookie with connections to organized crime offered New York fullback Merle Hapes and quarterback Frank Filchock $2,500 each to throw the championship game, plus an additional $1,000 each if Chicago beat the spread and won the game by more than 10 points. That morning New York Mayor William O'Dwyer told Commissioner Bert Bell of the allegations. Bell informed Jack and Wellington Mara, owners of the Giants, of the charges. Bell then moved quickly to control the damage.

Commissioner Bell, in town for the championship game, summoned both players to Gracie Mansion in Manhattan. Hapes admitted being offered a bribe but denied accepting any money. Filchock denied any knowledge of the matter. Filchock played that day (throwing six interceptions), but the commissioner suspended Hapes for failing to report an attempted bribe.

By game time the weather was clear and cold. The Bears scored 14 points in the first quarter, but the Giants fought back to tie it up. This contest was as rough as anyone could remember. Ed Sprinkle of the Bears crushed Frankie Filchock's nose with a wicked left-hand hook. Filchock played the game with packing in his nose, and then went to the hospital for treatment. Giants fullback Frank Reagan was carried off the field in the first quarter with a broken nose and a concussion. After the game both sides were bruised and bloody. The scene behind the New York bench looked like a field hospital during the war.

The score was 14–14 late in the fourth quarter when Giants kicker Howie Livingston shanked a punt that traveled only 16 yards. The Bears took full advantage and drove the ball downfield. Soon they had a first down on the Giants' 19, and the scene was set for the most famous play of the game. Sid Luckman, who *never* ran the ball, surprised everyone in the stadium by faking a handoff to George McAfee, sticking the ball on his hip and taking off around the Bears' right end. He even fooled the referees who thought McAfee had the ball and almost whistled the play dead when a Giant defender knocked the running back to the ground. Still, Luckman was almost nailed for a loss, but a crushing block by Bulldog Turner sprung the quarterback on a bootleg play that turned into a 19-yard touchdown run. Chicago kicked a late field goal and beat the Giants 24–14. The margin of victory was 10 points—the gamblers' precise betting line.

Despite the controversy that surrounded it, the game itself was a financial bonanza that helped solidify the future of the NFL. The gate grossed $282,955.22—the largest gate ever. Each Chicago player received $1,975.82 from the players' pool. Each Giant received $1,295.57.[15]

That weekend in New York, Bulldog and the Bears celebrated their fourth championship in seven years. The party lasted throughout the night, and it was fitting because the franchise would not get the chance to celebrate a championship again until a team led by Mike Ditka, Bill George, Doug Atkins, Willie Gallimore, Billy Wade, and Ronnie Bull won it all in 1963.

Several hours after the 1946 championship game, New York police arrested Alvin J. Parks, the bookie in question. At the trial both Hapes and Filchock strongly denied taking bribe money. The judge at the trial was sympathetic, especially to Filchock, saying he "was not an accomplice and was in fact an unfortunate victim of circumstances." But any association with gambling and organized crime was the unpardonable sin for professional sports, and the League had no choice but to come down hard on Hapes and Filchock. If the public ever became convinced that NFL games were fixed, the sport was doomed. A postseason investigation by the League found that, although neither man had taken a bribe, Merle Hapes and Frank Filchock had consorted with gamblers and were "guilty of actions detrimental to the welfare of the NFL." Commissioner Bell suspended them indefinitely. Neither man played in the NFL again.

The excitement of the 1946 NFL Championship still lingered on the streets of the Windy City in the spring and summer of 1947. There was little else for a Chicago sports fan to get excited about. The Cubs muddled along at the bottom of their division and would finish the season at 69–85—sixth place in the National League. The White Sox were better, but just barely, with a record of 70–84—sixth place in the American League. The Blackhawks were dead last in the NHL with a record of 20–34.

With so little excitement on the field, some of the biggest sports news in Chicago that spring was on the society page with the announcement that Bulldog Turner married Gladys Webber from Bartlesville, Oklahoma. Gladys was a blonde beauty with a strong will. She was the perfect mate for Bulldog. He adored her, and she took care of him. She rarely left his side for the next 40 years. Their marriage was long and successful because they understood each other. In public, Gladys stayed in the background and let Bulldog take the lead, but in private her influence was considerable. When Gladys spoke, Bulldog listened. Bulldog Turner had never been happier.

As defending NFL champions, the Chicago Bears prepared to play the College All-Stars in August 1947. Everyone expected a good turn-out, but the interest in the 1947 College All-Star game caught even the starry-eyed optimists by surprise. The event sold out in less than a week. There were 225,000 requests for tickets from 36 states and Cuba. The staff at Soldier Field added 3,000 additional seating plus room for 3,000 standing spectators bringing the capacity of Soldier Field to 106,000.

Doc Blanchard and Glenn Davis of Army were the headliners for the All-Stars supported by running back Bob Fenimore—an All-American from Oklahoma A&M. But the star of the show was little Buddy Young from Illinois (5'4", 170 pounds). Young ran for 165 yards. The All-Stars beat the Bears 16–0.

Chapter 9

On the Way Down

N o one was more excited than George Halas in December 1946. His team had just won the NFL Championship, and with two first-round selections in the draft, he had the chance to stay on top for years to come. But drafting is not an exact science. A little luck is involved.

The Bears selected Bob Fenimore from Oklahoma A&M, as their number one selection in the 1947 NFL draft. Fenimore, "The Blonde Bomber," was big and fast. He led the nation in total offense in 1944 and 1945, but sat out most of his senior year with injuries. The Bears took a chance on him anyway. He played one season in Chicago before injuries ended his career. The Bears then took Don Kindt, a halfback from Wisconsin, as the last player selected in the first round. Kindt had a good career in the NFL, but he was never the star Halas hoped he would be.

Most of the notables in the 1947 draft came in the later rounds, and some of them were noted more for coaching than playing. The Giants selected Tom Landry (Hall of Fame 1990), a halfback from Texas, in round 20 and Art Donovan (Hall of Fame 1968), a tackle from Boston College, in round 22. The Rams took Dante Lavelli (Hall of Fame 1975), a halfback from Ohio State, in round 12. The number two pick in the 1947 draft was Glenn Davis, "Mr. Outside," from Army. Davis played one year for the Los Angeles Rams, dated Elizabeth Taylor, injured a knee, and left the game. The Pittsburgh Steelers selected

Ara Parseghian, a halfback from Miami (Ohio) in round 13. Parseghian is best known as the head coach at Notre Dame from 1964 to 1974. In those 11 seasons the Fighting Irish won 97 games and two national titles.

But the Bears' run of good luck had petered out. Not only was the draft class relatively unproductive, the 1947 season did not start well for the defending champions. The Bears lost the first game of the year to the Green Bay Packers and the second game to the Chicago Cardinals. After four weeks the Bears were 2–2 and sucking wind.

Then on October 26, 1947 the Bears played the Redskins in Washington. For the Bears, the frustrations of the season came out in the form of 16 penalties for 130 yards. The Washington quarterbacks, Sammy Baugh and Jim Youel, threw for a combined 411 yards (26 of 46), but Chicago scored six touchdowns in the second half and won the game 56–20. In the third quarter Bulldog Turner intercepted a Sammy Baugh pass at the Bears' three-yard line and went 97 yards for a touchdown—the third longest touchdown run after an interception in League history at that time. But Bulldog didn't make the trip alone. He carried some extra cargo on his long trip to the end zone.

"I started weaving up that field and picking up blockers," Bulldog said. "First thing I know, I'm about in the clear and I got up a head of steam. I'm coming down that sideline, getting my blockers and weaving around. I finally decided I'd just dart over to my left, and I did. About that time somebody hit me in the back of the head and jumped on me. Well, it was Sammy Baugh. He was on my back and I was carrying him. I carried him for about seven yards, and I got the ball over the goal line and I looked up and said, 'Sammy, I can outrun you. How did you get back there?'"

"Well, Bulldog," Baugh replied. "You just cut back one too many times."

"Now that's the truth," Bulldog told a *Sports Illustrated* reporter. "It shows in the films. I went 97 yards for a touchdown, the last seven with Sammy Baugh from Sweetwater High on my back."[1]

Bulldog's interception and touchdown run held up as a team record until Richie Pettibone returned an interception 101 yards against the Los Angeles Rams in 1962. Pettibone's interception was another chapter in the sometimes bitter rivalry between the Rams and the

Bears that extended back to the days when the Rams were in Cleveland. But when the team moved to Los Angeles in 1946, the heated contests between the blue-collar Bears and the suntanned Southern Californians took on a new intensity. Some games looked more like insurrections and featured more fist fights than touchdowns.

The most unforgettable uprising occurred on November 16, 1947 at the Coliseum in Los Angeles. Officials knew they were in for a long afternoon when, in a pregame shouting match, the participants exchanged salutations in words not suitable for dinnertime conversation. The game itself was tense but without excessive brutality for the first 15 minutes. Then in the second quarter Ed Sprinkle threw a wicked left forearm at Rams quarterback Bob Waterfield (husband of actress Jane Russell). The blow hit Waterfield under the chin and broke his jaw. (In a game two years earlier, Waterfield threw an elbow that broke Sprinkle's jaw, but Sprinkle denied that his hit was in retaliation for his own injury. "It was just a part of the game," he said.) After Waterfield went down, all decorum disappeared. The referees were like policemen in the middle of a riot after a soccer game. Red flags flew like beads at Mardi Gras. By the end of the game officials had issued numerous warnings and ejected five players—three Bears and two Rams. The Bears alone had 114 yards in penalties. Sprinkle was thrown out of the game, not for breaking Bob Waterfield's jaw, but for throwing a punch at Dante Magnani.

When the clock ran out, the game ended but not the fight. Jack Matheson of the Bears (who had already been penalized three times during the game for unnecessary roughness) saw Harold "Bud" Leininger, the Rams' assistant trainer and equipment manager, carrying off what Matheson thought was the game ball. Matheson went to get it back. When Leininger (5'2" and 100 lbs.) refused to give it up, Matheson (6'2" and 230 lbs.) socked him in the eye. Rams coaches Bob Snyder and George Trafton (both ex-Bears and no strangers to trouble) intervened. Intermittent scuffling continued as players from both teams mingled on their way down the exit ramp. While angry players crowded the door of the Rams' locker room, Snyder suddenly whirled and landed a solid right to Matheson's jaw, knocking him through the door and into the training room. The shoving and cussing then became general, and security had to call in reinforcements to separate the two groups of large angry men.

But Bulldog Turner wasn't finished. "Some big guy on our team knocked him (Leininger) down and took the ball away from him," Bulldog recalled. "I thought it wasn't quite right." So Bulldog and Ken Kavanaugh walked straight into the Rams' dressing room where emotions were high and tempers still blazed. When the Rams saw Bulldog walk through the door, there was a general rush in his direction.

"Whoa down a minute," Bulldog roared. "I still ain't satisfied with the outcome of all those fights on the field, and I'll accommodate any or all of you guys. But I came here for another purpose." And he pushed his way through the scowling Rams and apologized to Bob Snyder and then to Bud Leininger for the actions of his teammate. "We'll take care of Matheson ourselves," Bulldog promised.[2] Leininger never forgot what Bulldog Turner did that day, and 20 years later he got a chance to show his appreciation. On Monday the Commissioner suspended Matheson without pay for one game and fined the five ejected players (including Ed Sprinkle) $50 each for their actions on the field.

It was later that same season that Bulldog invented one of the most familiar plays in football. On a cold day in Green Bay, Wisconsin, Bulldog discovered that Green Bay linebacker Charles "Buckets" Goldenberg (born in 1911 in Czarist Russia) was reading the quarterback. Every time Sid Luckman called a pass play, Buckets immediately dropped back into his middle zone.

"Somehow he could tell when Sid was going to pass," Bulldog explained. "As soon as that ball was snapped, Buckets Goldenberg would pull back and start covering the pass. So I said, 'Let's fake a pass and give the ball to the fullback and let him run up here where I am, 'cause there's nobody here but me.' The next year we put in the play, and it averaged 33 yards a try. The fullback would run plumb to the safety man before they knew he had the ball."[3] Today every football team from junior high to the pros uses the draw play, invented by Bulldog Turner on a cold afternoon in Green Bay.

As he got older, Bulldog delighted in proving to rookies that experience and treachery trumped youth and enthusiasm. Rocco Canale, a rookie with the Philadelphia Eagles, recalled the time Bulldog hoodwinked him in a game at Wrigley Field after Canale broke through the line clean and dropped Hank Margarita of the Bears with a jarring tackle. Margarita had to be carried from the field.

"It was purely accidental," Rocco said, "but those Bears sure gave me the business. 'We are going to get you, Canale,' threatened Bulldog Turner while the rest of them were growling at me under their breath."

Canale was not easily intimidated and was eager to prove it. "On the very next play," he recalled, "a hole opened up, and I charged through. Bulldog hit me just enough to swerve me, and the Bear fullback barreled up the middle for 55 yards and a touchdown. I'd been suckered into a perfect trap play."

"As Turner passed me on the way back, he grinned and said, 'Rookie, you're going to learn something out of this game yet.'"[4]

Bulldog would do just about anything to get an edge on the competition. He excelled at trash talk—especially when directed at rookies. "If opposing players thought they could throw you off or get a psychological advantage by making fun of your heritage, your religion, your girlfriend or your mother, they did it," said J. R. Boone. "Bulldog was the master. I've seen him use threats and insults to rattle a rookie and take him plumb out of the game."[5]

Bulldog's bag of tricks was as big as a tow sack. One Sunday afternoon the Bears played the Lions in Detroit. There had been a snowstorm the night before and flurries throughout the game dusted the field. The Bears were on the Lions' four-yard line and driving for a touchdown when a delay on the field momentarily suspended play. Bulldog, in a playful mood and bored by the delay, carefully molded a snowball and hurled it into the crowd behind the north goal. The spectators fired back, throwing so many snowballs onto the field that the referee felt it necessary to intervene. As the home team, the Lions were responsible for what the rule book called a "palpably unfair act by a non-player." The referee, who did not see Bulldog throw the first snowball, penalized the Lions half the distance to the goal. The Bears scored on the next play and won the game 28–7.[6]

"I also originated a play that got me even with Ed Neal for beating my head off," Bulldog remembered. "There in the late 1940s he played at Green Bay, and by this time they had put in the 5–4 defense. They put the biggest, toughest guy they had right in front of the center, and I was expected to block him either way, according to which way the play went. Well, Ed Neal weighed 303 pounds stripped. His arms were as big as my leg and just as hard as that table. He could tell when I was going to center the ball, and he'd get right over it and hit me in the face. You didn't have a face guard then, and so Ed Neal broke my nose seven times. Yes, that's right. No—he broke my nose five times. I got it broke seven times, but five times he broke it."[7]

In the old days, before face guards, the battle in the trenches was little more than a glorified bare-knuckles street fight. Only rookies had straight noses and all their incisors. Ed Neal would "bring that forearm across the bridge of my nose," Bulldog remembered. "Afterwards, I was always looking for my teeth."[8]

But Neal's aggressive style could be exploited. "I said to Halas one day, 'You can run somebody right through there, 'cause Ed Neal is busy whupping my head.' I suggested that we put in a sucker play—we called it 32 sucker—where we double teamed both of their tackles and I would just relax and let Neal knock me on my back and fall all over me. It'd make a hole from here to that fireplace. Man, you could really run through it, and we did all day. Later Ralph Jones, who had once been a Bears coach and was coaching a little college team, told me he brought his whole team down to watch the Bears play the Packers that day, and he told them, 'Boys, I want you to see the greatest football player that ever lived, Bulldog Turner. I want you to watch this man on every play and see how he handles those guys.' But ol' Ralph didn't know about the sucker play, and later he told me, 'Damn, if you wasn't flat on your back all day.'"[9]

"Anyway, I got to where I'd center the ball and duck my head," Bulldog said, "so then he (Neal) started hitting me on top of the headgear. He would beat hell out of my head. We had those headgears that were made out of composition of some kind—some sort of fiber—and I used to take three of them to Green Bay. Those headgear would just crack when he'd hit 'em—they'd just ripple across there like lightning had struck them." At the time Bulldog was field testing the first plastic helmet for Wilson Sporting Goods.

"So there one day," Bulldog continued, "every time Neal went by me I'd grab him by the leg. And then I began to get him worried. He said, 'You s.o.b., quit holding me!' I said, 'If you'll quit hitting me on the head, I'll quit holding you.' And Neal said, 'That's a deal 'cause I ain't making no tackles.' So the second half of that game we got along good, and later I got Halas to trade for him."[10]

Bulldog welcomed Big Ed Neal to the Bears. "It was a relief to have him on my side," Bulldog confided.[11]

"Ed Neal used to beat on Bulldog," Ed Sprinkle remembered. "He outweighed Bulldog by quite a bit and he'd line up over center, and I mean he'd whack Bulldog on the nose. And they'd fight. But as for Ed Neal breaking free and making a tackle, Bulldog was usually able to handle him pretty good."[12]

"The smaller, quick guy that would try to get around you was the toughest to block," Bulldog explained. "I never had much trouble with the ones that tried to run over me."[13] Then one day he squared off with a tough young nose guard from Cleveland.

"Actually the first guy who convinced me that I couldn't handle anybody I ever met was Bill Willis, who played for Cleveland, and I was on my way down then. They called him The Cat. He was skinny and he didn't look like he should be playing middle guard, but he'd jump right over you. . . . [B]ut I'll tell you the only way I could block him was I'd squat and when he'd try to jump over me I'd come up and catch him. Every time, my nose would be right in his armpit—and later I'd tell my wife, 'Damn, Gladys, that man perspires. I can't stand it.' But that guy was a football player, and don't think he wasn't. Oh, he was a warhorse, that Willis."[14]

Bill Willis made the Hall of Fame, but in the beginning he had two things going against him: his size and the color of his skin. He was a 210-pound defensive lineman and a pioneer who broke down social and racial barriers as one of the few black players in professional football. A handful of black stars had played in the National Football League from its inception in 1920, but during the Great Depression there was a lockout, often attributed to the influence of George Preston Marshall of the Washington Redskins. Marshall, who acquired the franchise in 1932, was a racist who refused to have black players on his team and used his influence to keep them out of the League. George Halas, Art Rooney, Bert Bell, Tim Mara, and others went along—a sad chapter not mentioned in the official League history. As a result there were no black players in the NFL between 1933 and 1946, and unlike baseball, no viable Negro football league emerged. The economics were too precarious.

Then when the Cleveland Rams wanted to move to Los Angeles in 1946, their contract with the Los Angeles Coliseum stipulated that the club would integrate. To comply with the contract, the Rams signed two UCLA teammates then playing in the minor leagues: Kenny Washington and Woody Strode. Washington had a short career in the NFL. After football, Strode became an actor—playing parts opposite John Wayne in John Ford westerns.

The same year that Kenny Washington and Woody Strode signed with the Rams, Bill Willis, who played college ball at Ohio State, signed a contract with the Cleveland Browns of the All-American Football Conference, a full year before Jackie Robinson signed a baseball contract with Branch Rickey and the Brooklyn Dodgers. A few days after signing Willis, the Browns signed Marion Motley, an African-American fullback (Hall of Fame 1968). Their rookie year, Willis and Motley were forbidden by law from playing against white players in the South and were required to sit out the game with the Miami Sea-hawks. Coach Paul Brown paid each man an extra $500 and told them he would take care of the problem. The next year Miami disappeared from the League. Then in 1950 the Browns moved to the NFL. Still, integration was slow, especially in Washington, D.C. George Preston Marshall did not sign a Black player until forced to do so in 1962 when the Kennedy administration threatened to revoke his lease on D.C. Stadium. That year Marshall grudgingly drafted Ernie Davis of Syracuse, who said, "I won't play for that S.O.B.," so Marshall traded Davis to Cleveland for Bobby Mitchell.

Times were changing. Football was changing too, and the Chicago Bears, winners of four World Championships in the 1940s, struggled to keep up. The Monsters of the Midway were getting old. Still, there were glimmers of hope and promise. From the 1946 draft, the Bears got Johnny Lujack (round one, number four), a spectacular quarter-back from Notre Dame and George Connor (originally drafted round one, number five by the Giants). In 1948 Chicago drafted Bobby Layne from Texas (round one, number three) and J. R. Boone, a running back from Tulsa (round 22, number 203). Lujack left the game after four seasons while Connor had a Hall of Fame career with the Bears.

Chicago Bears center-linebacker Clyde "Bulldog" Turner (66) poses for a photo during training camp at St. Joseph's College in Rensselaer, Ind., Aug. 9, 1948. Reprinted by permission of AP Photo/Football Hall of Fame.

George Halas dealt Layne to a rival league. A year later Layne joined Doak Walker, Lou Creekmur, and Cloyce Box in Detroit, and led the Lions to a string of NFL Championships. Boone played six years in the NFL with the Bears, 49ers, and Packers.

Most observers thought J. R. Boone would never make it in the NFL. He was only 5'6" and weighed 160. On the practice field he looked like he was playing among giants. The first time he carried the ball at training camp, Fred Davis (245 pounds) stopped him cold. The next time he carried the ball, Bulldog Turner crushed him. The third time he carried the ball, he went 75 yards for a touchdown. He was small, but he had blazing speed. When George Halas had concerns about his ability to play halfback on defense, Boone's college coach told Halas not to worry. "He gets real tall when covering pass receivers." Halas put Boone and George McAfee back to field punts, causing some punters to kick the ball out of bounds rather than put it in the hands of the twin lightning bolts from Chicago. Boone and Bulldog roomed together on the road and became life-long friends.

Meanwhile the 1948 Chicago Bears were a very respectable 10–2 but finished second in their division to the Cardinals. The Bears won 9 and lost 3 in 1949 but again finished second, this time to the Los Angeles Rams. After that they ran out of gas finishing 5–7 in 1950, 7–5 in 1951, and 5–7 in 1952. Even in those lean years, George Halas was publicly optimistic, claiming that the Bears were only three men away from having a great team—to which a wisecrack reporter in the back responded, "Yeah, the Father, Son and Holy Ghost."

In the early 1950s an article in the *Chicago Tribune* praised Bulldog Turner as "that Old Warrior of the Texas Plains." Older fans remembered when Bulldog and the Bears were the "Monsters of the Midway"—perhaps the greatest collection of football talent ever assembled. But time, and losing, makes people forget. Luckman, Lujack, Fortmann, and Stydahar were already gone, and Bulldog Turner had been eclipsed by a crop of young centers, like Chuck Bednarik of the Philadelphia Eagles, who learned to play watching the Bulldog in his prime. The old West Texas warrior still had plenty in his tank, but he was no longer invincible. He wasn't what he used to be, and he knew it. Most younger fans knew Bulldog's name but were too young to remember what a magnificent warrior he used to be.

There was a chill in the air in Chicago on December 14, 1952. The temperature was 45 degrees with a stiff breeze coming off Lake Michigan. In the damp concrete locker room below the grandstands at Wrigley, Bulldog Turner put on his Bears uniform for the last time. He was 33 years old—a senior citizen by football standards. He had played 12 full seasons on both sides of the ball—the equivalent of a 24-year career in today's terms. He played in 207 games for the Bears, eclipsing George Trafton's record. In some of those games he never left the field. That kind of playing time is hard to imagine to people who only know professional football in the era of television.

Bulldog tried to quit after the 1951 season and announced that the Cardinals game that year would be his last. There was a big celebration at Wrigley Field before the game. Friends and fans cheered him and said goodbye. The Bears gave Bulldog a new car—a Mercury "Woodie" station wagon. Money to buy the car came from the "Turner Fund"; an account set up at the Belmont National Bank in Chicago, but donations fell short. "They worked long and hard to come up with the money to pay for the car," Bulldog said, "but they didn't quite make it, so I had to pay for half of it."[15]

Bulldog expected to walk away in 1951, but said he would return "if the Bears wanted him." That opening was all George Halas needed to get Bulldog to return as a player-coach with an emphasis on the coaching. Specifically, Halas wanted Bulldog to groom a new center: Wayne Hansen from Texas Western. Hansen was very good so Bulldog moved to right tackle, where his reduced mobility was not so noticeable, and started there throughout his final season.

Professional football is a violent, grueling game that, unlike baseball or golf, does not invite older guys to hang around past their prime. Still, leaving the Bears was one of the toughest things Bulldog ever did. He was most alive on the football field. He loved the life, the travel, and the camaraderie of teammates in the sanctuary of the locker room. He loved Chicago. He loved the attention, which was what attracted him to the game in the first place. As his last game approached, he suddenly felt old and a little scared. Football had been the focus of his life since he stepped on the field in Sweetwater, Texas in 1934. Now it was almost over. What was he supposed to do on Sunday afternoons?

Bulldog Turner and his Mercury "Woodie" wagon on Bulldog Turner Day, 1951. Courtesy of Pat Turner.

Outside Chicago there was not a great deal of interest in the 1952 Bears-Cardinals game—two losing teams just trying to finish the season on a high note. The odds makers had them at even money. A gambler would have to invest $6 on a $5 return if his team won.

Because the celebration had already taken place, there was no announcement of Bulldog's retirement prior to the game. And in a way it was a melancholy affair. The Bears beat the Cardinals 10–7, and Bulldog Turner, the best lineman of his era, was finished. Still he could take pride in a string of successful seasons unequaled by any lineman in history. He was a six-time All-Pro whose teams won five divisional titles and four NFL Championships (1940, 1941, 1943, and 1946).

Rumors that Bulldog might return in 1953 were put to rest when in January he joined the coaching staff at Baylor University in Waco. It was a good job; about an hour's drive from his ranch at Pidcoke.

And Baylor gave him everything he wanted. He coached centers and linebackers, he had no recruiting duties, and he only coached during football season. The rest of the time he raised cattle, sheep, goats, and horses on his ranch. But Bulldog didn't enjoy his tenure at Baylor, and he left after a year. Baylor needed a recruiter, and Bulldog wasn't interested. "My one-year contract has not been renewed," he told a reporter, "and I'm looking for a part-time connection."[16]

There were rumors that he would succeed Murray Evans as the head coach at Hardin-Simmons in 1955. (Sammy Baugh took the job.) Another rumor had him taking the job as the head coach of the Chicago Bears when George Halas stepped down briefly in 1956. (That job went to Paddy Driscoll.) Still, Bulldog was not yet ready to leave the game, and when George Halas offered him a position in Chicago coaching centers and linebackers, Bulldog quickly accepted.

He spent the next five football seasons as a coach in Chicago where he learned that retired players, even the great ones, fade from the collective memory at warp speed. There was a time when Bulldog Turner was the most popular man in Chicago; then barely a year after he retired, a young wet-behind-the-ears reporter for the Galesburg (Illinois) *Register-Mail* wrote, "George Turner, a Bear great of former years, was in camp to help coach the centers." The worst part was that no one caught the error.

As the years passed, fewer people remembered. One day in 1976, Guy Mainella, host of a sports talk show on WBZ in Boston, reported as a joke that the New England Patriots traded quarterback Jim Plunkett to Chicago for George Halas, Richard Daley, and Bulldog Turner. The phones at the sports department at the *Boston Globe* lit up like a Christmas tree with calls from people wanting to know more about the players now on their way from Chicago to New England.[17]

Then in 1961 came an opportunity of a lifetime. A chance meeting in New York gave Bulldog the break he had been looking for since retiring as an active player. Bulldog Turner got his chance to be a head coach in professional football.

Chapter 10

High Jinks on the Hudson

The year 1959 was a milestone in the history of professional football. In that year a rival league emerged that had sufficient capital to challenge the NFL and bid against the established league for talent. The price for athletic services was about to hit the stratosphere. Yes, the American Football League (AFL) had money to burn. Lamar Hunt, a Dallas oil man and the leader of the new league, could have purchased the entire NFL out of petty cash. He had tried before to bring professional football to Dallas, only to be snubbed by the NFL. So he started another league. The AFL changed the landscape of sports and gave some West Texans an unexpected second chance at professional football.

On August 14, 1959 a group of prospective owners held the first organizational meeting of the AFL in Chicago. At that meeting the leadership of the new league awarded franchises to New York, Dallas, Los Angeles, Boston, Buffalo, Denver, Houston, and Minneapolis. Then in January 1960, yielding to significant pressure from the NFL, the Minneapolis ownership group forfeited its bond and its AFL membership to become the NFL's 14th team. Subsequently, the eighth AFL franchise went to Oakland.

The cost to purchase an AFL franchise in 1959 was $1 million. Each owner also had to put up a $100,000 performance bond to be forfeited should his team drop out of the league. Owners had to be well-heeled because all new businesses lose money in the beginning. The trick would be to have enough start-up money socked away to weather the lean times.

By all indications, the AFL ownership met the financial qualification with room to spare. In addition to Lamar Hunt, the league awarded the Los Angeles franchise to Baron Hilton, son of hotel magnet Conrad Hilton, and the Houston franchise to K. S. "Bud" Adams, a Houston oil man and the son of Boots Adams, CEO of Phillips Petroleum.

The AFL awarded the coveted New York franchise to Harry Wismer—the same Harry Wismer who told George Richards that Gus Henderson passed on Bulldog Turner in the first round of the 1940 NFL draft. Wismer was a former network sportscaster for Michigan State before working for George Richards and the Detroit Lions. In 1940 George Preston Marshall hired Wismer to be the voice of the Washington Redskins. Wismer's first game for the Redskins was the 73–0 blowout in the 1940 NFL Championship game.

Wismer named his new team the Titans after the Titan missile, a recent addition to the nation's strategic arsenal. But publicly he often added that "Titans are bigger and stronger than Giants," a slap at the NFL team playing nearby in Yankee Stadium. Wismer chose blue and gold as his team colors. In December 1959, he hired Slingin' Sammy Baugh as head coach and signed him to a three-year contract for $20,000 a year.

The new AFL did many things right, but awarding the New York franchise to Harry Wismer wasn't one of them. "Hairbreadth" Harry turned out to be more con man than businessman. He didn't have enough money for a regular office. The Titans' office was Wismer's suite at the Park Plaza Hotel in New York. The coaches met in the dining room and had to walk through the bathroom to get to the mimeograph machine. In addition to being the owner, Harry was the ticket agent. When the coaches reported for work in the morning, they stepped over and waded through stacks of tickets strewn across the business office—also known as Harry's living room. Of course, the coaches soon learned that selling tickets to Titan games was only a part-time job.

Harry Wismer talked big and fast for someone who lived one jump ahead of the banker. His pockets weren't very deep, and as a result the Titans were undercapitalized during his entire tenure as owner. He had significant cash flow problems, and his checks bounced. Every week was a new drama. On payday the players rushed to the bank to see if their payroll checks were good. Sometimes they weren't. His quarterback quit the team because Harry hadn't paid him for his summer job. Every spring the Titans would train at a different site. They couldn't go back to the place they trained the previous year because the owner didn't pay the bills.

The Titans had other problems besides the owner. They had to compete against the Giants for paying customers, and the Giants had a loyal and established fan base and a prestigious home in Yankee Stadium. The Titans played at the Polo Grounds, and by 1960 the fabled old arena was rotten and falling down. There were rats in the locker room. Taking a shower was dangerous. "You flush a commode while a guy is taking a shower," a player remembered, "and the guy gets the hell scalded out of him."[1] The new Shea Stadium in Queens was to be the saving grace of the Titans. The facility was supposed to be ready for the 1962 football season, but cost overruns and construction delays moved the opening to 1963. Some people speculated that if Harry could have held on until the move to Shea, he could have saved the Titans from default. But that was not to be. His fingernails weren't long enough.

The Titans' biggest problem in those early years was a lack of paying customers. Their first home game in 1960 against Buffalo drew a whopping 5,727 fans—more of a group than a crowd. The Titans won the game 23–7. That first year under Sammy Baugh the franchise went 7–7 and failed to make the playoffs. In 1961 the Titans went 7–7 again. Harry Wismer thought the team was better than that and plotted to replace Baugh with a head coach who could win championships. Winning would draw crowds and make the franchise profitable.

There were other issues between the coach and the owner that went beyond winning and losing. Baugh hated New York and quickly lost interest in the Titans after the last game. Wismer wanted a year-round coach, but Sammy lit out for West Texas as soon as the season ended. Baugh accused Wismer of making player deals behind his back. Wismer claimed Baugh violated the loyalty clause in his contract. By Christmas 1961, the owner and the coach were not on speaking terms.[2]

And so began one of most unbelievable years of madcap mismanagement in the history of sports. A case can be made that the 1962 New York Titans were the worst-managed football team ever. The players, the coaching staff, and the fans endured one of the zaniest years of any professional sports team on record. It is a story marked by humor and sadness and an owner's shattered dreams. A Texas rancher from Cowhouse Creek was in the thick of it.

"I'd just been up in New York for the (College Football) Hall of Fame ceremonies," Bulldog Turner remembered. "There were a lot of politicians and business types around, and that's where I met Harry Wismer. Well, Harry owned the New York Titans back then, and we got to talking, and he asked me what it would take for me to be his head coach. So I gave him what I think is an outrageous figure—$20,000, I think it was—and I came back home, figuring that was the end of it. So I'm tending to business, and one day Harry calls and says 'When can you start?' When we're done he tells me to be in New York the next day for a press conference.

"The only problem was that Baugh had been the coach before and Harry . . . well, Harry hadn't gotten around to firing him."[3]

Sammy still had a contract, and he refused to resign, so Wismer announced at the press conference that Baugh was demoted from head coach to "consultant in charge of kicking and punting and would go on the field when asked." Wismer thought Sammy would be humiliated and quit, but Sammy showed up for work anyway. He still had a $20,000 contract and wasn't about to forfeit his paycheck. "I knew what Wismer was doing," Baugh explained, "and didn't want him to get away with it."[4]

The *New York Times* reported that a "280-pound Texas cattle rancher became head coach of the New York Titans. He is Clyde (Bulldog) Turner, generally regarded as the greatest center in the history of professional football. . . . The former Chicago Bear succeeds another Texas rancher, Sammy Baugh, who guided the Titans to second-place and third-place finishes in the Eastern Division of the AFL in 1960 and 1961, respectively. Baugh's original three-year contract still has a year to run. He will remain with the club as a consultant for the same salary he received as coach. . . . Turner signed a two-year pact calling for $20,000 a season."

Bulldog's contract stated that he would spend at least 10 months of the year in New York. His off-season duties included making speeches and doing public relations work for the club. Baugh had refused to do public relations work or even attend the team's weekly press luncheons. Bulldog liked New York, at least in the beginning. Wismer was so happy with his new coach that he named Bulldog to the club's executive committee as vice-president and director.

Some sportswriters believed better days were ahead for the Titans. Bulldog had a reputation as a fair man who could get along with players from different races and backgrounds. He was also considered a disciplinarian, something the Titans needed after the laid-back style of Sammy Baugh. It is certainly true that under Baugh, discipline was lax and administration was loose. Some players complained to the press that practices were poorly organized. Players were late for meetings and practice. One player claimed that teammates "passed out bennies (amphetamines) in a doughnut box like they were salt tablets." Don Maynard recalled when "one old boy got cut and lived in the dorm four weeks before they caught him."[5]

Turner, it was widely believed, would be a good administrator, would tighten discipline and would take no lip from Harry Wismer. Bud Shrake of the *Dallas News* wrote: "If Harry Wismer ever took advice from anywhere other than his own mirror, he ought to consider the warning from Morris Frank. 'I never try to say anything funny about Bulldog Turner,' Morris told the crowd at College Football Hall of Fame Luncheon in New York. 'When I look at him, I forget it.' And this from a man who would insult Castro in the lobby of the Havana Hilton."

Shrake continued: "Turner, the new coach of the New York Titans, is truly a thoughtful sight. He makes most men look like girls. If he played for Russia, we'd be a 6-point underdog. When he stands there in his cowboy boots and broken nose, a person who averaged 55 minutes per game through an entire National Football League season, you can understand why there's been a strange silence in Manhattan since Turner was hired . . ."[6]

Despite their awkward situation, Baugh and Turner made the best of it. "I have the highest respect for Baugh and will welcome any help he can give me," Bulldog said. "We will go over our player personnel as soon as possible and start making plans for 1962."[7]

Turner added, "I don't know how he feels about it though." The deposed coach was unavailable for comment. However, a week earlier when Harry Wismer threatened to demote him to an assistant coach, Sammy retorted, "That's wonderful. I'd like to be an assistant at these prices."[8] Later Baugh added, "I hope I'll be taking up tickets because I'm a little lazy and that would be the biggest snap of all"—a not so subtle reference to the small bus load of fans that usually turned out for Titans' home games.[9]

Not to be outdone, Wismer never missed a chance to throw verbal darts at Baugh in the press. After hiring Bulldog Turner, Wismer told a reporter that he "settled" for Baugh when other coaches were not available. "Turner was my first choice for head coach when I organized this club," Wismer said. "My second choice was Otto Graham, my third choice was Frank Leahy and my fourth choice was Sammy Baugh."[10]

Baugh responded by telling reporters that Harry Wismer did not know what he was doing. "Wismer makes a big fuss over name players," said Baugh. "He puts out publicity about the big money he's going to pay them. And while we're fooling around with the big names, the NFL is picking off the top players which we had a chance of signing."[11]

The case of Ed Blaine, a big lineman from Missouri, is a good example. Wismer really wanted Blaine and invited the big man to his New York apartment to convince him to be a Titan. Ed was not impressed. When Ed said he didn't think he would be interested in playing in New York (he signed with Green Bay instead), Harry started throwing glasses at the wall. Blaine made a hasty exit declaring, "I don't want to be around that man."[12]

"Wismer wasn't quite honest with us," Baugh continued. "Before we went to training camp, Harry wrote that he had enough players signed that we shouldn't have any trouble winning the championship. Well, only two of those players finished the season for us. We had to cut the rest. Almost all of our team was picked up after the season started from other clubs."[13]

Despite the high jinks on the Hudson, there were no hard feelings between Bulldog Turner and Sammy Baugh. "Bulldog knows football," said Sammy, "and I'm sure he'll make a fine coach. I know I'll be able to work with him and I just hope he and Wismer get along good together."[14]

Bulldog and Baugh remained the best of friends the rest of their lives. In private they joked about the hay and horse feed they bought with Harry Wismer's money. When the Texas Sports Hall of Fame inducted Bulldog in December 1961, Sammy was there to present the plaque.

Meanwhile in New York, Harry Wismer gave his new head coach a two-year contract with assurances that Bulldog would have full power in assembling a team that would be competitive in the AFL. "I am enthusiastic over this chance to get back into coaching, and I have full confidence in the new American League," Bulldog said. He also assured reporters that "I will coach the team the way I see fit. I have gotten into the winning habit and I'm far too old now to change."[15]

In April 1962 Bulldog made a quick trip to Texas and a brief stop at his ranch to pick up a few things before hopping in his Cadillac and speeding away to catch a plane to New York. While in town he told John Frank Post, writer for the *Gatesville Messenger*, that he was happy with his job but was worried about his club's failure to sign more promising young players.

"We'll just have to out-fox our opponents this fall," he said with a nervous grin.[16] Perhaps he was trying to convince himself. Perhaps he didn't realize exactly what he had gotten himself into.

When the players reported for training camp, Bulldog did his best to impose discipline but many of the players did not take kindly to it. He insisted on punctuality and hard work. And just like his mentor in Chicago, he laid down the law on waistlines.

"Well," he explained, "some other coaches were telling me what a great end Art Powell was when they saw him, at a time when he weighed 190. Those who didn't have such nice things to say were talking about when he weighed 220."[17]

Bulldog quickly learned that playing football was a lot more fun than being the head coach. With his new job came responsibility. The coach, especially the head coach, had to be the heavy, and as a result he wasn't the same old Bulldog he used to be. Responsibility took a toll on his good humor. "Clyde 'Bulldog' Turner is in town," a reporter wrote, "and in a grouchy mood. When the Bulldog is snappish, keep your hands in your pockets, your hat pulled low, head the other way, and keep walking. When this Bulldog barks, he bites."[18]

In the meantime, Harry Wismer finally agreed to pay off Sammy Baugh and send him back to West Texas, although where Wismer got the money is anybody's guess because by spring 1962 he had very little cash and his line of credit was stretched to the limit. By now everyone knew that Harry was a terrible businessman. No honest person or reputable institution would invest in the Titans with Harry running the show. When Harry failed in all attempts to attract new investors, he borrowed $200,000 from Mercantile Bank of Chicago. Officials of the bank reluctantly agreed to the loan as long as the AFL front office paid the Titans' share of the ABC television contract money, which amounted to $190,000, directly to the bank. That left Harry to take care of the remaining $10,000 plus interest. The loan enabled the Titans to start the 1962 season but wasn't enough to see them through to the end.[19]

Then Harry made the best financial decision of his life. He married the widow of Abner "Longy" Zwillman, a New Jersey racketeer, but even Longy's extortion money couldn't help the Titans achieve respectability or financial stability. It was too little too late.

Since the new Mrs. Wismer controlled the purse strings, Harry appointed her the president of the club. "She is the boss," Harry explained, "and will do all the talking from now on." She was never heard from again.

Legally the team's finances were separate from Harry's personal assets, but as the Titans continued to lose money, Harry pumped more of his personal funds into the organization. In a cost-cutting measure, Harry ordered the general manager, George Sauer, the former athletic director at Baylor, to double as the backfield coach making Sauer Bulldog Turner's assistant and his boss. But Harry would have to do more than that to save the Titans. By the summer of 1962, Harry's bank account hit rock bottom. He had no more funds to invest in his team.

If all that wasn't enough evidence that the Titans were in serious trouble, the draft day debacle was proof that the team was spiraling out of control. Bulldog Turner was unable to call in the Titans' draft choices to the League office because the phones didn't work. Wismer hadn't paid the phone bill.

Every day was a new adventure. When the players and coaches reported to training camp in July 1962, the groundskeeper at East Stroudsburg State College in Pennsylvania was surprised to see them. Harry hadn't told him the Titans were coming. The field was bare as a bowling ball. It hadn't been watered all summer and was hard as a granite countertop. Records show that when the Titans filed for bankruptcy later that year they still owed the college $4,034.04. Bankruptcy papers also listed many other unpaid bills from doctors, hotels, restaurants, hospitals, and other businesses in the East Stroudsburg area. As the season wore on, businesses learned to collect from the Titans in advance.[20]

Sixty-three players reported to the Titans' training camp that summer in 1962. A few of them were talented athletes, but most were an odd collection of dreamers and rejects. Many of them were players who had been cut by the NFL and were looking for one last chance before giving up entirely on the game. Because the owner's financial difficulties were so well known, the team had trouble signing draft choices. No one wanted to board a sinking ship. That year the Titans signed only one draft pick—Alex Kroll—an All-American center from Rutgers.

On the opening day of training camp both Bulldog Turner and Sammy Baugh were on the field. Bulldog took charge, and Baugh, to his credit, did not interfere. He only came because he did not want to jeopardize his salary by not showing up for work. In a moment of wisdom Harry Wismer finally concluded that "Baugh's presence might become embarrassing for Turner," and agreed to pay Sam for *not* coaching the New York Titans. With that bit of news Baugh cleaned out his locker, stopped by the bank to make sure the check was good, picked up his two suitcases and flew back to Texas, happy to be out of New York and back on his West Texas ranch. He lived another 40 years, but he never went to New York again.

In July a reporter from the *New York Times* interviewed the Titans' new coach. Bulldog tried to put a positive spin on an ugly situation, but he was too honest to hide his feelings. He admitted that he needed linebackers in the worst way. He also needed offensive tackles, defensive ends, and defensive backs. He diplomatically described the quarterback situation as "good but not exactly great." In the course of the season Bulldog would use six quarterbacks: Johnny Green, Lee Grosscup, Dean Look, Butch Songin, Hayseed Stephens, and Bob Scrabis. At best the entire group produced a few isolated moments of acceptable performance. None of them earned the lasting confidence of his teammates. "Green would be calling signals," running back Bob Mathis remembered, "and Bob Mischak, the left guard, would turn around and argue with him."[21]

Still, hopes soared in preseason, as hopes always do, but as losses mounted, optimism quickly faded like a new pair of Wranglers. On Saturday, August 12, 1962, Marilyn Monroe died, and the Titans played the Buffalo Bills in a preseason game at a high school field in New Haven, Connecticut. Bill Mathis of the Titans scored on an 83-yard touchdown run in the first quarter, but the Bills won the game 21–10. The next preseason game with the Boston Patriots, scheduled to be played in Atlanta, was moved to a high school field in Lowell, Massachusetts, because of poor ticket sales.

"I don't think not getting paid on time was funny."

Art Powell, wide receiver, New York Titans

The persistent money problem raised its ugly head again when the team traveled to the West Coast in the preseason. A player was supposed to receive $50 for each preseason game, but the contest in Oakland came and went with no sign of a paycheck. The players held a team meeting and issued an ultimatum. "No pay, no play." The phrase had a nice sound and became the team slogan. The players told Bulldog of their decision and Bulldog told Wismer to pay up. Wismer threatened to put the entire team, including the coaches, on waivers. Team morale was low. The Titans finished the preseason 0–4.

The regular season started on a high note as the Titans beat the Raiders in Oakland. The second game was against the Chargers at Balboa Stadium in San Diego. The team did not travel back to New York that week but stayed in Southern California. The Titans booked rooms in a motel near downtown San Diego and practiced at a high school field 45 minutes away by bus. Every afternoon the temperature hovered near 100.

Still, everything went well, all things considered, until the end of the week. Then after practice on Friday the bus that shuttled the team between the motel and practice field didn't show. At first the players thought the bus was simply late, but after an hour they faced reality. The bus wasn't coming because the company hadn't been paid.

Bulldog Turner was one of the first to fully understand the situation. He leaped into a sportswriter's car and yelled, "I'll see you at the pool," as he drove away. As for the rest of the coaches and the players, it was every man for himself. The people of Southern California had never seen such a sight—25 sweaty professional football players, in full pads, hitching rides through the streets of San Diego.[22] In the game on Sunday the Chargers beat the Titans 40–14. Jack Kemp threw two touchdown passes to Lance Alworth.

As the season wore on the Titans tried to make a go of it with a few good players and a host of NFL rejects. Bulldog's biggest concern was that he had no stability at quarterback. Then Wismer signed Lee Grosscup, a pro quarterback who played behind Y. A. Tittle and Charlie Conerly with the New York Giants. Grosscup joined the Titans on a Friday before the Sunday game at Oakland. Normally a new quarterback would take months, even years, to learn the system of his new team, but there was no time for that. Bulldog Turner was having lunch in the hotel dining room when Grosscup walked in and introduced himself. Bulldog gave Grosscup the Oakland game plan on a linen table cloth.

"We signed him on a Friday," Bulldog recalled, "gave him six plays to work on for the opening game against the Oakland Raiders on Sunday, and he won it for us."[23] Grosscup threw three touchdown passes against the Raiders—two touchdowns came the first two times he touched the ball.

But financial troubles sucked all the joy out of victory. When the Titans returned to New York after taking a beating from the Chargers in week two of the season, paychecks were late again. "The league rule," Guard Bob Mischak a co-captain said in a team meeting, "clearly states that paychecks have to be delivered within 24 hours of a game." He looked at his watch. "Our paychecks are now 194 hours overdue."[24] This time the players said they wouldn't practice unless they got paid. "Wismer said OK," Larry Grantham recalled, "and told the coaches to take the rest of the week off."[25]

"We went up to Buffalo on our own," Grantham said. "So did the coaches. And we won." That Sunday, in the best game the Titans had played all year, New York beat Buffalo 17–6. Maybe the Titans were on to something.

The players knew better than anyone that the Titans were on the verge of financial collapse, but the leadership of the League understood the importance of a New York franchise. Larry Grantham recalled that "[t]he next week (after the Buffalo game) Lamar Hunt showed up, sat at a table in the locker room, asked each guy how much his paycheck was and wrote a personal check for that amount. That's how much he knew the A.F.L. needed a New York team."[26]

Despite the win in Buffalo, the Titans just didn't have the talent to compete successfully with most teams in the AFL. And the more games they lost, the more the fans' interest waned. In fact, "waned" is being kind. Free tickets couldn't draw a decent crowd. In an early game against Boston at the Polo Grounds, the players came out of the tunnel and onto the playing surface to the eerie sound of dead silence. They looked into the stands and saw nothing but a cavern of empty seats. Except for the players' wives, a small group of concessionaires in orange suits and a few curious spectators with nothing better to do, nobody else came to the game. Before the Titans took the field, Larry Grantham suggested that "instead of running through the goalposts for introductions, let's just go up and shake hands with everybody. It would be faster. It won't take more than one or two minutes." Eventually stadium officials threw open the gates and begged people on the street to come in and watch the game, just to fill up some of the seats. A few kids came in and sat in the premium seats on the 50-yard line. Newspapers had great fun with the inflated attendance figures. One paper quipped, "The announced attendance figure of 20,000 refers to arms and legs. Or else 15,000 of the 20,000 came disguised as empty seats."[27]

"We played a game against the Titans in the Polo Grounds," remembered Cotton Davidson of the Dallas Texans, "at 10 a.m. on Thanksgiving Day. There weren't 100 people in the stands, and most of them were the players' wives and kids."[28] For the entire 1962 season, the Titans drew less than 40,000 total for all home games. In 2013 the Dallas Cowboys will seat twice that many on a single Sunday afternoon at the new stadium in Arlington.

Bulldog Turner did his best to salvage something from the 1962 season. He hired Bud Leininger, the man he apologized to in the Rams' locker room, as the team trainer, and in the fourth week of the season he hired his good friend and former teammate Ed Sprinkle to coach the Titans' defensive line. Sprinkle resigned his job as the head coach of the Chicago Bulls, a semipro team, to take the position in New York.[29] Had Sprinkle known of the rocky financial condition of the franchise, he would have stayed in Chicago where paychecks were timely and didn't bounce.

The Denver Post reported that after the Broncos' game, "Turner barked insults at his own men in the dressing room." The report was understated.

After a particularly disappointing loss, Harry Wismer, in a fit of rage, put six starters on waivers, then withdrew them when all six were claimed.[30]

As midseason approached, the Titans suffered a rash of injuries. At the beginning of week five, only 15 players suited up for practice. That week a knee injury benched Lee Grosscup, and on October 4, 1962 the Titans called up Harold "Hayseed" Stephens to back up quarterback Butch Songin. Hayseed played on three state championship teams under legendary coach Chuck Moser at Abilene High School before Coach Sammy Baugh recruited Hayseed to play quarterback at Hardin-Simmons. During his senior year, Hayseed was the leading college passer in the nation on a team that lost every game. Recently Hayseed was the signal-caller for the Louisville Raiders, a semipro team, while fronting a country music band and selling life insurance on the side. Hayseed was in uniform on Sunday, October 7, when the Titans played the Boston Patriots at the Polo Grounds.[31] Later in the 1962 season, Bulldog Turner would switch Hayseed from quarterback to safety in a vain effort to shore up a defensive secondary that was not very good at tackling or playing pass defense.

During week six the team's only projector broke. There was no money to fix it.

During week seven the Titans played the Dallas Texans at the Cotton Bowl. There was a lot of pent-up anger on the New York side, not at the Texans in particular, but with the entire season in general. The Texans just happened to be in the line of fire. There were some shoving matches and lots of cussing, but the game remained a fairly civilized affair throughout the first half. Then in the third quarter officials called pass interference in the end zone against New York and penalized linebacker Larry Grantham for vigorously questioning the call. On the next play, Abner Haynes scored easily from the one-yard line with what some Titans thought was a little too much flair. After that the place was a brawl waiting to happen.

Then with three minutes left in the game, Haynes caught a pass from quarterback Len Dawson near the Dallas sideline. Linebacker Jerry Fields of the Titans tackled Haynes and knocked him out of bounds with a little extra forearm. Haynes, who was already spoiling for a fight, took exception to his treatment and got up swinging. A big brawl broke out, and it took officials quite a few minutes to restore order. Just as that fight was ending, another scuffle erupted. In the meantime Hayseed Stephens, the backup quarterback, wandered over from his place on the bench. Hayseed didn't want to fight, but there was a battle going on across the field, and he wanted a better view. This was the most excitement he had experienced since coming to New York.

After a long delay the officials separated the players and restored order. The referee ejected Haynes and went looking for Jerry Fields when Hubert Bobo of the Titans convinced the official that Hayseed Stephens was the main culprit. The official ejected Stephens, who was only an innocent bystander and had never been in the game. Afterwards in the locker room, Bobo explained that Hayseed was more expendable. "We only had three linebackers," Bobo said, "and didn't want to lose Fields, so I told the officials Fields didn't have anything to do with it. I accused them of not knowing who to throw out. Hayseed was standing there, so I told them he did it."

"I just came across the field to watch," Hayseed said, "and they put me out of the game."[32]

Towards the end of the 1962 season, Harry Wismer ran completely out of resources and the whole organization started to unravel. The team no longer kept the locker room stocked with toiletries. Bud

Leininger didn't have enough tape or aspirin. Towels, socks, and jocks were not laundered regularly.

Meanwhile, checks bounced and the franchise couldn't make payroll. The financial situation was so bad that only one teller at one branch of the Irving Trust Company at 39th Street and Madison Avenue in New York was authorized to cash Titan checks. As each player submitted his check, the teller subtracted that sum from Harry's balance. When the balance reached zero, which might be quickly if the quarterbacks and flankers got there ahead of the linemen, the teller closed the window.[33]

During week eight the Titans hosted the San Diego Chargers at the Polo Grounds. Just across the Harlem River, the NFL Giants played the Washington Redskins at sold-out Yankee Stadium. It was the first head-to-head pro football match in New York since 1949. The outcome was predictable. "We're going to get murdered at the gate," Wismer predicted. He was right. Adding insult to injury, the League decided to broadcast the Titans-Chargers game on national television. Harry was humiliated when television cameras panned the thousands of empty seats.

Had the cameras panned the parking lot they would have found it filled to its capacity of 2,000 cars, but most of the vehicles belonged to drivers who parked in Manhattan and walked across the bridge to Yankee Stadium in the Bronx. A full house of 62,844 watched Y. A. Tittle throw seven touchdown passes as the Giants beat the Redskins 49–34. Meanwhile at the Polo Grounds, the Titans announced the attendance as 21,467. The *New York Times* estimated the number of spectators at much closer to 7,500. The number of spectators who actually bought tickets was closer to 6,000. In the fourth quarter dusk settled over Manhattan, but Wismer couldn't pay the electric bill and refused to turn on the lights. The *New York Times* reported that "the crowd had some trouble seeing the ball and action during the fourth quarter." At the time the Titans were winning the game 14–10. Harry's only comment was, "We're doing good in the dark."[34]

During week 10 the public relations agency representing the Titans quit for lack of payment.

As the year wore on, press conferences were more painful. The coaching staff usually tried to paint a rosy picture for the press, but by November Bulldog Turner admitted to reporters that his team's morale was "the worst I've ever seen in football."[35]

That same month Harry Wismer announced his intention to sell the club for $2.5 million. Team spirits soared. Bolstered by the hope of a change in ownership, the Titans scored 84 points in a two-game stretch. But spirits sank like the Titanic when the deal fell through.[36] Then Harry tried to find another buyer. The price dropped to $2 million, then $1.5 million. There were still no takers.

During week 13 reports surfaced that the city had turned off the hot water and the electricity to the Polo Grounds. The Titans' officials, standing in a dark room, denied those reports.

When the team played in Boston on week 13, a chartered bus picked up the Titans in front of their hotel to drive them to the stadium. After the players and coaches were aboard, George Sauer climbed on, sat down on the front seat, and said, "Let's go." But word had gotten around. The bus driver refused to release the parking brake. "Not until I get paid," he said. "Cash."[37]

By November there was a significant cash flow problem—the cash didn't flow—and on November 8, 1962, Wismer was unable to meet payroll again. This time the League assumed the cost of running the Titans until the end of the season after which the AFL would try to find a new owner. In the meantime the League took $40,000 from a special fund to pay the players and coaches for the final game of the season. The loan would be repaid when the sale of the Titans was complete.[38]

Then a miracle almost happened. On November 20, 1962, a group of investors led by Frank Leahy, the old coach at Notre Dame, made Wismer "a very good offer"—reportedly around $2 million. Under the proposed agreement, the Leahy group would acquire controlling interest in the club. Wismer would retain 25-percent ownership in the Titans—down from 80 percent. In addition to his ownership responsibilities, Leahy would become the head coach and general manager.[39] But soon the deal collapsed, probably after attorneys and accountants saw how bad off the Titans really were.

On December 15, 1962, the Titans played the Houston Oilers in the last football game at the historic Polo Grounds. In the locker room, Bulldog Turner gave an honest prophetic talk that summed up his frustrations for the year. No one ever accused Bulldog of pulling punches. "This is the final game of the season," he said to his team. "There probably won't even be any New York Titans next year. So most of you are playing your last pro game. Most of you aren't good enough to play anywhere else."[40] The Titans played down to expectations and lost the game 44–10. In the only newsworthy event that happened on the field, Wayne Fontes, a defensive back from Michigan State who would later coach the Detroit Lions, intercepted a pass and ran 83 yards for a touchdown. That play stood as a club record for 26 years.

By January even Harry Wismer had to come down out of the clouds and face reality. Both he and the Titans were busted. In February 1963, the debt-ridden Titans filed for bankruptcy in Federal District Court in New York. The papers listed the Titans' assets at $271,990 with $1,341,000 in liabilities.[41]

Then a ray of hope. A last-minute buyer emerged but then withdrew. Wismer, angry and desperate, promptly filed a $2.5 million lawsuit against the man, charging fraud, misrepresentation, and slander.

On March 28, 1963 a five-man syndicate led by David "Sonny" (as in "show me the money") Werblin, an entertainment executive, and Leon Hess, CEO of Amerada-Hess Oil Company, bought the New York AFL franchise for $1 million, changed its name to the Jets, fired Bulldog Turner, and signed Wilbur "Weeb" Eubank to a three-year $100,000 contract as head coach and general manager. Eubank was optimistic. The franchise had nowhere to go but up. "I've seen sicker cows than this get well," he said. Two years later the Jets drafted Joe Willie Namath, a quarterback from Alabama, and paid him the astronomical salary of $430,000 a year. But Joe was worth every penny. The Jets won the Super Bowl in 1967, just as Broadway Joe predicted.

Bulldog won five games and lost nine in his one and only year as a head coach in the pros. The Titans beat Oakland (twice), Buffalo, San Diego, and Denver. The team only had one real star—flanker Don Maynard. Maynard was a West Texan who rode Joe Namath's arm all the way to the Hall of Fame. The rest of the roster included such household names as Hubert Bobo, Thurlow Cooper, Proverb Jacobs, LaVerne Torczon, "Bones" Taylor, Dainard Paulson, and Hayseed Stephens.

Bulldog wanted to be a head coach in the NFL, but his tenure with the Titans effectively ended any chance of that. Years later Bulldog confided to a journalist that the only regret of his career was taking the head coaching job with the New York Titans. "I didn't know the situation there," he said. "I found out after I got there that the team was broke. I jeopardized my entire career. Once I got finished up there I didn't have any chance of being a coach anywhere.

"I couldn't hire my own assistants. Everything went wrong. In training camp we didn't have any uniforms because the cleaning people hadn't been paid. We had to go through a travel agency to fly because we still owed the airlines money from the year before."[42]

"I suppose the whole deal in New York finished me in coaching," Bulldog added. "But it was changing by then. Drugs were coming in, and there was no such thing as discipline anymore. It was time to get out."[43]

Ed Sprinkle, Bulldog's straight-talking friend and assistant coach, did not have fond memories of his time with the Titans. "Harry Wismer was a drunk," Sprinkle remembered. "His checks were no good. I went up to New York in 1962 to help Bulldog with the coaching. Harry wouldn't pay me. When the League took over the Titans, Commissioner Joe Foss made sure I got paid. If it had been up to Harry, I wouldn't have made a dime."[44]

As soon as the 1962 AFL season ended, Bulldog and Sprinkle flew to Corpus Christi, Texas to take part in another football contest that had financial disaster written all over it. The Southwest Challenge Bowl matched a team of college seniors from the Southwest against a team of college seniors from the rest of the country. The idea came from a group of former Southwest Conference football stars at a meeting in Austin. The Southwest Challenge Bowl, Inc., the group organized to promote the event, hired Sid Gillman of the San Diego Chargers assisted by Al Davis of the Oakland Raiders, to coach the National All-Stars, and Bulldog Turner, assisted by Ed Sprinkle, to coach the Southwest All-Stars.

The game was never the star-studded extravaganza it was advertised to be, in part because of the bad blood between the NFL and the AFL. The National Football League strongly discouraged its players signed after the recent draft to participate in a contest so closely associated with the upstart AFL. Still, the 1963 Southwest Challenge Bowl did attract the likes of Jerry Hopkins, a center and linebacker from Texas A&M who played professionally with Denver, Miami, and Oakland; and Winston Hill, a tackle from Texas Southern who played for the Jets and Rams. Perhaps the biggest name on the roster was Lee Roy Caffey from Thorndale and Texas A&M. In his pro career, Caffey played linebacker next to Ray Nitschke for the Green Bay Packers of the 1960s and earned three Superbowl rings (Packers and Cowboys).

Originally the Southwest Challenge Bowl was to be played at Alamo Stadium in San Antonio, but ticket sales were "sluggish." Just weeks before the game, promoters moved the contest from San Antonio to the 21,000-seat Buccaneer Stadium in Corpus Christi. With the move to Corpus Christi came a $20,000 television deal. Fourteen stations got hookups by cable to broadcast the game live on New Year's Day.

Promoters figured they needed 12,000 to 14,000 paid spectators to make the Southwest Challenge Bowl profitable. Only 7,100 showed up. The game was supposed to showcase the superiority of football in the Southwest, but someone forgot to tell the National All-Stars. The Nationals won the game 33–13. The contract stated that each player on the winning team would get $800 while each player on the losing team would get $600, but more problems with cash flow caused a change of plans. The promoter told the players they would get their checks at the awards ceremony following the game but then changed his mind and announced he would mail the checks to the players. The players didn't trust the promoter and staged a boycott of the awards ceremony.[45]

The event was a financial failure. Investors lost upwards of $35,000. Then a group of Corpus Christi businessmen, wanting to protect the city's financial reputation, raised the money to pay everyone and square all accounts.

Despite the financial challenges, promoters had high hopes for the second Southwest Challenge Bowl, but the event lost a bundle again in 1964. That year the National All-Stars, bolstered by Black athletes who could not play in the Southwest Conference, trounced the Southwest All-Stars 66–14, foiling again the original premise behind the contest—namely that football in Texas and the Southwest was superior to football in other regions of the country. After two years the event mercifully died and was never resurrected.

On January 2, 1963, the day after the inaugural Southwest Challenge Bowl, Bulldog Turner, who had been a part of organized football for over 25 years, hung up his whistle and clipboard, retreated to his Texas ranch and never played or coached again.

He wasn't reclusive, but he could be hard to pin down. When Pat Turner called her dad one day in September 1966, no one answered the phone. She called again the next day with the same result. Bulldog was missing. Not that Pat was worried. Bulldog was probably at the horse races or playing in a celebrity golf tournament somewhere on the West Coast. Then a few days later Pat's phone rang, and Bulldog was on the other end. "I'm in Omaha," he said, "and I need you to pick me up at Love Field. I'm on my way back from Canton, Ohio."

"That," Pat said, "was how I found out my father was in the Pro Football Hall of Fame."[46]

On that day in Canton, eight players joined 31 other men previously elected to the Pro Football Hall of Fame. The new inductees were "Bullet Bill" Dudley (a halfback for the Steelers, Lions, and Redskins), Joe Guyon (from Carlisle—a blocker for Jim Thorpe—and later an NFL star), Artie Herber (a quarterback who teamed with Don Hutson to form one of pro football's greatest passing combinations), Walt Kiesling (the Pittsburgh coach who kicked Bulldog in the butt), George McAfee (Bulldog's teammate with the Bears), Steve Owen (for 23 years the head coach of the New York Giants), Hugh "Shorty" Ray (longtime supervisor of officials for the NFL), and Clyde "Bulldog" Turner. Each man was a unanimous selection. Dudley, Guyon, Herber, McAfee, and Turner were there in person. Kiesling, Owen, and Ray were deceased.

The induction ceremony at Canton on September 17, 1966 was a royal affair. The inductees were guests of honor in a two and a half–hour parade that included 28 marching bands. The parade terminated at the Hall of Fame complex on George Halas Drive. Many of the 31 members, in their gold Hall of Fame jackets, were present for the ceremony. Ed Healey (Chicago Bears, Hall of Fame, 1964) presented the bust to Bulldog Turner and helped him into his gold jacket. In a short acceptance speech, Bulldog gave credit for his success to his family and his coaches, especially George Halas and Frank Kimbrough. After Bulldog's induction, the large gathering of football fans gave him a standing ovation. This was the supreme moment of his life, worth all the years of hard work. As he stood on the podium and surveyed the crowd, his eyes froze on a familiar face. It was his old hero Mel Hein.

"I wasn't too impressed with going up there (to Canton) 'til I got there," Bulldog remembered. "But now I wish I had taken every kin I had up there. That's a very touching thing. That is the top. That's a Mecca that a football player can achieve."[47]

Bulldog had already been inducted into the College Football Hall of Fame in a ceremony at the Waldorf Astoria Hotel on Park Avenue in downtown New York City. Former President Herbert Hoover, a student manager for the football team during his college days at Stanford, was the guest of honor that night. Hoover received the gold medal for outstanding contribution to sports. The date was December 6, 1960. Also present were that year's College Football Hall of Fame inductees including Ki Aldrich (TCU), Sid Luckman (Columbia), Johnny Lujack (Notre Dame), and Bulldog Turner.

In 1961 the Texas Sports Hall of Fame (then in Grand Prairie but later moved to a beautiful facility on the banks of the Brazos River in Waco) added Bulldog Turner to its list of inductees. Other Texas legends enshrined there would eventually include Ki Aldrich, Sammy Baugh, Dana X. Bible, Eck Curtis, Lew Jenkins, Tom Landry, Bobby Layne, Don Maynard, Darrell Royal, Grant Teaff, Y. A. Tittle, Paul Tyson, Doak Walker, and Gordon Wood, to name a few.

In 1979 Hardin-Simmons University elected Bulldog to its athletic hall of fame. The list of athletes enshrined there would eventually include Ed Sprinkle, coaching legend Owen Goodnight, Frank Kimbrough, Sammy Baugh, Harold "Hayseed" Stephens, Warren Woodson, Gordon Wood, and track and basketball star Doyle Brunson (from Longworth, 20 miles north of Sweetwater) who, under the name "Texas Dolly," became the most famous poker player in the world.

In the summer of 1986, Bulldog opened his mail to find a special invitation to attend that year's Pro Football Hall of Fame ceremonies in Canton to be held on August 2. The occasion was the 20th anniversary of his own induction. The two other living members of the Class of 1966, George McAfee and Bullet Bill Dudley, also attended. The Class of 1986 included Paul Hornung, Ken Houston, Willie Lanier, Fran Tarkenton, and Bulldog's old deer hunting buddy Doak Walker.

Chapter 11
Practicing Poverty

I t may be shocking to fans of modern professional sports to learn that Bulldog Turner never made a lot of money playing football. His highest salary as a player, $14,000 in each of his final two seasons, is beer money—a sum that today wouldn't pay his green fees. In the 2011 season, Ben Roethlisberger, quarterback for the Pittsburgh Steelers, made $13,381.25 every minute of every regular season game.

Of course the financial landscape of professional sports has changed considerably since the advent of television, collective bargaining, and free agency. Today the biggest stars of the NFL make fortunes in a short time. In 2009 the average median yearly salary across the NFL was $1.4 million. Even for a lowly offensive lineman, the average median salary in 2009 was $1.2 million per year. In 2011, a first-round draft pick, regardless of the position he plays, can expect to earn at least $20 million in a multiyear deal.

But when it came to money, Bulldog Turner was a day late and a dollar short. His player's salary from the Bears never carried him to the start of the next season. "Damn near every year I'd get in a little bit of financial trouble," he explained, "and I'd need money during the off-season."[1]

In the old days most players had some kind of spring and summer job to make ends meet, but seasonal work was not easy to find. Employers wanted someone to work all year, not just January to June.

"The fact was that you couldn't get a job because you were already working six months out of the year at football," Bulldog said. "It was hard to get a job. About all I'd do, I'd take some kind of little salesman job or something."

He could have stayed in Chicago year-around, but Texas was in his blood. "I came back to Texas all the time," Bulldog explained, "and that was probably the wrong thing to do. There was a lot more money to be made in Chicago, some pretty good jobs with political connections, but I wanted to come back to Texas."[2]

Even when he had a good job he couldn't crawl out from under a mountain of debt. He once confided to a friend that, "I have thrown away several fortunes in my life, but I wouldn't change a thing."[3] He accepted his fate philosophically. "I drove a new car every year," he once said about his playing days with the Chicago Bears, "and I didn't run out of money until March." And he had no regrets. "I don't remember any bad days playing football," he said.[4]

But bad days were ahead. When Bulldog retired as a player there was no pension and no benefits from the NFL. He was completely on his own. He had his ranch on Cowhouse Creek, but the bank held the mortgage. Still, he could survive as long as he was young enough to work and generate income. Between coaching and other jobs, Bulldog could pay the bills. The real financial difficulties did not begin until he got too old to work and had to live on Social Security.

In addition to his coaching duties with the Bears and Titans, Bulldog worked in sales for several companies in Nebraska and Illinois, and he sold used cars in Lubbock—first at Jarmon Motors (19th and Avenue J) and later at his own business, Turner Motor Company, at 2401 Texas Avenue. For a time he worked at a brokerage house in Chicago. All he had to do was sit there and take orders over the phone, but the job was too confining for a West Texas cowboy. He could have a lot more fun chasing cattle around his Texas ranch or losing money at the race track. He liked to gamble, particularly on horse races, and he sometimes lost his shirt.

"I never did save any money out of football," Bulldog once said. "I never could save enough money to buy a place. I'd buy one, then have to pay it out. I always owed a lot of money. Some of our guys had good jobs in the off season. They'd go to work for somebody that wanted to hire them because they were players. But I never did capitalize on being a football player. I always came back to Texas and practiced poverty. But I liked it here and I got a lot of happiness out of coming back. I can't regret doing it.[5]

"I didn't try to capitalize on my name and reputation when I retired," he explained, "and I probably should have. The way I was brought up, I thought I was supposed to come back to Texas and get my own piece of land and settle down on my own place. That was my goal all the time I was playing, so that's what I did. I'm just Clyde down here and I'm Bulldog up in Chicago. I didn't realize I could have set myself up for life."

Does he wish he had played pro football about three decades later?

"Every minute of every day," he said with a chuckle. "Of course, mostly for the money. They play just a few years now and make big money and get themselves set up for life. I think of that part of it a lot."[6]

Some of Bulldog's teammates did well after retiring as players. Danny Fortmann, a Phi Beta Kappa from Fordham, went to med school and became a surgeon in Los Angeles. Bill Osmanski became a dentist in Chicago. Sid Luckman, a graduate of Columbia, worked for a company in Chicago that manufactured cellophane—eventually becoming its president. Ed Sprinkle ran a successful tile company in suburban Chicago. Lee Artoe was a chemical engineer. Joe Stydahar was a policeman. Johnny Lujack worked in the booth at college football games for ABC and CBS. Someone once asked Bulldog what is was like to play with guys who were so successful as business executives, dentists, and doctors. As usual he joked about it. "I was in medical school once," he quipped, "for observation."

When he tried to make money his efforts often fell flat. In the 1940s, when he was at the top of his game, a sportswriter persuaded him to write a book called *Playing the Line*, but Bulldog finished it during one of those periods in his life when he was broke. He sold the rights to the book for $1,500. The book reportedly made $5,000 the first day it went on sale.

About the same time he wrote a book called *Mr. Football*, about his relationship with George Halas, but the book never went to the publisher. (Years later, Bulldog said the manuscript was "still around here

Bulldog Turner on *The Steve Allen Show*, 1961. Courtesy of Pat Turner.

somewhere.") Bulldog wrote the story as a screenplay, and enlisted his friend in Hollywood, Shotgun Britton, to find a producer. Shotgun showed Bulldog's screenplay to Robert Mitchum, the man they both wanted to play the lead if Bulldog himself was counted out, but in the end nothing came of it.[7]

About as close as Bulldog got to the movies was a spot on *The Steve Allen Show* in 1961 and a few appearances on a television show called *Sports Challenge*—a weekly syndicated program on NBC hosted by Dick Enberg. The show ran from 1971 to 1979 on Saturday afternoons and featured two teams of three current or former players representing a sports franchise. The teams competed against each other answering sports trivia questions. The Chicago Bears team featured Sid Luckman, Hampton Pool, and Bulldog Turner.

In the off season and after retirement, Bulldog filled a part of his spare time at the golf course. "I could play a little better golf than I looked like I could," he explained. "I had me one 'sucker' that didn't think I could beat him playing golf. And we would play every day for six months out of the year. He couldn't get out there early enough to try me again.

"We'd start out betting a dollar and then we'd start pressing the bet. We'd play the last hole for about $25. And that last hole (at the Abilene Country Club) happened to be a dog-leg left and I could cut across and be real close to the green. But he had to come down the fairway and then come in. You'd think he'd learn after a while. . . ." He never did.[8]

With his size, strength, quickness, and athletic ability, Bulldog could drive the ball a long way. Few people could out hit him off the tee. A case in point is the first hole at the Abilene Country Club—a 495-yard par 5. With a driver and a tailwind, Bulldog could hit the ball 400 yards, and then use an eight iron to pitch it on the green in two.[9]

Bulldog appreciated the athletic part of golf, but it was really the human side of the game that made it fun. Golf was an excuse for men to get together—to drink and laugh and talk dirty and verbally abuse each other. The game made no sense without the bragging, the joking, and the boozing that went along with it.

One day on a golf course in Southern California, Shotgun Britton introduced Bulldog Turner to Bob Hope. Shotgun and Hope were old friends having met years before at the Lakeside Country Club Golf Course in California. Like everyone else, Bob Hope was captivated by Shotgun's rowdy ways and colorful personality. The two men became friends for life. Hope insisted they play golf once a week because, as Hope said, "It's the only way I can get material for my next show."[10] Later, through Shotgun and Hope, Bulldog met the actor and comedian Joe E. Brown and got reacquainted with Bing Crosby, whom Bulldog had first met in Los Angeles in 1936. Bulldog played regularly at the Bing Crosby Pro-Am Golf Tournament at Pebble Beach and the Bob Hope Desert Classic. He drank beer with sports celebrities and movie stars at the barbecues in Bing's back yard, next to the 13th green at Pebble Beach. Bulldog's golf game wasn't the best, especially his shot game, but even the pros crowded in close to watch him crush the ball off the tee with his driver.

Bulldog Turner is on the right; at far left, Whitey Ford; at center, Mickey Mantle; and Bobby Layne in the plaid jacket. Seated between Bulldog Turner and Bobby Layne is Doak Walker. Photo taken at a celebrity golf tournament in Las Vegas. Courtesy of Pat Turner.

Bulldog's friendship with Bob Hope, Joe E. Brown, and Bing Crosby made him a regular at celebrity golf tournaments in California and Las Vegas where Bulldog was a member of some of celebrity golf's legendary foursomes, known particularly for their play at the 19th hole.

"I've got a picture that I couldn't find a while ago," Bulldog recalled, "but it's one I'm most proud of. It's Doak Walker, Bobby Layne, Mickey Mantle, Whitey Ford, and myself. It was a Hall of Fame golf tournament in Las Vegas. The same group always wound up together all three or four nights we were up there."[11]

What a wild weekend that must have been. In three or four nights that group could have worn out a whole shift of cocktail waitresses and several bartenders.

Doak Walker and Bulldog were especially good friends. Doak liked to hunt deer at Bulldog's place at Pidcoke.

Doak was a three time All-American at SMU and a Heisman Trophy winner. He and Bobby Layne were high school teammates at Highland Park High School and later were stars on the great Detroit Lions teams of the 1950s.

Walker had it all. He was handsome, smart, and talented. Rick Reilly of *Sports Illustrated* wrote that Doak "had perfectly even teeth and a jaw as square as a deck of cards and a mop of brown hair that made girls bite their necklaces. He was so shifty you couldn't have tackled him in a phone booth, yet so humble that he wrote the Associated Press a thank-you note for naming him an All-American."

Walker only played six professional seasons, and his career statistics are not spectacular by today's standards. The great Barry Sanders gained more yards in a season than Doak Walker gained in his entire career. But Doak and his Lions won championships—something Barry and his teammates never did. And watching Doak Walker carry the ball was like watching Fred Astaire dance with a hat rack. Doak was that good. He was inducted into the Pro Football Hall of Fame in 1986. Bulldog was there.

One cool December night after a Central Texas deer hunt, Bulldog Turner and some hunting buddies stopped in for a few beers at a honky-tonk outside Gatesville called the Shandar Club. The front part of the building housed the bar and a few pool tables. The dance hall was in back. As Roy Robbins and the Availables played in the background, Bulldog's group stood drinking at the bar when a local man who knew Bulldog started up a conversation with a member of the hunting party who was drinking Coke instead of Lone Star. The local man introduced himself, and the Coke drinker stuck out his hand.

"I'm the cook and designated driver," he said. "I'm Doak Walker."[12]

The rowdy crowd at the Shandar Club was in the presence of football royalty that night. Too bad most of them were in no condition to appreciate it.

"In the thirties," Bulldog recalled, "you know, we had that big drought, my dad was in the cattle business, and we kept moving east where there was more rainfall. We bought a place in Hamilton County and some guy came along and wanted it worse that we did so we sold it to him."[13]

After the sale of the Hamilton County property, Bulldog and his family bought a ranch near Pidcoke in the edge of the Hill Country between Gatesville and Lampasas. On August 9, 1950, Bulldog signed a contract to pay $27,000 for 1,300 acres along the east bank of Cowhouse Creek. He named the property the Triple T Ranch.

Bulldog bought the place from Daisy Perryman Hampton. Daisy Hampton had a niece named Phyllis Perryman, the daughter of Daisy's brother Verne who lived on a ranch just up the creek from Bulldog Turner's place. Phyllis married a young man from Christoval named Jack Pardee who played football for Bear Bryant at Texas A&M in the 1950s. After college, Pardee had a long career as a player in the National Football League (Rams and Redskins). Like Bulldog Turner, Pardee was a linebacker. He once had three interceptions in a game in St. Louis. And like Bulldog, Pardee became a coach (Florida Blazers, Washington Redskins, Houston Gamblers, University of Houston Cougars, and Houston Oilers). For three years, from 1975 to 1977, Jack Pardee was the head coach of Bulldog's team, the Chicago Bears. The remarkable coincidence of two old Chicago Bears crossing paths on Cowhouse Creek was not lost on Coach Pardee.

"It was interesting how it all came about," Pardee explained. "When I was a senior at A&M, I had two college buddies who were married to sisters. Dean Meeks was married to Margaret Perryman and John Henry was married to Margaret's sister Dixie. Margaret and Dixie's father was Verne Perryman who lived on Cowhouse Creek in Coryell County just up the road from Bulldog Turner's place. Well, Dean and John talked me into going on a blind date with Margaret and Dixie's sister. Her name was Phyllis, and she was a twirler at TCU. We got married six months later.

"After Phyllis and I married I would stop by and see Bulldog once in a while, whenever I was in Coryell County. He was stove up by then and had a hard time getting around. But he was a character. He told some great stories about the old days."[14]

The Triple T Ranch was Bulldog's refuge, and after the fiasco in New York, he spent more time in Pidcoke. He raised sheep, goats, Angus cattle, and registered quarter horses. He had been attracted to

Bulldog with Mai-Don D at Sunland Park, New Mexico. Courtesy of Pat Turner.

horse racing since the day he saw his first race at Fair Park in Abilene in the 1930s. His quarter horse business was what Bulldog called a "15 minute-a-day hobby that has turned into a full-time job." He raced his horses at Junction, Goliad, Fredericksburg, New Braunfels, and Columbus—some of the few Texas towns that still had tracks after the state declared parimutuel betting illegal in 1937. He also took his horses out of state to Louisiana, Oklahoma, and California. In the 1960s, he kept 25 animals at a 40-acre training facility in the mountains outside Tularosa, New Mexico. He and Gladys lived in Tularosa during the racing season at Sunland Park near El Paso and at Ruidoso Downs. His silks were navy blue and burnt orange—the colors of the Chicago Bears. Bulldog loved racing horses but never made much money at it. Still, the action at the track was the only thing he ever found that came close to the excitement of living in Chicago and winning championships for the Bears.

Bulldog first raced his horses in the "bushes" as a hobby in the 1950s. Back then the sport was little better than a backwoods cock fight. It was relatively unregulated and amateurish, and it enjoyed a less than sterling reputation. Rules were not uniform, which mattered little because they weren't enforced anyway. Wagering on horse races was illegal in Texas so betting was done under the table. The winner of a close race was sometimes settled by a fist fight at the finish line. There were rumors of widespread "doping" of horses.

Bulldog Turner helped change that seedy image. He was a good ambassador, and his association with the sport gave it legitimacy. Slowly the sport became respectable. It adopted uniform rules and regulations and moved from the outhouse into the parlor.

Bulldog began breeding race horses as a serious business in 1961 and two years later sent his first animal to the starting post. "The money is in selling the horses," he confessed, "but the fun is in racing." In the beginning he sent his horses elsewhere to be trained, but Gladys persuaded Bulldog to do his own training with help from his brother-in-law Leroy Hairston. Their first win came on July 24, 1965 when Little Red Demon, a three-year-old quarter horse, won by a nose at Ruidoso Downs. There were five wins, three seconds, and four thirds in 12 starts that season. Then a mare named "Hurihomhoni" won at Sunland.[15] Bulldog was on a roll. He bought a new truck and matching horse trailer.

Bulldog Turner Day at Sunland Park Racetrack in New Mexico, March 5, 1966. Kneeling to Bulldog's right is Johnny Unitas. Kneeling to Bulldog's left is Bobby Layne. Standing behind with Gladys Turner are Don Maynard—Titans and Jets, Carlton "Stretch" Elliott—Packers, Paul Barry—Rams, Jesse Whittenton—Packers, and Wayne Hansen—Bears. Courtesy of Pat Turner.

To show appreciation for its best-known ambassador, Sunland Park Racetrack in New Mexico celebrated "Bulldog Turner Day" on March 5, 1966. Former New Mexico Governor John Burroughs was there. Track officials gave Bulldog a silver trophy and a monogrammed blanket. There were flowers and a silver tray for Gladys. George Halas wired a telegram of congratulations. Then organizers of the event brought a real bulldog into the winner's circle to pose with Turner and a group of special NFL friends including Johnny Unitas, Bobby Layne, Carlton (Stretch) Elliot (Packers), Paul Barry (Rams), Don Maynard (Titans and Jets), Jesse Whittenton (Packers), and Wayne Hansen (Bears).

"This is a great day for me," Bulldog said with a grin. "Let's do it again next week."[16]

A good-sized crowd surrounded the winner's circle for the ceremony. At its conclusion a group of autograph seekers brushed past Bulldog and mobbed Johnny Unitas.[17]

When the day was over, Bulldog sat down on a bale of hay, lit a smoke, popped opened a cold Lone Star, and relaxed. A reporter asked him if there were similarities between coaching football players and training horses. "Yes," Bulldog replied, taking a long drag on a Marlboro, "except that horses are easier to get along with."[18]

"Horses are real competitors," he went on to say. "I believe you will find horses will give you better effort every day than people. They've got great heart. Why, I've seen a horse try to grab a jockey on another horse with its teeth before letting that other horse go by it in a race. They like to run, and once they've learned what it means to win, they don't want to be beaten."[19]

For the moment, Bulldog was living the good life, but those closest to him knew he was struggling financially, despite the recent winning streak. Horse racing is great sport for a wealthy gentleman who just wants to have fun at the track, but a risky business for a man with limited resources. It's like playing the lottery. Bulldog was living for a big fat payoff that never came. While he waited, he mortgaged just about everything he owned and borrowed heavily to pay his bills. After a few trips to the winner's circle came a long dry spell. His new truck disappeared, and his matching horse trailer sat on the parking lot at the bank with a "for sale" sign on it. Then some revelations to a newspaper reporter suggested that his life was not all beer and steak. When asked if he made any money from horse racing, Bulldog, who was too honest for his own good, quipped, "Are you kidding?"

"I may not manage money very well," he confessed. "In fact, I'm about as close to being broke now as I ever was. Not that we're starving, but just about everything Gladys and I have is mortgaged to the hilt. But we do have just about everything we need, though most of our resources are tied up in property."[20]

At least he had his health. Then on August 28, 1974, while in Chicago on business for the Interstate Steel Company of Omaha, Nebraska, Bulldog collapsed in the lobby of the Landers Hyatt Chalet Hotel in suburban Elk Grove Village. He was unconscious when he arrived by ambulance at Northwest Community Hospital in nearby Arlington Heights. Nurses learned his identity from a Chicago Bears identification card in his pocket.[21]

Doctors said Bulldog suffered a stroke, and he spent the next week in the hospital. At the end of his stay he announced he had "some stiffness in my right arm, but otherwise I feel fine." He eventually recovered, but the treatment was expensive. He had trouble paying his bill. His health problems made news and his financial difficulties leaked to the media and focused attention for the first time on the plight of some of the NFL old-timers who retired without a pension or any benefits from the NFL. By the 1970s sports fans had grown accustomed to outrageous salaries paid to NFL players and were shocked to learn that the great Bulldog Turner had financial problems. His story would eventually bring shame to the NFL and change the pension system.

The world of professional football that Bulldog Turner knew had no job security and no benefits. Players had to work in the off-season just to make ends meet. Salaries were low, even for established stars and future Hall of Famers. Nobody got rich playing football. When their athletic careers ended, players went to work full-time. Professional football had all kinds of players: doctors, lawyers, engineers, teachers, and businessmen of all sorts. Some players made a good living after leaving the NFL. Others didn't.

It is hard to imagine today, but in Bulldog's time, professional football was not the great money-making machine it is in the twenty-first century. Back then baseball stood unchallenged as the national pastime. College football was big. Boxing was front-page news. But pro football was not very important. Bulldog didn't even know pro football existed when he started playing the game at Sweetwater in the 1930s.

Of course things have changed a great deal since then. In 1962 Bulldog created a furor when he predicted, "Pretty soon, it won't be long, the colleges will just be a proving ground for the pros. When the fans get used to seeing pro football games, they will quit going to college football games."[22] He wasn't exactly a prophet, but he was half right.

While millions still attend college games, the pro game long ago surpassed college football in fan interest. Today pro football is far and away the most popular sport in the United States. Half of all American males over the age of 12 list professional football as their favorite sport. With the rise in popularity came recognition and money. Today when a professional football player retires, he has a pension, and he can use his fame to earn a living.

Things were different when Bulldog retired. There was no pension and precious little fame. "I had some first cousins down here in Texas," Bulldog said, "who knew I was up in Chicago playing ball, but they didn't know whether it was baseball or football or what. I don't think anybody was impressed down here in Texas."[23]

Even while he played, Bulldog tried to cash in on what fame he had, but not much money came his way. He didn't score enough touchdowns. "Once I endorsed Vicks Cough Drops," Bulldog remembered, "and I think I got $35 out of that. It was a short subject for movie houses. It showed me coming out of a game, sitting down all sweaty and dirty, and having trouble breathing. I pick up a box of Vicks Cough Drops and hold it so you can read the label and put one in my mouth."

"I had one other deal," he recalled, "with Phillips 66 gasoline. I can't remember how much I got out of it. My football number was 66; that's how I got that one. I think Gillette Razor Company used a Bears' squad picture, and I believe we got a dollar apiece for it. That's how big the endorsements were then."[24]

Football cards first appeared in packages of bubble gum in the 1930s, but the players made no money from them. For almost 20 years the cards were free-booted. The bubble gum company made money, but the players got nothing. Then in 1951, NFL Commissioner Bert Bell began collecting a fee from the gum manufacturer for the rights to use players' pictures. Royalties from baseball cards went to the players, but pro football card royalties went into a League fund. In 1958 the NFL Players Association assumed control of that fund. A lot of people got a Bulldog Turner football card with their bubble gum, but Bulldog never made a dime.[25]

In the old days, when players retired from the NFL, they were completely on their own. Many of them had bad backs and busted knees. Some suffered concussions and brain injuries that would cause serious problems later in life. But they got no help from the NFL to defray medical expenses. There were no retirement benefits at all for retired players for the first four decades of the NFL.

Then in 1956 the players began to organize. In that year players from Cleveland and Green Bay formed a union to demand that owners provide a list of items that are taken for granted today including a minimum League-wide salary, per diem for out of town games, uniforms and equipment paid for by the club, and continued payment of salaries while players were injured and unable to play. Leaders of the players union would eventually include Don Shula, Frank Gifford, Sam Huff, and Norm Van Brocklin. Although the owners refused to bargain with the union (to do so would legitimize its existence) or formally respond to its proposals, the players eventually gained some concessions from the owners including some minimal health insurance, a basic salary structure, and compensation for exhibition games. But some of the owners were less than magnanimous, and a few were downright stingy and resentful. Don Colo, a defensive end for the Cleveland Browns, claimed, "The owners started giving us $50 an exhibition game, then took it out of our first paycheck."[26]

The organization that began in Cleveland and Green Bay evolved into the National Football League Players Association and slowly encompassed a majority of the players on every team in the league. Even though the owners still would not recognize the union, the NFL-PA exerted enough pressure to obtain the first pension agreement in 1962. The pension was a small monthly annuity paid to certain retired players who left the game in 1959 or later. Players like Bulldog Turner, who retired before 1959, received nothing at all.

As salaries, and pension dues, climbed higher in the 1960s, the NFL Players Association grew stronger. The union obtained its first collective bargaining contract in 1968, and in 1970 the NFLPA hammered out an agreement with the owners that set up the present structure of the pension plan. By then the owners were no longer struggling. Fat televisions contracts made them a lot of money. Under the new pension plan, retired players (but still not the pre-59ers) would receive monthly annuities based not on their salaries as active players but on the number of years they played in the League.

The plan, called the Bert Bell/Pete Rozelle Retirement Plan, worked this way. A player who played in three or more games in a year received credit for a season. Players who earned five benefit credits— by playing in at least three games a year for five years—were vested and entitled to a pension when they reached 55 years of age. (A 1977 collective bargaining agreement reduced the number of years from five to four. Still later the number of years dropped from four to three.) At the time, players received $60 a month for each credited season. A 10-year veteran could get a $600 (gross) monthly annuity starting at age 55. The annuity had certain options like a reduced pension starting at age 45, a lump sum option, and an increased monthly annuity for players who waited until they turned 65. Still the old guys were left out, and some of them, like Bulldog Turner, really needed the money.

In 1987 another collective bargaining agreement left the annuity amount at $60 a month for players who retired between 1959 and 1966 but gave vested players who retired after 1966 $150 a month for each credited season. In 1989 the NFL pension plan came under the complete control of the owners, and in that year the monthly annuity multiple for an accredited season increased from $60 to $80 for vested players who retired between 1959 and 1966 and from $150 to $210 for eligible retirees who retired after 1966. The particulars of the pension seemed fair to the men who structured it because the explosion in salaries was caused by the performances of men like Joe Namath, Joe Montana, Roger Staubach, and Lawrence Taylor, so those players should get most of the pension riches.

The current benefit package for an NFL retiree is $470 per benefit credit and is designed to promote a lifetime of financial security. It is a good plan, but not as generous as some might think. (A comparable Major League Baseball pension is much higher.) For example, a 10-

year NFL veteran can gross $56,400 a year at age 55. (The average career lasts only 3.5 years.) If he waits until age 65, his yearly income increases to $147,000 a year. He will also receive $455,000 from an annuity plan, $132,000 from a 401K plan, five years of free health insurance, and $300,000 from a health reimbursement plan that kicks in after the five years of free health insurance have expired.[27] The severance package pays any player with at least two accredited seasons (on the active roster, the injured reserve, or the physically unable to perform list for three games in each of two seasons) $10,000 for every year played between 1993 and 1999 and $12,500 for every year from 2000 on.

But those men who retired before 1959 didn't even get a thank-you. The current players gave themselves raises while the old-timers, some living below the poverty line, got nothing. The old guys were confused and hurt, especially by the indifference displayed by the NFLPA. Years went by, and still nothing was done.

The beginning of the big push for an old-timer's pension goes back to 1966. The idea began with Ed Sprinkle, the former Chicago Bear and Bulldog Turner's friend from Hardin-Simmons. Sprinkle asked Harold "Bud" Leininger, the Los Angeles assistant trainer who Bulldog Turner apologized to in the hostile Rams locker room, to help. In the spring of 1967, Sprinkle, Leininger, and a veterans delegation representing an estimated 500 pre-59ers not covered under the current pension plan, presented their concerns at the NFL annual meeting in Hawaii. Not much came of that effort. Leininger had already talked with many active players and correctly predicted that current players would resist the effort to include old-timers in the pension. "They're a bunch of upstarts," he explained, "who don't realize what these former players did for them."[28]

"It's a heck of a thing the kind of money the fellows make today while the old-timers who made it possible got nothing, and some of them got nothing when they played," Sprinkle added.[29]

Sprinkle and Leininger knew that persuasion was their only recourse. "We don't have a legal leg to stand on," Leininger said, "but we have moral law and moral law is even stronger than legal law."[30]

Marion Motley, a Hall of Fame running back for the Browns and the Steelers expressed the hurt and the anger felt by the old guys.

"The young players don't seem to want anything to do with us. Ed Garvey (a labor lawyer and director of the NFLPA) doesn't want them to associate with us. Garvey is the reason we haven't come to some kind of understanding."[31]

But some men in a position to help understood and took notice. In 1982, Cloyce Box, a former NFL star from Jonesboro, Texas who made a fortune after football in the oil and gas business, organized a reunion of the 1952 NFL Champion Detroit Lions in conjunction with Super Bowl XVI in Pontiac, Michigan. Box anticipated a celebration but was shocked at what he found. When he greeted his old friends, some for the first time in 30 years, he saw once incredible athletes with broken bodies but no money for medical treatment. He saw men with bad teeth who couldn't afford a dentist, and he saw men whose sharp minds had been hijacked by head injuries.

"It was hard for him to accept the conditions [in which] he found some of the players," Box's son Tom explained. "They didn't have pensions. To think of their lives in tattered old houses or in lonely places out in the country was just horrible. There were lots of players living in poverty, a lot of pros having fallen on hard times. When my father heard some of their stories, he just felt something had to be done."[32]

A few weeks later Cloyce Box quietly used over a million dollars of his own money to establish a trust fund—the interest to be used to give assistance to help destitute old-timers, including Bulldog Turner, pay their bills. Before its liquidation, the Box Fund paid out over $300,000.

"We also provided wheelchairs, other medical equipment, and in-house medical care," Tom Box added. "It all depended on what someone needs. In one instance, a former player wrote us saying he needed tires for his car. We got him tires."[33]

"I was there the day he (Cloyce Box) and Doak Walker and Bobby Layne met and agreed to start the old-timers' fund," Maurice Campbell, Box's attorney and friend, recalled. "Not long after that Cloyce went to Bulldog Turner's house near Gatesville and gave him a substantial sum of money. He did it quietly. He didn't want to embarrass anybody. He really cared about those old guys and didn't want them to suffer."[34]

Mike Ditka, another former NFL player and coach, founded the Gridiron Greats Assistance Fund to help retired NFL players who couldn't pay their bills. The fund provided money for food, housing, transportation, clothing, and other basic needs to football pioneers who made the NFL what it is today.

In the meantime, the NFL Alumni Association, formed in 1967, led efforts to include players who retired before 1959 in the League's pension plan, but progress was painfully slow. Dante Lavelli, formerly of the Cleveland Browns, led the alumni organization that was founded in part with a $5,000 donation from the owners. Still, for some owners, the money was nothing more than an effort to pacify the old-timers because the owners and the players association fought, tooth and nail, every effort by the Alumni Association to include the old-timers in the pension. There was suspicion, but no proof, that on two occasions the League used its influence to keep the Alumni Association from getting a tax exemption. Finally, the Alumni Association sued the NFL, asking that the pre-59ers be included in the pension plan. The suit asked for $200 a month for each of the old-timers—a modest amount that represented a fraction of what the average modern player got at the age of 55. The court ruled in favor of the League.[35]

The legal setback caused the NFL Alumni Association to change its tactics. Rather than depending on the owners or the union for financing, the association raised its own funds by holding celebrity golf tournaments and the sale of merchandise. Then in 1983 a group called Pro Legends, Inc., a subsidiary of the NFL Alumni Association, distributed $500 royalty checks to 135 former NFL players who retired before 1959. The first check went to Red Grange, then in retirement near Tampa, Florida. Among others who received checks were Sammy Baugh, Don Hutson, Sid Luckman, Marion Motley, Bronko Nagurski, and Bulldog Turner.[36]

In 1988, the Alumni Association founded Pro Advisor—a service that helped former players with health, legal, tax, and social problems. That same year the Association started the Dire Need program for former players whose needs were desperate. But some old-timers whose needs were dire, like Bulldog Turner and Bronko Nagurski, refused to apply out of pride.[37]

Meanwhile, Bulldog did what he could to make ends meet. In the winter he sold firewood. The ad in *The Gatesville Messenger* read, "You don't have to cut it. Just load it. Call Bulldog Turner." Gladys raised and sold Chihuahuas commercially. Their house was filled with dogs.

When he got too old to work, the only thing between Bulldog and the poor house was Social Security. He had never been the kind to look too far ahead. He had no retirement plan and no savings. The ranch never brought in much money and the quarter horse business came up lame. When Bulldog and Gladys got sick and the medical bills mounted, Social Security and Medicare didn't cover everything. Bulldog Turner was broke. He had borrowed against everything and had nothing left to collateralize. He owed more money than he was worth.

"Dad lived in the moment," daughter Pat recalled. "He didn't plan much for the future."[38]

Then Gladys got lung cancer and had part of a lung removed. After that she never ventured far from her oxygen machine in the back of the house. Bulldog and Gladys had all kinds of trouble getting the insurance company to pay the doctor bills. They sued the company and finally recovered some money. They sold off parts of the Triple T Ranch to pay the doctors and the hospital. By the 1980s only 250 acres remained of the original 1,300.

In the meantime, Bulldog had his own health problems. He contracted emphysema. In 1984 he had a tumor removed from his lip— the result of too many hours in the hot Texas sun. He had suffered from diabetes since childhood. Doctors told him to quit drinking and smoking, but he wouldn't listen. Gladys nagged him when he drank, so Bulldog kept his beer in a small rock outbuilding once used as a deer hunter cabin. He didn't hide his drinking, but he kept his beer out of the big house out of respect for his wife. His weight dropped to under 200 pounds. But even as he faced life-threatening issues he couldn't put down those Marlboro cigarettes, and he had too many "three Lone Star lunches" at the Shandar Club.[39]

Gladys loved to ride horses at the ranch. Before she got sick, she rode almost every day. When it was goat shearing time, Gladys would round up goats on horseback while Bulldog drank beer under the goat shearer's tarp. When Bulldog retired as an active player, the Chicago Bears gave Gladys a custom-made, hand-tooled saddle. She was proud of that saddle and used it on the ranch for years. But a time came when Bulldog and Gladys needed money, so Bulldog swallowed his pride and sold the saddle to Dr. Tom Williams, a Gatesville dentist, for $250.[40] For years Gladys Turner's saddle was on display with other Western artifacts at Poco Automotive on Main Street in Gatesville. How hard it must have been for Gladys to part with that saddle, but not nearly as hard as watching her proud husband forced to sell their most prized possessions just to pay the bills.

Gossip in a small town spreads quickly and intensifies when the object of the gossip is a prominent person who is down on his luck. One story made the rounds that Bulldog had a $3,000 note at the bank in Gatesville. The note was past due, and the bank needed its money. An officer of the bank called Bulldog and reminded him that the note needed to be paid.

A few weeks later Bulldog stood before the officer's desk to pay his note. In his hand he had three $500 dollar bills—an unusual thing since $500 bills had not been printed for decades. Along with the cash, Bulldog had a check for $500 from the Chicago Bears, a $500 check from Mike Ditka, and a $500 personal check from Mike McCaskey, George Halas's son-in-law and the president of the Chicago Bears.

Another story was about a telephone company technician sent to cut off Bulldog Turner's service after Bulldog couldn't pay his phone bill. The technician knew Bulldog only by his surly reputation and feared for his life. "I'm sorry, Mr. Turner," he said when Bulldog came to the door, "but I'm here to cut off your phone."

"Well, come on in," Bulldog growled. The man from the phone company was a sports fan and nervously commented on a picture that hung on the living room wall. For the next hour, Bulldog showed him pictures and told stories about the old days. Then he stood up. "Well son," he said. "Do what ya gotta do." The man disconnected the phone and left.

By the 1980s the old ranch house was in disrepair, but there was no money to fix it up. Still, Bulldog and Gladys had plans. They bought a mobile home to live in while fixing up the big house, but the repairs they planned never happened. Medical expenses ate up the money until nothing was left. Then Gladys's health failed. After she died on October 27, 1988, Bulldog lost all interest in improving the big house.

Even a mansion would be empty without Gladys. When Gladys died, Bulldog buried her in Greenbriar Cemetery. Mike Ditka and the Chicago Bears paid for the funeral.[41]

Then in the late 1980s more stories about Bulldog Turner's health problems and financial difficulties appeared in the national press. This time the stories featured a sense of urgency. The media used Bulldog's story again to call attention to NFL pioneers, some of whom were destitute and dying, who received no benefits from the League and missed out on the windfall of the television era. Journalists wrote of a shameful and unjust system that made instant millionaires of untested rookies while Bulldog Turner, Bronko Nagurski, Dick Lane, and other gridiron immortals lived in poverty.

"Bronko lives in International Falls, Minnesota," Ed Sprinkle recalled. "He ran a gas station there for years. He doesn't get around much now. He's had problems with his eyesight.

"Bulldog had a ranch down in Texas and had a rough time of it," Sprinkle continued. "They had a drought. He was the same type of guy (as Nagurski), very proud. He didn't want to go on Dire Need.

"Things got so bad that Bulldog had just about lost the desire to live or do anything. He told me the bank had foreclosed on his mortgage."[42]

Dick "Night Train" Lane, a Hall of Fame defensive back and husband of jazz singer Dinah Washington, died penniless in an Austin, Texas nursing home—a sad end to a proud life. Mike Ditka used the proceeds from his golf tournament to pay for Lane's funeral and tombstone.[43]

The sad part is that the League could have taken care of the old guys but chose to ignore them. By the 1970s the NFL had lots of money and could have funded benefits for the pre-59ers without overdrawing on the regular pension fund. Television had made professional football a billion-dollar business. The pigskin and the picture tube were made for each other, and television rewarded professional football with staggering revenues.

In 1962, the 14 NFL teams authorized Commissioner Pete Rozelle to negotiate a single network TV deal, pitting the three major networks, NBC, ABC, and CBS against each other. CBS won the bid, paying the league $4.65 million a year for two years for the rights to televise League games—the money to be split evenly among the teams. The NFL Championship game was not a part of the package. The contract to televise the 1963 Championship game went to NBC in a separate deal for $926,000. In the 1980s CBS paid $420 million for the right to televise NFL games. In 1993, Rupert Murdoch and Fox won the television rights with a bid of $4.4 billion for 4 years.

The networks were willing to pay such outrageous prices because on any given Sunday, 28 million men between the ages of 18 and 49 plopped down in their recliners to watch pro football, and that age group represented the most important demographic of all for advertisers. Other sports could only dream of pro football's ratings. And those ratings translated into windfall profits for owners and players. There was reportedly a billion dollars in the NFL benefits fund in the 1990s. The League could have easily taken care of the men who founded the game.

"When I see the kind of salaries they make today it makes me sick," Bulldog once said. "Not just because I wish I could have made that kind of money, but because I don't think these guys appreciate how good they have it now."[44]

But it was more than just money. The old-timers wanted to be included. "We feel like we started the League," said Bear Hall of Famer George Musso. "Any kind of pension makes us feel a part of it all."

Alex Wojciechowicz, one of Fordham's seven blocks of granite (Vince Lombardi was another) and an early star in the NFL, agreed. "When I first started in 1938, the Giants were drawing 10,000 to 15,000 per game. We helped build it up to 50,000."[45]

Finally the publicity generated by Bulldog Turner and some other destitute old-timers put enough pressure on the NFLPA and the owners to include the pre-59ers in their pension plan. In 1993 the pension system for the first time included the sport's founding fathers with an $80 benefit credit for all vested retirees who left the game prior to 1966. Many of the pre-59ers give credit to Gene Upshaw. They say when Upshaw became executive director of the players' union, he included the old-timers' pension among a list of union demands.[46] There is a possibility that a meeting Upshaw had with Bulldog Turner in 1975, when both men were members of the all-time Texas professional football team, influenced Upshaw's opinion of the old-timers.

"I didn't think much about it when I was chosen," Upshaw told a reporter, "but then I got to meet Bulldog Turner, Bobby Layne and the rest of them and heard the stories they tell.

"Heck, those guys built football. I was thinking that when we walked into Texas Stadium. Those guys are responsible for all the fantastic new stadiums we have, and they never got to play in them."[47]

Still, some old-timers were skeptical of the motives. "We wouldn't be getting anything if the players fund wasn't overfunded," said Bulldog's old teammate Ray Nolting. He may have been right.

In 1993, the players fund contained so much money that the owners, instead of making their usual $500,000 payments to the players' fund, contributed $100,000 each to create a special needs fund for the pre-59ers. The old-timers' money was in a separate account so that the regular players' pension fund, which pays its members a lot more than the old-timers get and has widows and survivors benefits, was not diluted.[48]

But at least one old-timer didn't complain. At 74 years of age, after years of living off Social Security checks, Bulldog Turner received a pension of $960 a month. In 1998, not long before his death, his monthly annuity increased to $1,200 per month.

"That probably doesn't sound like a lot to some, but we've run out of money," Bulldog conceded. "We're busted.

"It's really been a good life. We couldn't have had more fun. I never felt anyone owed us anything. We played because we wanted to, and no one promised us anything.

"But it sure will be nice to get that first check."[49]

"He's got 12 or 13 years of service," Ed Sprinkle explained, "so he'll be getting $720 to $780 a month for this. That's a lot of money to people like this. He'd told me he was living on Social Security, $440 a month. You add $720, and he should be just about able to make it."[50]

"I figured I'd saved enough for retirement," Bulldog said with a grin but added, "then I went and lived more than 2 days."[51]

Ed Sprinkle was more indignant. "I'm going to make them suffer," he said with a laugh. "I'm going to live till I'm 90."[52] (He's 87 and counting.)

Chapter 12
Fourth and Long

"It's quiet," Bulldog Turner said of his last years. "Not many people remember anymore. To be honest with you, it's a little lonesome sometimes."[1]

After Gladys died, Bulldog's health declined. He didn't get out much. He had been an active man all his life, but now he rarely left his bedroom. He liked to watch the squirrels, turkeys, and deer from his bedroom window. In the fall he watched a lot of football on TV—college on Saturday and the pros on Sunday.

"I wouldn't walk across the street to see a game," he confided, "but I watch them all on TV. Football is a lot faster and better game than when I played. It's a lot more entertaining."[2]

"Some of these announcers have a greater knowledge of what's going on than the radio men when I was playing," he added. John Madden was his favorite. "They're good. They tip you off on what to look for. They sure must get information from the coaching staff. I remember our coaching staff on the Bears wouldn't put out anything to announcers when I was playing."[3]

"I'm a pretty good fan of TV," he said. "I enjoy the game. It's good for me. But I like to bitch about the rule changes. There just aren't many places you can hit a guy anymore."[4] And there were parts of the modern game that didn't seem right to an old warrior of the Texas plains. "Of course there's artificial turf. I can't say I like that. I just don't think the game should be played on carpet and tennis shoes."[5]

Still, some of the youngsters impressed him—especially a pair of

Chicago linebackers. "Butkus was probably my favorite of all time at that position," he said. "But I was always kind of impressed with (Mike) Singletary. He didn't seem all that big, but he sure got the job done."[6]

Bulldog's pension gave him a steady income. He had an agent, and he made some extra cash signing pictures and footballs for dealers of collectibles. Bulldog Turner memorabilia still sold well in Chicago. He also received an inheritance from a childless aunt in West Texas. During her lifetime Aunt Pearl received royalties from oil wells on the family property near Tokio in Yoakum County, and when she died, she left the royalties to her nieces and nephews. Bulldog used his share of the money to fix up his house and pay his debts. For the first time in a long while he didn't have to worry about money.

But his physical condition was a great concern and by the spring of 1998, it was fourth and long for Bulldog Turner. He was in bad health with no prospects of getting better. In March he was diagnosed with lung cancer, but there was little the doctors could do. Complications from that disease would kill him before the end of the year. He had a terrible cough most of the time. He took oxygen from a bottle that was never far from his bed. He didn't go outside anymore. When he was young he was the fastest big man in the NFL. Now his movements were ponderous, deliberate, and slow. He needed help and every ounce of energy to get from the living room to the kitchen or the bathroom. His daughter Pat did her best to make her father comfortable, but he was a big man and not easy to care for.

Ed Sprinkle called regularly. So did J. R. Boone and George McAfee, some of the few Bears still alive from the old days. Dan Edwards and Cotton Davidson, both former professional football players, came by every few weeks. But Bulldog had recently lost some important people in his life, and the sadness was almost unbearable. Bill Bishop, Bulldog's friend and teammate with the Bears, died in May. Sid Luckman died on July 5, and Doak Walker died on September 27 from injuries suffered in a skiing accident.

Meanwhile Bulldog grew weaker. Every day he found each breath harder to come by. In October 1998, the family accepted the inevitable and arranged for hospice care—a service Bulldog would need for only a short time.

On October 28, 1998, Cotton Davidson stopped by the Triple T ranch house to visit with Bulldog. They talked about the old days. For a while that afternoon it was Chicago again in the 1940s, and Bulldog Turner was the toast of the town. Pat could hear the two of them in the other room, laughing and talking like a couple of rookies at training camp.

Cotton recalled the meeting in detail. "He sat on the edge of the bed, and I sat in a chair in front of him. We talked a long time. He signed a few pictures for me with an unsteady hand. He had a bad cough and was in pretty bad shape. He would take a few hits of oxygen and smoke a cigarette. He told me some stories about the old days, and we laughed a lot. He didn't have long to live, and I think he knew it. But we had a great visit that afternoon."[7]

Then on October 30, 1998, Bulldog tried to get out of bed. His knees buckled, and he collapsed. The man who once lapped Parramore Field with a 350-pound calf on his shoulders didn't have the strength to get off the floor. His family helped him get back in bed, but his time had run out. There was an urgent phone call to family members in other parts of Texas. "Daddy's not doing good," Pat told them. "You need to get here in a hurry."

A few hours later, Bulldog Turner died.

As soon as word of Bulldog Turner's death made the news, his friends Ed Sprinkle, J. R. Boone, and other Chicago Bears teammates began raising money to help with funeral expenses and to buy a granite memorial to mark the final resting place of one of the greatest football players in history. Miller Robinson, a local Baptist preacher, conducted the funeral. The pall bearers were not celebrities, Hall of Famers, or ex-NFL stars, but Bulldog's friends and fence neighbors from Coryell County. That's the way he wanted it.

The men and women who knew him best remembered him not as a legend of the gridiron but as a good neighbor and a true and loyal friend. A neighbor in Pidcoke described Bulldog as "the most generous man I ever knew. He was too generous and too trusting. He had a kind heart. If you were his friend, he would give you the shirt off his back and his last dollar."[8] No one had anything bad to say about Bulldog Turner.

Bulldog is buried in the shade of a live oak tree in Greenbriar Cemetery. He lies next to Gladys, and a few feet away from his brother Dugie. For a time only a small metal marker placed there by Scott's Funeral Home marked the grave.

"It wasn't that Daddy didn't have the money to buy a tombstone." Pat recalled. "In the last years of his life he had his pension and his inheritance. He was debt-free. But he insisted that he didn't want to mark the grave until after he died. Ed Sprinkle and the Bears offered to buy the marker. It seemed important to them, so I let them do it."[9] A few months later, a truck rolled up to the fence and workers lowered a beautiful red granite monument into place. On the back of the monument is a football with the following inscription: "In Memory of Bulldog Turner from the Chicago Bears Teammates."

Some years earlier, before Gladys died, Pat Turner took inventory of her father's things. Some items were missing. "I have an engraved watch from the 1940 NFL Championship game," she said, "and I have his Hall of Fame ring. I have a lot of his old photographs. Most of the other stuff is gone. I'm not sure where his Hall of Fame bust is. But I can tell you this: It didn't favor him at all."

One possession in particular had a special meaning for Bulldog, and Pat Turner knew exactly where to find it—hanging in the closet. "His gold Hall of Fame jacket was his most prized possession," Pat said. "He was so proud of that jacket. I buried him in it."[10]

Greenbriar Cemetery lies on the north side of a narrow tree-lined lane that cuts through ranch country outside Gatesville. The road runs from the top of South Mountain in an easterly direction down into the valley of Coryell Creek and the Leon River. The road and the cemetery get their names from Greenbriar Creek. The scenery is what many people would say is typical Texas: grazing land with gently rolling hills, plenty of live oak trees for shade, and white-faced cattle chewing nonchalantly on knee-high grass. Cottontail rabbits scurry along the pavement, and white-tail deer pop out of the thick brush along the sides of the road. To an old warrior of the dusty plains, who knew the excitement of the big city but always returned to the country where he belonged, this part of Texas looked a lot like heaven.

Heaven is a place where rain is plentiful, cows are fat, horses are fast, beer is cold, bank accounts are never overdrawn, legends are not forgotten, and a lineman can always get his name in the paper.

The Frenchman Jules Renard once wrote, "On earth there is no heaven but there are pieces of it." Bulldog Turner found a little piece of heaven in Chicago and a little piece of heaven in West Texas.

Photo by the author.

Endnotes

Chapter 1: The Short End of the Stick

1. *Radio Post* (Gatesville, Texas), November 10, 1994.
2. Myron Cope, *The Game That Was—The Early Days of Pro Football* (Omaha, NE: World Publishing Company, 1970).
3. *Radio Post*, November 10, 1994.
4. *Abilene Reporter-News*, September 17, 1953.
5. *Chicago Tribune,* October 31, 1998.
6. Bill Sullivan, "The Dry Days of Bulldog Turner," *Texas Sportsworld*, January 1985, 56. Also see George Herbert Allen, *Pro Football's 100 Greatest Players: Rating the Stars of Past and Present* (Indianapolis: Bobs-Merrill, 1982).
7. *Chronicle Telegram* (Elyria, Ohio), August 31, 1995.
8. *The New Braunfels Herald Zeitung*, September 23, 1988.
9. Robert W. Peterson, *Pigskin: The Early Years of Pro Football* (New York: Oxford University Press, 1997), 129-30.
10. Richard Whittingham, *What a Game They Played* (New York: Harper and Row, 1984), 100.
11. *Waterloo Daily Courier*, September 14, 1941.
12. *Abilene Reporter-News*, July 1, 1939.
13. Ed Sprinkle, interview by author, December 20, 2007.
14. Ibid.
15. *Chicago Tribune*, November 1, 1998.
16. Sprinkle, interview, 2007.
17. *Charleston Daily Mail*, December 28, 1967.
18. *The Gatesville Messenger*, July 30, 1965.

19. Ibid., May 28, 1970.
20. J. R. Boone, interview by author, April 26, 2008.
21. Ed Sprinkle, interview by author, May 30, 2008.
22. Bob Curran, *Pro Football's Rag Days* (Englewood Cliffs, NJ: Prentice-Hall, 1969), 158.
23. *Billings Gazette,* October 24, 1948.
24. *Radio Post*, November 10, 1994.
25. Jim Dent, *Monster of the Midway* (New York: Thomas Dunne Books, 2003), 277.
26. *Pasadena Star-News*, January 12, 1959.
27. *Chicago Tribune*, August 21, 1944.
28. Myron Cope, "A Life for Two Tough Texans," *Sports Illustrated*, October 20, 1969.
29. *Radio Post*, November 10, 1994.

Chapter 2: A Tough Row to Hoe

1. *The Handbook of Texas* (Austin: Texas State Historical Association, 2013).
2. Cope, "Two Tough Texans."
3. Ibid.
4. *Abilene Reporter-News*, April 17, 1945.
5. Ilene Turner Hairston, interview by author, April 12, 2008.
6. Ibid.
7. *Abilene Reporter-News*, May 11, 1945.
8. Turner Hairston, interview.
9. Ibid.
10. Ibid.
11. Ibid.
12. Cope, "Two Tough Texans."
13. *Radio Post*, November 10, 1994.
14. Turner Hairston, interview.
15. Bill Sullivan, "The Dry Days of Bulldog Turner," *Texas Sportsworld*, January 1985. 56.
16. Cope, "Two Tough Texans."
17. Ibid.
18. *Abilene Reporter-News*, October 3, 1971.
19. Ibid., October 12, 1926.
20. *Charleston Daily Mail*, January 25, 1930.
21. *San Antonio Express*, January 27, 1938. Also see *Chester Times*, November 16, 1940.
22. *Sandusky Star Journal*, December 5, 1934.

23. *Portsmouth Times*, September 11, 1939.
24. Ibid., August 21, 1933.
25. *Abilene Reporter-News*, October 3, 1971.
26. Cope, "Two Tough Texans."

Chapter 3: A Silver Lining in a Funnel Cloud

1. Cope, "Two Tough Texans."
2. Ibid.
3. Ibid.
4. Ibid.
5. Ibid.
6. *Amarillo Globe-News*, March 30, 1966.
7. *Radio Post*, November 10, 1994.
8. Ibid.
9. Ibid.
10. Peterson, *Pigskin*, 129.
11. *Radio Post*, November 10, 1994.
12. Sullivan, "Dry Days," 56.
13. Ibid., 56-57.
14. *The Brand*, October 9, 1937.
15. Todd Patterson, "A Talk with HOFer Bulldog Turner," *Sports Collectors Digest*, October 25, 1991, 301.
16. Sullivan, "Dry Days," 57.
17. *Abilene Reporter-News*, September 7, 1973.
18. *The Brand*, October 22, 1938.
19. *Amarillo Globe-News*, March 30, 1966.
20. *Chicago Daily Tribune*, August 24, 1949.
21. *The Brand*, September 8, 1937.
22. *Abilene Reporter-News*, July 1, 1939.
23. Ibid., July 1, 1977.
24. J. D. Sandefer, interview by author, June 17, 2011.
25. *Abilene Reporter-News*, October 7, 1973.
26. *The Brand*, May 22, 1937.
27. *Abilene Reporter-News*, October 7, 1973.
28. *Hardin-Simmons University Yearbook*, 1937.
29. *Abilene Morning News*, February 13, 1930.
30. Ibid.
31. *Ogden Standard Examiner*, July 11, 1938.
32. *San Antonio Express*, July 11, 1938.
33. *San Antonio Light*, August 4, 1938.

34. *Hutchinson News*, June 20, 1982. Also see *Salt Lake Tribune*, September 22, 1946.
35. *Altoona Mirror*, September 1, 1950. Also see *San Antonio Express*, February 7, 1952.
36. *Abilene Reporter-News*, October 3, 1938.
37. Ibid., October 9, 1939.
38. *Abilene Reporter-News*, October 18, 1938.
39. *Arizona Republic*, April 11, 1968.
40. *Abilene Reporter-News*, November 21, 1938.
41. Ibid.
42. *Hardin-Simmons University Yearbook*, 1937.
43. *Lubbock Avalanche-Journal*, December 7, 1960.

Chapter 4: Young Hercules

1. *Radio Post*, November 10, 1994.
2. *Abilene Reporter-News*, February 12, 1937.
3. Ibid., September 21, 1938.
4. Ibid., July 1, 1939.
5. Ibid., September 4, 1938.
6. Edwin Shrake, "The Mad Hatter in Photoland," *Sports Illustrated*, September 21, 1964.
7. *Radio Post*, November 10, 1994.
8. *The Brand*, September 24, 1938.
9. *Abilene Reporter-News*, December 17, 1939.
10. *The Brand*, September 30, 1939.
11. *Abilene Reporter-News*, December 16, 1938.
12. *The Brand*, February 24, 1940.
13. Ibid., September 23, 1939.
14. *Abilene Reporter-News*, March 16, 1939.
15. Ibid., October 24, 1939 and March 27, 1939.
16. Ibid., March 19, 1939.
17. *The Brand*, October 16, 1937.
18. Ibid., September 15, 1939.
19. Ibid., December 8, 1937.
20. Ibid., February 25, 1939.
21. Ibid., Cut Throat Edition, April 1, 1939.
22. *The Brand*, March 25, 1939.
23. *Abilene Reporter-News*, March 16, 1939.
24. *The Brand*, March 4, 1939.
25. *Abilene Reporter-News*, March 28, 1939.

26. Ilene Turner Hairston, interview by author, April 12, 2008.

27. *Abilene Reporter-News*, March 28, 1939.

28. *The Brand*, April 1, 1939.

29. Ibid., May 6, 1939.

30. Ibid., October 28, 1939.

31. Ibid., November 18, 1939.

32. Ibid., September 15, 1939.

33. Ibid.

34. *Oakland Tribune*, December 15, 1939.

35. Ibid., December 10, 1939.

36. J. R. Boone, interview by author, April 26, 2008.

37. Steve Springer, "The No-Funds League," *Los Angeles Times*, July 29, 2000.

38. Don Smith, "Gino Marchetti," *The Coffin Corner*, vol. 18 (1996).

39. *Pacific Stars and Stripes*, September 2, 1974.

40. Whittingham, *What a Game*, 28.

41. *Sports Illustrated*, "The Game That Was," January 13, 1969.

42. Cope, "Two Tough Texans."

43. *Capital Times* (Madison, WI), April 5, 1940.

44. *El Paso Herald-Post*, December 11, 1939.

45. *The Brand*, September 30, 1939.

46. *Freeport Journal-Standard*, November 25, 1939.

47. Cope, "Two Tough Texans."

48. Ibid.

49. *Abilene Reporter-News*, December 17, 1939.

50. *The Brand*, December 16, 1940.

51. *Paris News*, December 24, 1939.

52. *The Brand*, December 4, 1937.

Chapter 5: The Roughest Team on the Planet

1. *Abilene Reporter-News*, December 10, 1939.

2. Patterson, "A Talk with HOFer Bulldog Turner," 301.

3. *San Antonio Light*, July 9, 1940.

4. *San Antonio Express*, December 11, 1963.

5. Pat Turner, interview by author, April 12, 2008.

6. *Mexia Daily News*, September 6, 1951.

7. *The Brand*, March 9, 1940. Also see *San Antonio Light*, March 2, 1940.

8. *Salt Lake Tribune*, October 1, 1943.

9. Turner, interview.

10. *Chicago Tribune*, April 26, 1940.

11. *Radio Post*, November 10, 1994.
12. Ibid.
13. *European Stars and Stripes*, February 2, 1971.
14. Sullivan, "Dry Days," 57.
15. *Chicago Tribune*, June 7, 1987.
16. Patterson, "A Talk with HOFer Bulldog Turner," 302.
17. *Daily Herald* (Illinois), October 10, 1995.
18. Whittingham, *What a Game*, 104.
19. George Blanda and Jack Olsen, "I Keep Getting My Kicks," *Sports Illustrated*, July 19, 1971.
20. *Waukesha Daily Freeman*, August 1, 1950.
21. *Radio Post*, November 10, 1994.
22. Ed Sprinkle, interview, 2007.
23. Ibid.
24. Jack Drees and James C. Mullen, *Where Is He Now?* (New York: Jonathon David Publishers, 1973), 110.
25. Sullivan, "Dry Days," 57.
26. *Radio Post*, November 10, 1994.
27. *Lake Charles American Press*, August 28, 1963.
28. Drees and Mullen, *Where Is He Now?*, 108.
29. Cope, "Two Tough Texans."
30. *Radio Post*, November 10, 1994.
31. *The Brand*, December 4, 1937.

Chapter 6: The Worst Thrashing in History

1. Peterson, *Pigskin*, 131-32.
2. Cope, "Two Tough Texans."
3. *The Brand*, December 14, 1940.
4. *San Antonio Light*, December 9, 1940.
5. Cope, "Two Tough Texans."
6. *Chicago Tribune,* June 7, 1987.
7. Ibid.
8. Cope, "Two Tough Texans."
9. *Radio Post*, November 10, 1994.
10. *Arizona Independent Republic*, December 9, 1940.
11. *Pacific Stars and Stripes*, August 2, 1974.
12. *Lubbock Avalanche-Journal*, December 7, 1960.
13. *Redlands Daily Facts*, September 17, 1974.
14. Whittingham, *What a Game*, 180.
15. *The Brand*, December 14, 1940.
16. Ibid.

17. *Radio Post*, November 10, 1994.

18. Sullivan, "Dry Days," 57.

19. *Waterloo Daily Courier*, January 25, 1955.

20. Ed Sprinkle, interview by author, May 30, 2008.

21. *Abilene Reporter-News*, December 19, 1942 and December 23, 1945.

Chapter 7: Bombs and Blitzes

1. *Charleston Gazette*, May 8, 1940.

2. *Oakland Tribune*, December 5, 1973.

3. *Provo Daily Herald*, June 11, 1943.

4. *Abilene Reporter-News*, May 24, 1945. In 1951 Lew Jenkins joined the Army, a move he credited with saving his life. He won decorations for bravery in Korea. When he came home he married and had a son. He took a job as a groundskeeper at a California golf course. He finally found the peace he had been searching for all his life. When he died he was buried with full military honors at Arlington National Cemetery.

5. *San Antonio Light*, December 22, 1941.

6. *New York Times*, January 2, 1942.

7. *Titusville Herald*, November 25, 1942.

8. *Abilene Reporter-News*, December 23, 1942.

9. *Laredo Times*, December 25, 1942.

10. *Abilene Reporter-News*, February 17, 1943.

11. *New York Times*, September 24, 1943.

12. *Chicago Tribune*, October 17, 1943.

13. Jim Dent, *Monster of the Midway* (New York: Thomas Dunne Books, 2003), 237.

14. *Manitowac* (Wisconsin) *Herald Times*, December 27, 1943.

15. Myron Cope, "The Game That Was," 1970.

16. *Abilene Reporter-News*, December 23, 1944.

17. J. R. Boone, interview by author, April 26, 2008.

18. Ed Sprinkle, interview by author, December 20, 2007.

19. *Abilene Reporter-News*, February 6, 1944.

20. *Big Spring Daily Herald*, July 20, 1944.

21. *San Antonio Light*, January 26, 1945.

22. Peterson, "Pigskin," 141.

Chapter 8: The Master of His Trade

1. *Oakland Times*, February 8, 1967.

2. After leaving professional football, Clarkson took a job as assistant coach at Sugarland High School. On October 26, 1957, Stuart Clarkson col-

lapsed of a heart attack and died on the sideline while Sugarland played Hitchcock. He was 38 years old.

3. Ed Sprinkle, interview by author, December 20, 2007.
4. Ibid.
5. Ibid.
6. *Abilene Reporter-News*, April 15, 1947.
7. Ed Sprinkle, interview by author, December 20, 2007.
8. Ibid.
9. Ibid., May 30, 2008.
10. *Abilene Reporter-News*, November 27, 1955.
11. Ed Sprinkle, interview by author, May 30, 2008.
12. Cotton Davidson, interview by author, September 7, 2008.
13. *Abilene Reporter-News*, April 15, 1947.
14. *The Brand*, November 2, 1946.
15. *Abilene Reporter-News*, December 16, 1946.

Chapter 9: On the Way Down

1. Cope, "Two Tough Texans." Also see *New York Times*, November 2, 1998.
2. *Press-Courier* (Oxnard), June 11, 1962. Also see *Salt Lake Tribune*, November 17, 1947, *Long Beach Press-Telegram*, November 17, 1947, and the *New York Times*, November 17, 1947.
3. Whittingham, *What a Game*, 221. Also see Dent, *Monster of the Midway*, 238.
4. *Post-Standard* (Syracuse), December 6, 1964.
5. J. R. Boone, interview by author, April 26, 2008.
6. *San Antonio Light*, November 30, 1949.
7. Cope, "Two Tough Texans." Ed Neal was a big man, even as a teenager. When he played for the Wichita Falls High School Coyotes in the 1930s, he was 6'4" and weighed 280 pounds. After high school, Neal bounced around at several colleges, including New Mexico State, Tulane University, and Louisiana State University, before settling at Ouachita Baptist College in Arkadelphia, Arkansas.

In 1942 he tried out for the Philadelphia Eagles. He made the team and signed a contract for $100 a game. Then the Eagles traded him to Green Bay. For seven seasons he played center and defensive tackle for the Packers. He was a warrior with the strength of a giant. He could bend bottle caps between his fingers and bust helmets wide open with his bare hands.

After football, Neal returned to Wichita Falls and worked for the water department. For 20 years he diligently watched over the pumps at

Lake Kickapoo—the city's only source of water at the time. In 1962 the city named him water superintendent.

Neal bought a lot on the lake and dreamed of building a cabin there. But money was tight. Ed retired from the NFL too early to get a pension, and his wife Vera didn't make much as a waitress in Burkburnett. Like many people raised during the Depression, Neal hated debt, so he built his cabin a little at a time, as he could afford it. The process took 30 years.

At some point in his life Ed Neal unknowingly contracted hepatitis. The disease damaged his liver and caused complications when he injured his leg. Doctors had to amputate the leg just below the knee. The *Wichita Falls Record* quoted him as saying, "I've ridden bulls, played football for 17 years, been a deep sea diver, and jumped from one rig to another and never had to take an aspirin. That's what happens when you live to be a hundred."

He moved into his cabin on the lake in 1982. Two years later he died there.

8. *Abilene Reporter-News*, July 1, 1977.
9. Cope, "Two Tough Texans."
10. Ibid.
11. *Gatesville Messenger and Star Forum*, July 30, 1965.
12. Gary D'Amato and Cliff Christi, *Mudbaths and Bloodbaths: The Inside Story of the Bears-Packers Rivalry* (Boulder, CO: Prairie Oak Press, 1997).
13. *Abilene Reporter-News*, July 1, 1977.
14. Cope, "Two Tough Texans."
15. *Chicago Tribune*, December 12, 1951. Also see *Radio Post*, November 10, 1994.
16. *San Antonio Express*, February 9, 1954.
17. *Berkshire Eagle*, March 18, 1976.

Chapter 10: High Jinks on the Hudson

1. *Anniston Star*, June 12, 1974.
2. *Abilene Reporter-News*, December 19, 1961. Also see William J. Ryczek, *Crash of the Titans: The Early Years of New York Jets and the AFL* (Jefferson: McFarland and Company, 2009).
3. Sullivan, "Dry Days."
4. Ryczek, *Crash of the Titans*, 7.
5. *Anniston Star*, June 12, 1974.
6. *Gatesville Messenger and Star Forum*, January 5, 1962.
7. *The Brand*, January 2, 1962.
8. *New York Times*, December 19, 1961.

9. *The Brand*, January 5, 1962.

10. *Oshkosh Daily Northwestern*, December 19, 1961.

11. *The Brand*, January 2, 1962.

12. *Sandusky Register*, October 31, 1962.

13. *The Brand*, January 2, 1962.

14. Ibid.

15. *Lowell* (Massachusetts) *Sun*, December 19, 1961.

16. *Gatesville Messenger and Star Forum*, April 13, 1962.

17. *Redlands Daily Facts*, August 4, 1962.

18. *Oakland Daily Tribune*, September 5, 1962.

19. Jim Hogrogian, "The Last Fall of the Titans," *Coffin Corner*, vol. 13, no. 2 (1991).

20. Alex Kroll, "The Last of the Titans," *Sports Illustrated*, September 22, 1969.

21. *New York Times*, October 14, 2007.

22. Kroll, "Last of the Titans."

23. *Middleton* (New York) *Times Herald Record*, September 27, 1962.

24. Kroll, "Last of the Titans."

25. *Anniston Star*, June 12, 1974.

26. *New York Times*, October 14, 2007.

27. Kroll, "Last of the Titans."

28. Cotton Davidson, interview by author, September 7, 2008.

29. *Abilene Reporter-News*, September 26, 1962.

30. *Sandusky Register*, October 31, 1962.

31. *Abilene Reporter-News*, October 4, 1962.

32. *The Bee* (Danville, Virginia), October 22, 1962.

33. Kroll, "Last of the Titans."

34. *Anniston Star*, June 12, 1974.

35. *Bridgeport Times*, November 30, 1962.

36. Ibid.

37. Kroll, "Last of the Titans." Also see Hogrogian, "The Last Fall of the Titans."

38. *European Stars and Stripes*, November 11, 1962.

39. *San Antonio Light*, November 21, 1962.

40. Hogrogian, "Last Fall of the Titans."

41. *Abilene Reporter-News*, March 27, 1963.

42. Patterson, "A Talk with HOFer Bulldog Turner," 302.

43. Sullivan, "Dry Days," 59.

44. Ed Sprinkle, interview by author, May 30, 2008.

45. *Abilene Reporter-News*, November 29, 1962 and January 7, 1963.

46. Pat Turner, interview by author, April 12, 2008.
47. *Radio Post*, November 10, 1994.

Chapter 11: Practicing Poverty

1. Myron Cope, "The Game That Was," 1970.
2. *Radio Post*, November 10, 1994.
3. Jimmy Wood, interview by author, May 15, 2009.
4. *Radio Post,* November 10, 1994.
5. Cope, "Two Tough Texans."
6. Drees and Mullen, *Where Is He Now?*, 109.
7. *Abilene Reporter-News*, April 15, 1947.
8. *Radio Post*, November 10, 1994.
9. *Abilene Morning News*, February 23, 1942.
10. *The Brand*, May 17, 1947.
11. *Radio Post*, November 10, 1994.
12. Larry Pruitt, interview by author, April 23, 2007.
13. *Radio Post*, November 10, 1994.
14. Jack Pardee, interview by author, September 25, 2008.
15. *El Paso Herald-Post*, September 17, 1965.
16. Ibid., March 7, 1966.
17. Ibid.
18. *Sports Illustrated*, "People," April 4, 1966.
19. *El Paso Herald-Post*, September 17, 1965.
20. *Gatesville Messenger and Star Forum*, July 30, 1965.
21. *Cumberland News*, August 30, 1974. Also see *Chicago Tribune*, September 7, 1974.
22. *Abilene Reporter-News*, July 19, 1962.
23. Peterson, *Pigskin*, 207.
24. Ibid., 206.
25. *Sports Illustrated*, "Events and Discoveries," December 15, 1958.
26. *The Terra Haute Tribune-Star*, July 26, 1970.
27. Mark Gaughan, "Nixon, DeLamielleure Lead Pension Fight," BuffaloNews.com, August 26, 2010.
28. *Manitowac Herald Times*, February 3, 1967.
29. Ibid.
30. Ibid.
31. *Nevada State Journal*, March, 19, 1976.
32. Steve Springer, "The No-Funds League," *Los Angeles Times*, July 29, 2000.
33. Ibid.

34. Maurice Campbell, interview by author, March 20, 2009.
35. *The Capital* (Annapolis, Maryland), July 3, 1988.
36. *Wisconsin State Journal*, November 16, 1985.
37. *The Capital*, July 3, 1988.
38. Pat Turner, interview by author, June 23, 2011.
39. Sullivan, "Dry Days," 59.
40. Tom Williams, interview by author, September 1, 2008.
41. Pat Turner, interview by author, June 23, 2011.
42. *Los Angeles Times*, April 16, 1987.
43. *Baltimore Sun*, July 2, 2006
44. Sullivan, "Dry Days."
45. *Chicago Tribune*, June 7, 1987.
46. Ibid.
47. *Oakland Tribune*, November 13, 1975.
48. *Chicago Tribune*, June 7, 1987.
49. Ibid.
50. *Los Angeles Times*, April 16, 1987.
51. *Chicago Tribune*, November 1, 1998.
52. *Los Angeles Times*, April 16, 1987.

Chapter 12: Fourth and Long

1. Sullivan, "Dry Days," 55.
2. *San Antonio Light*, April 9, 1970.
3. Drees and Mullen, *Where Is He Now?*, 110.
4. Sullivan, "Dry Days," 59.
5. *Big Spring Herald*, November 11, 1995.
6. *Chicago Daily Herald*, September 6, 1993.
7. Cotton Davidson, interview by author, September 7, 2008, and Pat Turner, interview by author, April 12, 2008.
8. Jimmy Wood, interview by author, May 15, 2009.
9. Pat Turner, interview by author, April 25, 2011.
10. Ibid.

Bibliography

Books

Allen, George Herbert. *Pro Football's 100 Greatest Players: Rating the Stars of Past and Present.* Indianapolis: Bobs-Merrill, 1982.

Cope, Myron. *The Game that Was—The Early Days of Pro Football.* Omaha, NE: World Publishing Company, 1970.

Curran, Bob. *Pro Football's Rag Days.* Englewood Cliffs, NJ: Prentice-Hall, 1969.

D'Amato, Gary and Cliff Christi. *Mudbaths and Bloodbaths: The Inside Story of the Bears-Packers Rivalry.* Boulder, CO: Prairie Oak Press, 1997.

Dent, Jim. *Monster of the Midway.* New York: Thomas Dunne Books, 2003.

Drees, Jack and James C. Mullen. *Where Is He Now?* New York: Jonathon David Publishers, 1973.

Hardin-Simmons University Yearbook, 1937.

Peterson, Robert W. *Pigskin: The Early Years of Pro Football.* New York: Oxford University Press, 1997.

Ryczek, William J. *Crash of the Titans: The Early Years of the New York Jets and the AFL.* Jefferson: McFarland and Company, 2009.

The Handbook of Texas. Austin: The Texas State Historical Association, 2013.

Whittingham, Richard W. *What a Game They Played.* New York: Harper and Row, 1984.

Periodicals

Blanda, George and Jack Olsen. "I Keep Getting My Kicks." *Sports Illustrated.* July 19, 1971.

Cope, Myron. "A Life for Two Tough Texans." *Sports Illustrated*. October 20, 1969.

Gaughan, Mark. "Nixon, DeLamielleure Lead Pension Fight." BuffaloNews. com. August 26, 2010.

Hogrogian, Jim. "The Last Fall of the Titans." *Coffin Corner*, vol. 13, no. 2, 1991.

Kroll, Alex. "The Last of the Titans." *Sports Illustrated*. September 22, 1969.

Patterson, Todd. "A Talk with HOFer Bulldog Turner." *Sports Collectors Digest*. October 25, 1991.

Shrake, Edwin. "The Mad Hatter in Photoland." *Sports Illustrated*. September 21, 1964.

Smith, Don. "Gino Marchetti." *Coffin Corner*, vol. 18, no. 5, 1996.

Sports Illustrated. Events and Discoveries. December 15, 1958.

Sports Illustrated. People. April 4, 1966.

Sullivan, Bill. "The Dry Days of Bulldog Turner." *Texas Sportsworld*. January 1985.

Newspapers

Abilene Reporter-News

Altoona Mirror

Amarillo Globe-News

Anniston Star

Arizona Independent Republic

Baltimore Sun

Berkshire Eagle

Big Spring Daily Herald

Billings Gazette

Bridgeport Times

Capital Times (Madison)

Charleston Daily Mail

Chicago Tribune

Chronicle Telegram (Elyria)

Cumberland News

Daily Herald (Illinois)

El Paso Herald-Post

European Stars and Stripes

Freeport Journal-Standard

Gatesville Messenger and Star Forum

Hutchinson News

Lake Charles American Press

Long Beach Press-Telegram
Los Angeles Times
Lowell Sun
Lubbock Avalanche-Journal
Manitowoc Herald Times
Mexia Daily News
Nevada State Journal
New Braunfels Zeitung
New York Times
Oakland Tribune
Ogden Standard Examiner
Oshkosh Daily Northwestern
Pacific Stars and Stripes
Paris News
Pasadena Star-Times
Portsmouth Times
Press-Courier (Oxnard)
Provo Daily Herald
Racine Journal Times
Radio Post (Gatesville)
Redlands Daily Facts
Salt Lake Tribune
San Antonio Express
San Antonio Light
Sandusky Register
Sandusky Star Journal
Terre Haute Tribune-Star
The Bee (Danville)
The Brand (Hardin-Simmons University student newspaper)
The Capital (Annapolis)
Titusville Herald
Waterloo Daily Courier
Waukesha Daily Freeman
Wisconsin State Journal

Interviews

Boone, J. R. April 26, 2008.
Campbell, Maurice. March 20, 2009.
Davidson, Cotton. September 7, 2008.
Hairston, Ilene Turner. April 12, 2008.

Pardee, Jack. September 25, 2008.
Pruitt, Larry. April 23, 2007.
Sandifer, J. D. June 17, 2011.
Sprinkle, Ed. December 20, 2007, May 30, 2008.
Turner, Pat. April 12, 2008, April 25, 2011, June 23, 2011.
Williams, Tom. September 1, 2008.
Wood, Jimmy. May 15, 2009.

Archives

Bulldog Turner Collection. Texas Sports Hall of Fame. Waco, Texas.
West Texas Digital Archives. Hardin-Simmons University Library. Abilene,
    Texas.

Index